QUALITIES OF
effective
principals

QUALITIES OF
effective
principals

JAMES H. STRONGE

HOLLY B. RICHARD

NANCY CATANO

Alexandria, Virginia USA

ASCD

1703 N. Beauregard St. • Alexandria, VA 22311-1714 USA
Phone. 800 933-2723 or 703-578-9600 • Fax: 703-575-5400
Web site: www.ascd.org • E-mail: member@ascd.org
Author guidelines: www.ascd.org/write

Gene R. Carter, *Executive Director;* Nancy Modrak, *Publisher;* Julie Houtz, *Director of Book Editing & Production,* Leah Lakins, *Project Manager;* Mike Kalyan, *Production Manager;* Reece Quiñones, *Senior Graphic Designer;* Circle Graphics, *Typesetter*

PAPERBACK ISBN: 978-1-4166-0744-1   ASCD product #108003   n11/08
Also available as an e-book through ebrary, netLibrary, and many online booksellers (see Books in Print for the ISBNs).

Quantity discounts for the paperback edition only: 10–49 copies, 10%; 50+ copies, 15%; for 1,000 or more copies, call 800-933-2723, ext. 5634, or 703-575-5634. For desk copies: member@ascd.org.

Library of Congress Cataloging-in-Publication Data

Stronge, James H.
   Qualities of effective principals/James H. Stronge, Holly B. Richard, and Nancy Catano
     p. cm.
   Includes bibliographical references and index.
   ISBN 978-1-4166-0744-1   (pbk.:alk. paper)   1. School principals—United States.
2. School management and organization—United States.   3. Educational
leadership—United States.   I. Richard, Holly B.   II. Catano, Nancy.   III. Title.

   LB2831.92.S77 2008
   371.2'012—dc22

                                                                 2008032801

18 17 16 15 14 13 12 11   3 4 5 6 7 8 9 10 11 12

Qualities of Effective Principals isn't devoted to Hollywood-style heroic school leaders; it isn't even about them. In fact, Jim Collins (2001), in *Good to Great*, found that "larger-than-life, celebrity leaders who ride in from the outside are *negatively* correlated with taking a company from good to great" (p. 10). Instead, this book on what makes principals effective is concerned with the unsung heroes who do their jobs day after day, year after year, and make a difference in the lives of young people. Thus, we dedicate this book to all caring, committed, and capable school principals everywhere.

Qualities of Effective Principals

Acknowledgments

―――――――――

Developing a book of this nature can be a solitary achievement. However, in writing *Qualities of Effective Principals,* this was not the case. Moving from imagination to culmination required the encouragement, support, and assistance of many individuals. We would like to take this opportunity to acknowledge the contributions of many friends, generous colleagues, and capable students.

A number of colleagues provided invaluable support in the development of the book. In particular, Dr. Leslie Grant, Visiting Assistant Professor for the College of William and Mary's School of Education, provided a thorough review and edit of the entire text. Additionally, drawing on a variety of resources and in conjunction with Shelley Nowacek, Leslie developed the bulk of the material contained in Part 2 of the book, including checklists, quality indicators, and red flags. Dr. Jennifer Hindman, from Teacher Quality Resources, LLC, created scenarios that introduce selected chapters in Part 1 of the book. For the generous contributions of their technical expertise and creativity, we are most appreciative.

Several current and former doctoral students in the College of William and Mary's Educational Policy, Planning, and Leadership program are due substantial credit for their background research and writing that was adapted for the book. Specifically, John Caggiano, Ellen Turner, and Brig Lampert contributed content to selected sections of the book. Their work, along with the work of numerous other graduate students, has provided a solid connection between research and practice as the book has unfolded. Xu Xianxuan provided assistance in reviewing and refining annotations included in the annotated bibliography. Additionally, we wish to especially thank Shelley Nowacek for her careful review and organization of existing research on issues related to principal effectiveness. Her generous contributions of time and expertise were essential to the creation of the book.

JHS, HBR, and NC

Finally, I wish to acknowledge Scott Willis, director of Book Acquisitions for ASCD, for his confidence in my work and his support throughout the book development process—from initial proposal to completion. This is my fifth book published with ASCD, and it is the capable and conscientious professionals there that have made these publishing endeavors a pleasure. Thank you!

JHS

Introduction

D o principals factor into student success? In *Qualities of Effective Principals*, we answer this question with a resounding YES! In fact, among school factors, the effect of principals is considered second only to that of teachers in facilitating student learning (Leithwood, Seashore Louis, Anderson, & Wahlstrom, 2004; Marzano, Waters, & McNulty, 2005). Highly effective principals are considered "the key to initiating, implementing, and sustaining school success" (Tucker & Codding, 2002, p. 253) and "imperative to high student achievement" (Anthes, 2005, p. 1). Consequently, principals are expected to promote and develop the school vision, empowering stakeholders to build and maintain the conditions necessary for the success of all students.

The nature of the principal's role has changed significantly in the past two decades, from primarily managerial to that of management and leadership (Lashway, 2002b; Murphy, 2003; Shellard, 2003; Tucker & Codding, 2002). Despite the recent emphasis on instructional leadership, principals continue to be responsible for traditional duties such as facility management, budgeting, school safety, and student discipline—tasks that continue to absorb a considerable amount of their time (Doyle & Rice, 2002; Lashway, 2002b; Tirozzi & Ferrandino, 2001).

Due to the increasing number of responsibilities required of principals, it is not surprising to find that long hours are spent on the job. Elementary school principals work an average of 62 hours per week (Groff, 2001), while middle and high school principals spend successively greater amounts of time on the job (DiPaola & Tschannen-Moran, 2003). Although it is generally agreed that the principals' role has evolved in recent years, there is no clear definition of that role and no method to balance the responsibility of instructional leadership with the myriad of other demands on their time (Portin, Schneider, DeArmond, & Gundlach, 2003). Given the competing demands for precious time, it is imperative not only that principals do their work well, but also that they do the right work.

One essential ingredient for success in education or any business, for that matter, is effective leadership. Ken Chenault, CEO for American Express, captured this sentiment well: "Most companies maintain their office copiers better than they build the capabilities of their people, especially the ones who are supposed to be future leaders" (cited in Colvin, 2007, p. 100). If we are to succeed as an educational enterprise in a highly competitive world, then we must embrace leadership development—not in a cursory fashion, but rather in an ongoing, comprehensive, sustained manner. It is for this purpose—leadership development—that we have written *Qualities of Effective Principals*. We hope you find it of value to your organization and your leadership team.

Conceptual Framework for the Book

The framework for *Qualities of Effective Principals* is provided in Figure I, which outlines eight key qualities for understanding and prioritizing the principal's work.

Although we can comfortably identify the major components of the principal's work, interestingly, "we know much less about how—or how much principals carry out these functions on a daily basis" (Lashway, 2002a, p. 2; also, see Spillane, Halverson, & Diamond, 2001). Nonetheless, these qualities, based on our review, do capture well the essence of the principal's work.

Each quality serves as the basis of discussion for the eight chapters included in Part 1. Additionally, the style and format by which we present the findings are designed to be user-friendly, providing easy-to-use summaries and tools for reference.

Qualities of Effective Principals is based primarily on existing research, although we also include applicable policy and theoretical perspective. Specifically, the sources considered in creating this synthesis of principal effectiveness include empirical studies of principal practice as linked to student achievement, case studies of principals, meta-analyses of principal effectiveness, and other reviews of research.

Figure I **Qualities of Effective Principals**	
Principal Quality	**Description**
Quality 1: Instructional Leadership	The principal fosters the success of all students by facilitating the development, communication, implementation, and evaluation of a shared vision of learning that reflects excellence.
Quality 2: School Climate	The principal fosters the success of all students by advocating, nurturing, and sustaining a positive and safe school climate for all stakeholders.
Quality 3: Human Resource Administration	The principal fosters effective human resources administration through the selection, induction, support, and retention of quality instructional and support personnel.
Quality 4: Teacher Evaluation	The principal conducts meaningful, timely, and productive evaluations of teachers and other staff members in order to support ongoing performance effectiveness and school improvement.
Quality 5: Organizational Management	The principal fosters the success of all students by supporting, managing, and overseeing the school's organization, operation, and resources.
Quality 6: Communication and Community Relations	The principal fosters the success of all students by collaborating effectively with all stakeholders.
Quality 7: Professionalism	The principal fosters the success of all students by demonstrating integrity, fairness, and ethical behavior.
Quality 8: The Principal's Role in Student Achievement	The principal's leadership results in acceptable, measurable progress based on established standards.

The research findings and recommended practices identified in the book should be familiar to many school leaders. For effective principals, the book should serve as a review and reminder for continued improvement. For developing school leaders, the same findings serve to build awareness as they take steps to enhance their effectiveness. By focusing on principal effectiveness, our ultimate goal is to improve the educational experiences and achievement of the students we serve in our schools.

Parts of the Book

Qualities of Effective Principals is designed to serve as a resource and reference tool for school leaders and their supervisors. It identifies elements of effective leadership within eight broad categories and points readers interested in further exploration to the research studies and reviews used in the preparation of the text. The book is divided into two parts.

- Part 1 provides a research synthesis useful in developing a profile of what an effective principal should know and be able to do.
- Part 2 contains checklists for principal effectiveness, along with quality indicators and red flags that are tied to the eight identified qualities. It also provides an annotated bibliography for selected sources that we considered central to understanding the effective principal.

In Part 1, the first seven chapters address major aspects of a principal's job responsibilities and practices. In the final chapter, we turn our attention to the direct impact of principals on the ultimate goal of leadership—student success. Within each chapter, information is organized into categories of characteristics or behaviors that are supported by existing research on important aspects of principal effectiveness. Summaries of research are provided in a straightforward manner in each chapter, with a list of key references to guide the interested reader to further information on the topics.

Part 2 of the text provides checklists to assess principal skills, quality indicators to look for in effective principal performance, and red flags for inappropriate or ineffective principal performance. This portion of the book focuses on helping principals apply the qualities of effectiveness to improve— whether the improvement is self-diagnosed or the result of supervisor assistance. In particular, the checklists and qualities should be helpful in converting research findings into more effective practice. Part 2 also contains an annotated bibliography of selected sources, a matrix of those sources tying them back to the eight principal qualities, and a complete reference list. We hope that the annotations are useful for those who would like a convenient summary of the research.

Uses for the Book

By identifying and carefully considering the attributes of quality leadership, we can be better equipped to identify links between leadership processes and desirable school and student outcomes. Thus, *Qualities of Effective Principals* is aimed at improving the quality of principal performance and the learning community in which they work. In this effort, the book can be a valuable resource for the following audiences:

- Principals who desire to improve their own performance through analysis and reflective practice.
- Administrators who supervise and evaluate principals and assistant principals. Staff development specialists who plan and deliver training focused on improving school leadership.
- Human resource specialists who are responsible for recruiting and selecting high-quality principals and assistant principals.
- Professors of educational leadership who can employ the book's research synthesis in their leadership programs.
- Policymakers and their staffs who are responsible for developing tools and strategies for state or district leadership development programs and processes.

For any user of the book, we attempt to make clear that there are only two things, beyond safety, that really count in schools and school leadership: (1) teaching and learning, and (2) supporting teaching and learning. And it is to these ends that we hope you find *Qualities of Effective Principals* beneficial.

Related Resources: Anthes, 2005; Colvin, 2007; DiPaola & Tschannen-Moran, 2003; Doyle & Rice, 2002; Groff, 2001; Lashway, 2002a, 2002b; Leithwood, Seashore Louis, Anderson, & Wahlstrom, 2004; Marzano, Waters, & McNulty, 2005; Murphy, 2003; Portin, Schneider, DeArmond, & Gundlach, 2003; Shellard, 2003; Spillane, Halverson, & Diamond, 2001; Tirozzi & Ferrandino, 2001; Tucker & Codding, 2002.

Part 1

What It Means to Be an Effective Principal

Part 1 of *Qualities of Effective Principals* focuses on the research useful in developing a profile of an effective principal. Following the Introduction, the eight chapters of the text address major qualities of principal effectiveness. Chapters 1 through 7 provide an extensive review of the key roles and responsibilities of building-level school administrators. Chapter 8 serves as a culmination for the book by exploring the effect of effective principals on school improvement and student success.

1

Instructional Leadership: Supporting Best Practice

Beth entered the education profession as a middle school science teacher who wanted to make a difference in the lives of her students. After teaching for a number of years, she wanted to accomplish more than the work that she could do within her classroom and, thus, became a grade-level chair. Beth also worked on the district's science curriculum committee, and then began taking classes at the university at night to earn her administrative and supervision license. Beth was an outstanding teacher, and her first administrative position as the assistant principal for instruction seemed tailor-made for her strengths. Her instructional expertise and knowledge of curriculum provided her with a sound foundation for leading instructional efforts in her school. Beth's office walls looked like a strategic command center of data disaggregation and data tracking. She traveled through classrooms daily, observing instruction and student learning. Her observations helped her to identify classroom needs and strengths. She collaborated regularly with grade-level teams to monitor the needs of students and to determine strategies and resources that could better support students and teachers. And she continued to meet with students to talk about their education goals and progress. In essence, Beth is committed to make teaching and learning in her school the most positive experience it can be.

One major emphasis in the educational arena in the early 21st century has been the continuing demand for greater accountability to increase student performance. National and state expectations require schools to ensure that all students achieve mastery of curriculum objectives, and local schools focus on implementing those requirements to the best of their ability. As a result, leading instructional efforts in a school has evolved into a primary role for school principals.

In order to meet the challenges associated with national and state expectations, principals must focus on teaching and learning—especially in terms of measurable student progress—to a greater degree than heretofore. Consequently, today's principals concentrate on building a vision for their schools, sharing leadership with teachers, and influencing schools to operate as learning communities. Accomplishing these essential school improvement efforts requires gathering and assessing data to determine needs, and monitoring instruction and curriculum to determine if the identified needs are addressed. This chapter summarizes existing research related to instructional leadership and methods principals use to exhibit and harness that leadership to meet their school goals. In particular, we focus on the following goals:

- Building and sustaining a school vision
- Sharing leadership
- Leading a learning community
- Using data to make instructional decisions
- Monitoring curriculum and instruction

Figure 1.1, at the end of the chapter, outlines key references relating to these elements of instructional leadership.

Building and Sustaining a School Vision

If you are not sure of where you want to go, how will you ever get there? Furthermore, how will you know when and how to take corrective action along the way? And how will you know when you've arrived at the destination? A successful principal must have a clear vision that shows how all components of a school will operate at some point in the future. Having a clear image of their schools helps principals avoid becoming consumed by the administrative requirements of their jobs. In fact, principals may need two types of vision: one vision of their schools and the roles they play in those schools, and another vision of how the change process will proceed (Manasse, 1985).

Clearly, multiple role expectations exist for school leaders. All schools need principals to exercise their roles as instructional leaders who ensure the quality of instruction (Portin et al., 2003). Thus, there is a need to spend time in classrooms observing the process of teaching and learning while also balancing other needs such as student safety and parent relationships.

Fulfilling these multiple responsibilities well requires principals to possess an inner compass that consistently points them toward the future interests of the school, never losing sight of their schools' visions, missions, and goals.

Successful principals understand that it is important to establish clear learning goals and garner schoolwide—and even community-wide—commitment to these goals. The development of a clear vision and goals for learning is emphasized by principals of high-achieving schools (Leithwood & Riehl, 2003). They hold high expectations that teachers and students will meet these goals and hold themselves accountable for the success of the school. These principals provide emotional support for teachers and are viewed as possessing the ability to foster positive inter-personal relationships. They protect instructional time by limiting loud-speaker announcements and scheduling building maintenance to minimize disruptions. They ensure that student progress is monitored through the continual aggregation and disaggregation of student performance data that are directly related to the school's mission and goals. Principals of high-achieving schools are confident that they will accomplish their vision and goals despite challenges and setbacks and, thus, serve as role models for staff and students (Cotton, 2003). And when milestone achievements are reached, those successful results are celebrated.

The following conclusions can be drawn from the research related to the role of the principal and building and sustaining the school's vision:

- First and foremost, principals need to have a clear vision for their schools (Manasse, 1985; Zmuda, Kuklis, & Kline, 2004).
- Schools need principals who strive to ensure the quality of instruction in their schools (Harris, 2007; Marzano et al., 2005; Portin et al., 2003).
- Principals of high-achieving schools expect teachers and students to meet the schools' goals (Leithwood & Riehl, 2003).
- Principals of high-achieving schools are confident that their schools can meet their goals (Cotton, 2003).
- Principals who focus on school improvement have more effective schools (Shen & Hsieh, 1999).
- Principals of high-achieving schools communicate to all stakeholders that learning is the school's most important mission (Cotton, 2003; Marzano et al., 2005).

Sharing Leadership

Guiding a school staff to reach a common vision requires intensive and sustained collaboration. After all, it is the expertise of teachers upon which any quality educational system is built. Wise principals know that going it alone makes meeting instructional goals virtually impossible. A key responsibility of school leaders is to sustain learning, and this can best be accomplished through leading learning endeavors that are focused on long-term outcomes rather than short-term returns. Additionally, distributing leadership throughout a school and providing for leadership succession are indispensable to a school's success (Hargreaves & Fink, 2003). "Leaders influence others to understand and agree about what needs to be done and how. This process requires the facilitation of individual and shared efforts to accomplish common objectives" (Kyrtheotis & Pashiardis, 1998b, p. 3).

Tapping the Expertise of Teacher Leaders

There is no evidence of troubled schools turning around without the influence of strong leadership. Effective leadership sets the direction and influences members of the organization to work together toward meeting organizational goals. Principals can accomplish this essential responsibility by providing individual support, challenging teachers to examine their own practices, and securing models of best practice. Additionally, effective principals develop and depend on leadership contributions from a variety of stakeholders, including teachers and parents (Leithwood et al., 2004). As key instructional leaders, principals share their leadership with teachers to promote reflection and collaborative investigation to improve teaching and learning. Subsequently, teacher leaders lead change from the classroom by asking questions related to school improvement, and they feel empowered to help find the answer (Reason & Reason, 2007).

In practical terms, principals talk to teachers, provide staff development, and support lifelong learning about teaching and learning (Blase & Blase, 1999). They also create opportunities for teachers to work together and share teaching practices with one another. What they tend not to do, however, is to exhibit directive leadership styles (Mendel, Watson, & MacGregor, 2002). Consequently, principals are not the only instructional leaders in a school.

In sharing leadership, principals collaborate with teachers to evaluate issues related to curriculum, instruction, and assessment. As part of this collaborative process, teacher leaders provide valuable insight and ideas to principals as they work together toward school improvement. Principals who tap into the expertise of teachers throughout the process of transforming their schools and increasing the focus on learning are more successful. And a valuable byproduct for principals who collaboratively focus on instructional leadership is that they are less likely to burn out (Marks & Printy, 2003).

Collaborating in Leading

Interestingly, some evidence suggests that female elementary school principals participate more actively in instructional leadership than their male counterparts. Also, they spend more years in the classroom before entering their first administrative post and, consequently, may possess greater knowledge in instructional matters (Cotton, 2003; Hallinger, Bickman, & Davis, 1996). Perhaps most telling is the suggestion that because female administrators tend to assume a major instructional role as central to their work, they shape teachers' attitudes regarding students' ability to master subject matter, thus, having an indirect effect on student outcomes through their teachers (Cotton, 2003; Hallinger et al., 1996; Hallinger & Heck, 1996).

The research shows that effective principals (both men and women) facilitate shared leadership and collaboration among their staffs to include the following:

- Wise principals understand that they cannot reach instructional goals alone (Hargreaves & Fink, 2003).
- Attaining school goals requires individual and shared efforts (Kyrtheotis & Pashiardis, 1998b).
- Effective instructional leaders believe that staff should collaborate and openly discuss instruction and program administration collectively among all stakeholders (Blase & Blase, 1999).
- Principals who distribute leadership across their schools contribute to sustainable improvements within the school organization (Hargreaves & Fink, 2003).
- Highly successful principals develop and count on the expertise of teacher leaders to improve school effectiveness (Leithwood et al., 2004).
- Principals need to create opportunities for teachers to work together (Mendel et al., 2002).

- Principals need to tap the expertise of teacher leaders in their schools in order to enhance improvement efforts and results (Marks & Printy, 2003).
- Principals need to function as the chief instructional leader of their school while balancing multiple responsibilities. However, to effectively foster student learning requires the exercise of distributing leadership (Tucker & Tschannen-Moran, 2002).

Related Resources: Danielson, 2007; Donaldson, 2007; Dozier, 2007, Harrison & Killion, 2007; Lieberman & Friedrich, 2007; Wade & Ferriter, 2007.

Leading a Learning Community

Today's principals must become role models for learning while continually (or at least regularly) seeking tools and ideas that foster school improvement (Lashway, 2003). Simply put, schooling is organized around two key functions: (1) teaching and learning, and (2) organizing for teaching and learning. Thus, it seems clear that school principals need to manage the structures and processes of their schools around instruction.

Principals as Learners

Effective principals make student success pivotal to their work and, accordingly, pay attention to and communicate about instruction, curriculum, and student mastery of learning objectives, and are visible in the school. Learning needs to occur throughout an organization, and principals need to become participants in the learning process in order to shape and encourage the implementation of effective learning models in their schools. To illustrate, effective principals don't just arrange for professional development; rather, they participate in staff training provided to their staffs. Additionally, good principals foster the idea of working together as a valuable enterprise because they understand that this kind of collaborative learning community ultimately will build trust, collective responsibility, and a schoolwide focus on improved student learning (Prestine & Nelson, 2003).

Teachers as Learners

Keeping staff informed about current research and practice and possessing a belief system that schools are learning communities are crucial to school success. Principals use a variety of staff development tools to focus awareness on research-based strategies that facilitate improved instructional effectiveness (Blase & Blase, 1999). In an effort to infuse instructional know-how across the entire faculty, the concept of an instructional leader needs to become broadened beyond that of increasing student learning. Principals also need to mobilize teachers' energy and capacities. This requires a transformation of the learning cultures of schools—a capacity in which effective principals are adept (Fullan, 2002).

To summarize, principals—that is, effective principals—support instructional activities and programs by modeling expected behaviors and consistently prioritizing instructional concerns day-to-day. They strive to become a learner among learners. Involvement in curriculum, instruction, and assessment are crucial to the idea of instructional leadership. As part of their ongoing instructional leadership responsibilities, effective school principals are highly visible through contact and interaction with teachers, students, and parents, thus promoting the concept of a learning community (Marzano et al., 2005).

Particular features of effective principals and their role in leading the learning community include the following:

- Effective principals tend to the learning of all members of a school community (Lashway, 2003).
- Effective principals also serve as participatory learners with their staffs (Prestine & Nelson, 2003).
- Successful instructional leaders provide conditions through staff development that incorporate study of professional literature and successful programs, demonstration and practice of new skills, peer coaching, and use of action research focused on student data, and they study the effect of new strategies on students (Blase & Blase, 1999).
- Instructional leadership requires a broader view that incorporates the expertise of teachers (Fullan, 2002).
- Schools that work (i.e., that are successful by various measures) have leadership that provides meaningful staff development (Marzano et al., 2005).

Using Data to Make Instructional Decisions

Data sources inform and guide action, or at least they should. Without meaningful data it is impossible to monitor and evaluate the effectiveness of school initiatives. Effective principals skillfully gather information that determines how well a school organization is meeting goals and use that information to refine strategies designed to meet or extend the goals. Thus, they find themselves in a constant state of analysis, reflection, and refinement. They challenge their staff to reexamine assumptions about their work and how it can be performed. Beyond the ability to successfully gather and analyze school data, principals need to possess basic skills for using these data for setting directions, developing people, and reinventing the organization. The use of appropriate data helps to maintain a consistent focus on improving teaching and learning, and, consequently, effective principals accept no excuses for lack of success to improve student learning (Leithwood & Riehl, 2003).

Many proponents of school improvement stress the importance of data-driven decision making. Today, school districts collect demographic, achievement, instructional, and perceptual data in an effort to improve teaching and learning. For example, information is gathered to diagnose student learning and to prescribe interventions that will best support students in need (Education Commission of the States, 2002). At the building level it is vital that principals employ data-gathering processes to determine staff and student needs.

The demands that accompany high-stakes testing compel principals to guide their schools to learn from their results and experiences. Doing so will lead to coherence within a school and offer better opportunities to sustain results. Additionally, continuous improvement requires principals to examine data and find means to address inconsistencies with expected results (Fullan, 2005).

Useful and properly mined data can inform staff about the gaps between desired outcomes and the reality of the results. Furthermore, this knowledge should result in changes in practice. Encouraging staff to collect, analyze, and determine appropriate actions based upon the results should be a collective enterprise. When staff members assume an active role in the data analysis process, it promotes solutions and actions for improving results (Zmuda et al., 2004), and facilitating the active involvement of all staff in information gathering and analysis is the prerogative of the principal.

A summary of key indicators of the role of effective principals and gathering and using data in their schools is listed on the next page:

- Effective school leaders skillfully gather data and use them to determine school effectiveness (Leithwood & Riehl, 2003).
- Continuous improvement requires an examination of the data (Fullan, 2005).
- Greater results are achieved when principals encourage school staff to actively analyze data for improving results (Zmuda et al., 2004).

Related Resources: Brimijoin, Marquisse, & Tomlinson, 2003; Guskey, 2003; Marzano, 2003; Parsons, 2003; Schmoker, 2003.

Monitoring Curriculum and Instruction

There are good reasons to focus on school leadership. The importance of the principal's role has never been greater, taking into consideration national accountability standards for schools and the likelihood that principal job vacancies will increase in the near future. Not only do effective principals focus attention on curriculum and teaching, they also understand teaching and possess credibility in the eyes of their staff (Mazzeo, 2003). Schmoker (2006) suggested that too often school cultures discourage close scrutiny of instruction. He says that effective leaders can raise the level of importance by looking for evidence that curriculum standards are taught through the review of formative assessments, grade books, team lesson logs, and student work.

Principals support instructional activities and programs by modeling expected behaviors, participating in staff development (as noted earlier), and consistently prioritizing instructional concerns on a day-to-day basis. They strive to protect instructional time by removing issues that would detract teachers from their instructional responsibilities (Marzano et al., 2005). Moreover, principals in effective schools are involved in instruction and work to provide resources that keep teachers focused on student achievement. They are knowledgeable about curriculum and instruction and promote teacher reflection about instruction and its effect on student achievement (Cotton, 2003).

Visiting Classrooms

Principals build trust by supporting and nurturing teacher development by providing feedback that helps teachers to improve. This is more likely to occur when principals exercise the collegiality of leadership. Additionally, principals are in the best position to help teachers improve in areas of weakness and can accomplish this through observations and dialogue that shows respect for teachers as professionals (Cooper, Ehrensal, & Bromme, 2005). Ultimately, many principals spend too little time in classrooms or analyzing instruction with teachers. It is important to evaluate the quality of teaching in order to select and retain good teachers, which is discussed in more depth in Chapter 3. Principals must develop leadership skills that help them to build the intellectual capital that is necessary to make good curriculum choices, establish expectations for student work, and provide teachers with opportunities to learn the specifics of teaching well within their academic areas. As such, leadership skills and knowledge of instruction must be tied together (Fink & Resnick, 2001).

Monitoring the Curriculum

Some educators believe that if a school organization is not meeting curriculum expectations established by state and local policymakers, the problem is leadership. Principals must monitor how the curriculum is taught and participate in how it is developed. The knowledge that principals gain through this process can ensure that teachers understand the curriculum and have access to all the necessary tools and resources. They then can hold teachers, students, and themselves responsible for the results (Ruebling, Stow, Kayona, & Clarke, 2004). Not only do principals need adequate knowledge and skill to assess teacher performance, they also need a sense of self-efficacy that they can do so successfully. This is especially important when principals are faced with removing ineffective teachers. Knowing what is important about good teaching is different from the ability to use that knowledge well in stressful situations such as teacher removal. To do so successfully requires that principals are confident in their ability not only to assess the quality and effectiveness of teachers but also to take the necessary actions when instruction is weak (Painter, 2000). Evaluating teachers is addressed in more depth in Chapter 4. Existing research related to the role of the principal and monitoring curriculum and instruction indicates the following:

- Effective principals possess knowledge of the curriculum and good instructional practices (Cotton, 2003) and, subsequently, focus their attention in their schools on curriculum and instruction (Mazzeo, 2003).
- Effective principals monitor the implementation of curriculum standards and make sure they are taught (Schmoker, 2006).

- Effective principals model behaviors that they expect of school staff (Marzano et al., 2005).
- Principals are in a good position to support teacher effectiveness through observations and conversations with teachers (Cooper et al., 2005).
- Principals need to spend time in classrooms in order to effectively monitor and encourage curriculum implementation and quality instructional practices (Fink & Resnick, 2001; Pajak & McAfee, 1992; Ruebling et al., 2004).
- Teachers and principals feel it is important to have someone to steer the curriculum and prioritize staff development (Portin et al., 2003).
- Teachers too frequently view classroom observations as a means to satisfy contractual obligations rather than as a vehicle for improvement and professional growth (Cooper et al., 2005).
- In effective schools, principals are able to judge the quality of teaching and share a deep knowledge of instruction with teachers (Fink & Resnick, 2001).
- An effective leader promotes coherence in the instructional program where teachers and students follow a common curriculum framework (Leithwood & Riehl, 2003).
- Effective principals trust teachers to implement instruction effectively, but they also monitor instruction with frequent classroom visits to verify the results (Portin et al., 2003).

Related Resources: Armstrong, 2007; Wise, 2001.

A Final Word on the Power of Positive Instructional Leadership

Nothing in the principal's role is more important for ensuring successful student learning than effective instructional leadership. School principals who focus on a vision for their schools nurture the leadership capabilities of their teachers. Additionally, if their schools are moving in the right direction, they model effective leading and learning. Combining these efforts with using data appropriately, as well as monitoring what takes place at the classroom level, will increase the likelihood that schools will achieve their goals for student learning.

Figure 1.1 Key References for Instructional Leadership

Reference	Building a Vision	Sharing Leadership	Leading a Learning Community	Gathering Data	Monitoring Curriculum and Instruction
Armstrong, 2007					•
Blase & Blase, 1999		•	•		
Brimijoin et al., 2003				•	
Cooper et al., 2005					•
Cotton, 2003	•	•			•
Danielson, 2007		•			
Donaldson, 2007		•			
Dozier, 2007		•			
Education Commission of the States, 2002				•	
Fink & Resnick, 2001					•
Fullan, 2002			•		
Fullan, 2005				•	
Guskey, 2003		•		•	
Hallinger et al., 1996		•			
Hallinger & Heck, 1996		•			
Hargreaves & Fink, 2003		•			
Harris, 2007	•	•			
Harrison & Killion, 2007		•			
Kyrtheotis & Pashiardis, 1998b		•	•		
Lashway, 2003	•		•		
Leithwood et al., 2004		•			
Leithwood & Riehl, 2003	•			•	•
Lieberman & Friedrich, 2007		•			•
Manasse, 1985	•				
Marks & Printy, 2003		•			

Reference	Building a Vision	Sharing Leadership	Leading a Learning Community	Gathering Data	Monitoring Curriculum and Instruction
Marzano, 2003				•	
Marzano et al., 2005	•		•		•
Mazzeo, 2003					•
Mendel et al., 2002		•			
Painter, 2000					•
Pajak & McAfee, 1992					•
Parsons, 2003				•	•
Portin et al., 2003	•				
Prestine & Nelson, 2003			•		•
Reason & Reason, 2007		•		•	•
Ruebling et al., 2004					•
Schmoker, 2003				•	
Schmoker, 2006					•
Shen & Hsieh, 1999	•				
Tucker & Tschannen-Moran, 2002		•			
Wade & Ferriter, 2007		•			•
Wise, 2001	•				•
Zmuda et al., 2004				•	

Figure 1.1 **Key References for Instructional Leadership, cont.**

2

School Climate:
The Heart of the School

In preparation for development of their new school improvement plan, the school community and staff at Webber Elementary were required to conduct a school climate survey. The newly appointed principal, Helen Roberts, curious about the school climate factors at Webber, asked parents and staff at the monthly PTA board meeting to share their feelings on the topic. Parents commented that Webber was well-known for its excellent teachers and that parents felt welcome at the school. Another parent shared that her family had moved to the neighborhood because of the school's excellent academic reputation. Teachers responded that they felt supported and worked as a team. Several parents inquired about the steadily increasing student enrollment of the school, and whether growth would affect the learning environment and school safety. Helen thanked the group members for their comments, acknowledging that the school's positive climate and its culture of mutual respect and continual improvement would help ease the anticipated challenges that growth would bring.

It has often been said that one can tell the climate of a school simply by entering the building. How does the school feel? Are the school's vision, mission, and priorities clearly demonstrated? Do administrators and staff efficiently ensure that effective teaching and learning are taking place? Are members of the school community treated with respect? Is there a sense of pride in the school? Do staff members and stakeholders work as a team, a professional learning community? What level of community involvement is evident? When all is said and done, is there a sense that this school is a great place to learn and work? These and many other factors coexist to form the climate of a school. This chapter addresses the role of the effective principal relative to school climate. In particular, we address the following issues, in turn:

- The principal's role in fostering and sustaining school climate
- Internal and external dynamics at work in the school
- The importance of high expectations and respect
- School climate, conflict, and crisis management
- School climate and shared decision making

Figure 2.1, at the end of the chapter, indicates key references for these issues about school climate.

The Principal's Role in Fostering and Sustaining School Climate

Formally, school climate refers to the social and working relationships of staff and administrators. It is the school's collective personality or atmosphere (Deal & Kennedy, 1983), including student and staff behaviors that help or inhibit teaching and learning, or instructional climate (Hallinger, Bickman, & Davis, 1996). Because school climate affects teacher productivity, the instructional quality received by students may be affected (Villani, 1997). Likewise, the climate of a school affects its culture, or the belief system and manner in which tasks are accomplished—"the way we do things around here." Understandably, one of the more difficult tasks of the school leader is to change the prevailing culture of a school (Barth, 2002). As we consider the qualities of effective principals, we need to be able to answer the question: How do effective principals foster a positive school climate and culture with high expectations for student learning?

The Relationship Between the Principal and School Climate

It is well-established that there is a relationship between school leadership and climate, and that climate is a factor related to school effectiveness (Hallinger et al., 1996; Marzano et al., 2005). Although it may be possible for school leaders to enable school success without establishing a productive and academically rigorous climate in the short term, long-term sustainability is unlikely. Consequently, the effective school leader's role in relation to fostering and sustaining a positive school climate

- Involves students, staff, parents, and the community to create and sustain a positive and safe learning environment (Cotton, 2003).

- Uses knowledge of the social, cultural, leadership, and political dynamics of the school community to cultivate a positive learning environment (Piltch & Fredericks, 2005).
- Models high expectations and respect for students, staff, parents, and the community (Cotton, 2003; Council of Chief State School Officers, 2002; Harris & Lowery, 2002).
- Develops and implements a plan that manages conflict and crisis situations in an effective and timely manner (Cornell & Sheras, 1998; United States Department of Education, 2006).
- Utilizes shared decision making to maintain positive school morale (Fink & Resnick, 2001; Leithwood & Riehl, 2003).

Stakeholder Involvement in School Climate

In creating a positive and safe learning environment, the effective school leader involves the entire school community—students, staff, parents, central office personnel, and community members. Such a network of collaboration has the potential to strengthen the school in multiple ways through support of teaching and learning, by providing financial and volunteer resources, and by encouraging active involvement of students in the school and community, among many other benefits. It is essential, however, that this collaboration is focused on the right work—that which supports the vision and mission of the school (Marzano et al., 2005). The role of the school leader, therefore, is to ensure that relationships are established that promote focused and desirable outcomes (Fullan, 2001). Therefore, when others become part of a collaborative school effort, time is spent in discussion of school goals and norms to reach consensus on what will be done and how it will be accomplished. This process may require vigilance on the part of the school leader to redirect efforts that stray from the school's essential goals while acknowledging appreciation for time and effort spent and the input of others.

The importance of stakeholder involvement in school success is well documented. Cotton (2003) includes parent and community outreach as one of 26 essential traits of effective principals; parents and others in the community are viewed as valuable sources of input and assistance. Meta-analysis of school leadership research by Marzano and colleagues (2005) cite the building of professional relationships between school leaders and staff as a crucial administrative responsibility. A study of school administrators in

Cyprus confirmed the importance of positive parent-school relations as one of 10 factors evident in successful school leadership (Kythreotis & Pashiartis, 1998b). In essence, the effective principal demonstrates understanding that efforts to make interpersonal connections with students, staff, parents, and community members will pay large dividends in establishing a positive and productive school environment.

How does the school leader form these interpersonal bonds, and what are the benefits? Some examples include the following:

- Greeting students and parents by name creates validation.
- Listening attentively builds trust.
- Seeking the assistance of local scout troops, church groups, and athletic associations encourages positive community relations; groups can assist in school projects such as clean-up and beautification efforts at the school.
- Encouraging volunteerism creates potential benefits in student achievement, school safety, or other important areas within the school.
- Attending team or department meetings demonstrates interest and affirmation of teachers' work.
- Participating in parent conferences provides evidence of focus on student achievement, care for students, and willingness to address parent and teacher concerns.
- Showing interest in the personal lives and activities of teachers and support staff builds trust.
- Recognizing student and staff accomplishments encourages pride in performance and achievement.
- Being visible in the building shows interest and involvement in instruction and school activities.
- Holding orientation sessions for new students builds trust with families unfamiliar with the school.
- Providing necessary resources to staff to meet desired ends establishes credibility.
- Giving written feedback to staff in response to their efforts demonstrates appreciation, allowing two-way communication.
- Writing positive comments on student report cards and progress reports allows the leader to show interest in student work and achievement and builds trust with parents and pride in students.

Key Research Findings

- There is a positive relationship between school climate and leadership, which affects overall school effectiveness (Barth, 2002; Hallinger et al., 1996; Marzano et al., 2005; Villani, 1997).
- Attempting to change the prevailing culture of a school is one of the more difficult tasks of the school leader (Barth, 2002; Fullan, 2001).
- Relationship building and stakeholder involvement are of fundamental importance in establishing and sustaining school success (Cotton, 2003; Fullan, 2001; Kythreotis & Pashiartis, 1998b; Marzano et al., 2005).

Related Resources: Barth, 2002; Cotton, 2003; Deal & Kennedy, 1983; Fink & Resnick, 2003; Fullan, 2001; Hallinger, Bickman, & Davis, 1996; Kythreotis & Pashiardis, 1998a; Leithwood & Riehl, 2003; Marzano et al., 2005; Piltch & Fredericks, 2005; United States Department of Education, 2006; Villani, 1997.

Internal and External Dynamics at Work in the School

The successful administrator understands the importance of the social, cultural, political, and leadership factors in creating and sustaining a positive school climate. In an era of rapid change, it is imperative that leaders adapt and guide others through the change process while developing other school leaders. Through cultural change principals help create a school climate and culture that is conducive to learning (Fullan, 2002). According to research summarized by Kouzes and Posner (2002), a learning climate characterized by trust and openness is the foundation for any successful organizational change effort.

Establishing a Climate of Trust

There is one thing that is common to every individual, relationship, team, family, organization, nation, economy, and civilization throughout the world—one thing which, if removed, will destroy the most powerful government, the most successful business, the most thriving economy, the most influential leadership. . . . That one thing is trust. (Covey, 2006, p. 1)

Trust, in any relationship—organizational or individual—is absolutely indispensable to success. Without this simplest of ingredients in human interactions, we are bound for failure. Thus, it seems abundantly clear that school leaders have a responsibility to model and foster trust in the school setting. The issue of trust and professionalism is addressed in Chapter 7.

There are numerous facets of trust, including benevolence, openness, reliability, competence, and honesty (Tschannen-Moran, 2004), and in order to have credibility, school administrators must first demonstrate these qualities. Take honesty, for example. A worldwide survey that asked participants to name the most important qualities for leaders consistently revealed four factors that received over 50 percent of the vote—honest, competent, forward-looking, and inspiring (Kouzes & Posner, 2002). Of these, honesty has been identified as the single most important factor in the relationship of leader and constituents. Because of the principal's power to influence relationships in the school, the successful leader establishes and maintains a culture of trust by demonstrating honesty on a daily basis through words and actions (Tschannen-Moran, 2004). Subsequently, maintaining trust allows ongoing relationship-building between the leader and constituents, improving school climate as well as providing the foundation of trust necessary to permit the inevitable changes that will occur in schools. As Fullan (2002) stated:

> The single most important factor common to successful change is that relationships improve. If relationships improve, schools get better. If relationships remain the same or get worse, ground is lost. (p. 17)

How do effective school leaders demonstrate honesty and credibility, inspiring the trust of others? The old adage that actions speak louder than words is particularly applicable; leadership behaviors provide the evidence of a connection between the values and ethics of leaders and actual practices (Kouzes & Posner, 2002). Some of the ways that leaders demonstrate their sincerity include

- Listening to others (Fullan, 2001; Kouzes & Posner, 2002).
- Seeking input from stakeholders (Marzano et al., 2005).
- Doing what they say they will do (Kouzes & Posner, 2002).
- Ongoing visibility and participation in school activities and operations (Cotton, 2003; Marzano et al., 2005).
- Diagnosing the needs of the individual school and school community and seeking resources to address needs (Cotton, 2003; Marzano et al., 2005; Portin et al., 2003).
- Respecting existing school and community cultures and traditions (Cotton, 2003; Portin et al., 2003).
- Decision making based on student safety and achievement above all else (Cotton, 2003; Marzano et al., 2005).

- Understanding areas of change needed in the school (Fullan, 2002; Marzano et al., 2005).
- Not tolerating ineffective teaching (Fullan, 2005; Fullan, Bertani, & Quinn, 2004; Mendro, 1998), ensuring that "the right people are on the bus and in the right seats" and "the wrong people get off the bus" (Collins, 2001).
- Demonstrating confidence in school staff to assist in problem solving and leadership capacities (Cotton, 2003; Marzano et al., 2005; Spillane et al., 2001).
- Remaining current with best practices in education (Boris-Schacter & Merrifield, 2000; Kouzes & Posner, 2002).
- Supporting staff as professionals and as individuals (Cotton, 2003; Fullan, 2001; Portin et al., 2003).

It is not enough to communicate an inspiring vision; leaders must "walk the talk," modeling the importance of their beliefs. Of course, this will be insufficient if there is lack of evidence regarding the competency of the school leader. Every administrator brings his or her track record to the school—a knowledge base and the ability to effectively get things done while encouraging the leadership potential of others (Kouzes & Posner, 2002). Likewise, leaders must demonstrate that there are legitimate reasons for their actions and that these will contribute to the continual improvement of the school. Without establishing the ethical and moral reasoning behind decisions, or moral purpose (Fullan, 2001), there is little reason for stakeholder buy-in and support.

Navigating School Challenges

One of the more daunting challenges faced by school leaders may be navigating the political waters that influence the school—the ongoing and often competing demands of parents, community, school boards, central office, staff, and even students. While charged with adherence to school board policies, administrators must also be responsive to their school communities in a wide variety of situations. These may include student or staff disciplinary actions, enforcement of school attendance zone boundaries, equitably handling building rental with community or faith groups, responding to curriculum concerns of stakeholders, enforcement of policies for handling religious observations, and many more. In some cases, issues may force the principal into conflict management situations between stakeholders (e.g., a parent angry with a teacher, a teacher claiming injury from a student, or a community member concerned about a school or school board policy).

The effective school leader is prepared to handle difficult or challenging circumstances as a result of ongoing situational awareness. Situational awareness is one of 21 research-based leadership responsibilities described in the meta-analytic research of Marzano and colleagues (2005), and the responsibility with the highest correlation ($r = .33$) to student academic achievement. Thus, the effective school leader recognizes that continued awareness of the school environment is a crucial factor in school success. Such a leader maintains constant attention to the numerous details, relationships, and potential areas of conflict within the school and is proactive in addressing them. In fact, successful leaders not only are able to manage conflict but also view challenges as opportunities for growth (Boris-Schacter & Merrifield, 2000). They learn from their failures as well as from their successes and create a framework for positive relationships and trust among members of the school community (Tschannen-Moran, 2004).

The Effect of Internal and External Dynamics

At best, situations involving conflict may create stress and absorb valuable administrative time; at worst, they may result in administrators leaving the profession—whether by choice or not. A qualitative study examined the exit of 12 principals during the 2003 school year, three of whom had left voluntarily and nine of whom had left involuntarily. Participants cited several significant areas of political or cultural difficulty that they did not miss after leaving the position, including

- School culture issues (e.g., difficulty working with faculty members who were resistant to change).
- Workload (e.g., time spent on the job and attending school functions).
- Bureaucracy (e.g., central office mandates and dealing with legal issues).
- Student discipline and parent confrontations (e.g., time-consuming and sometimes hostile interpersonal issues) (Johnson, 2005).

Recommendations resulting from the study include (1) adjustment of the degree of accountability expected of principals as compared to the relative lack of influence, (2) redistribution or reduction of principal workloads, (3) increased effort to reduce principal isolation, and (4) improvement of principal internship experiences to better prepare school leaders (Johnson, 2005). Similarly, recommendations for anticipating and managing school political factors provided by former principals include the following:

- Communicate and provide staff training in school district policies and procedures.
- Create and follow consistent and equitable disciplinary procedures.
- Observe classes regularly.
- Provide regular communication with teacher, parent, and community groups.
- Demonstrate honesty.
- Designate and communicate who will act in the principal's absence.
- Maintain opportunities for open communication.
- Provide timely notification regarding significant school situations (Piltch & Fredericks, 2005, pp. 12–13).

Key Research Findings

- Establishing a climate of trust is essential in promoting organizational change (Kouzes & Posner, 2002; Tschannen-Moran, 2004).
- In order to inspire the confidence of others, leaders must first demonstrate honesty and credibility (Cotton, 2003; Kouzes & Posner, 2002; Tschannen-Moran, 2004).
- Continual monitoring of internal and external factors affecting the school—situational awareness—is the responsibility of school leaders that has the highest relationship to student achievement (Marzano et al., 2005).

Related Resources: Boris-Schacter & Merrifield, 2000; Collins, 2001; Cotton, 2003; Fullan, 2002; Fullan, 2005; Fullan, Bertani, & Quinn, 2004; Johnson, 2005; Kouzes & Posner, 2002; Marzano et al., 2005; Piltch & Fredericks, 2005; Portin et al., 2003 Tschannen-Moran, 2004.

The Importance of High Expectations and Respect

The ability of the school leader to establish a learning environment based on high expectations and respect for all is critical. In a survey of 123 teachers enrolled in a university principal preparation program, teachers listed the following principal behaviors as most valuable in establishing a positive school climate:

- Respect for students
- Communication with students
- Support of students (Harris & Lowery, 2002, pp. 64–65)

Specific behaviors noted were treating students fairly, frequent interaction and encouragement, advocacy for students, and providing students with a safe and secure learning environment. Cotton (2003) confirmed that caring and love for children are essential principal traits necessary for a positive school climate.

In addition, respect and recognition of staff, parents, and members of the school community are important factors in school success. Regardless of school demographic conditions, the principal sets the expectation of success for all students—no matter what it takes. Staff, parents, and community members are partners in school success; without the active involvement of stakeholders, administrators will likely find it difficult to meet school goals. Such involvement creates success through shared commitment and purpose with others rather than top-down leadership mandates. This is particularly important in areas such as enforcement of student attendance and discipline policies and procedures, both of which are related to academic achievement. While the type of leadership may vary depending on the school context, a study of three elementary school leadership styles—directive, nondirective, and collaborative—revealed that schools were rated higher in the area of school climate when principals used a collaborative leadership style (Mendel, Watson, & MacGregor, 2002). Thus, involvement of the school community—or lack of it—has important implications for school climate. This, in turn, is likely to affect the long-term success, or sustainability, of school reform efforts.

Various reviews of existing research have led to the conclusion that the influence of principals on student achievement is indirect in nature (see, for example, Hallinger & Heck, 1996; Leithwood & Riehl, 2003). There is evidence, however, that principals play a major role in shaping teacher attitudes toward student learning and that principal involvement influences student opportunity to learn (Hallinger et al., 1996). Thus, at the core of the principal's role is the ability to provide direction and influence others (Leithwood & Riehl, 2003). Yet, school leaders also support staff members by demonstrating concern and care for their personal needs (Leithwood & Riehl, 2003). In short, the effective school leader demonstrates an ethic of care with students, staff, and those in the school community.

Key Research Findings

- Respect, support, and caring for students are essential leadership responsibilities that positively affect school climate (Cotton, 2003; Harris & Lowery, 2002).
- Although the effect of school leadership is indirect in relation to student achievement, principals shape teacher attitudes and influence student opportunities to learn (Hallinger et al., 1996; Hallinger & Heck, 1996; Leithwood & Riehl, 2003).
- A collaborative leadership style is related to positive school climate (Mendel et al., 2002).

Related Resources: Cotton, 2003; Hallinger et al., 1996; Hallinger & Heck, 1996; Harris & Lowery, 2002; Leithwood & Riehl, 2003; Mendel et al., 2002.

School Climate, Conflict, and Crisis Management

No school is immune from conflict and crisis, whether it originates within or outside the school. The range of possible incidents may include disputes or health and safety issues among students, staff members, parents, and visitors attending school functions. Other incidents may include injury or death of persons in the school community, child custody situation, weather-related emergencies, and even problems in the community that affect school safety. When such situations arise, school leaders must respond quickly and effectively to manage the impact on those in the school community. The effective school leader remains informed of possible internal and external concerns and is proactive in establishing and implementing a school plan to address them. A common mistake of school personnel is to respond in a reactive mode (United States Department of Education, 2006). While it may be impossible to anticipate every type of emergency or conflict, a thorough crisis management plan—with roles assigned to school personnel—is essential.

In addition to development of a school crisis plan, the manner in which the plan is implemented is equally important. Leadership, teamwork, and responsibility are critical elements of a successful plan (Cornell & Sheras, 1998). Contact information for community resources such as police, safety resource officers assigned to schools, fire department personnel, and psychological and social services departments may prove invaluable during emergency situations and should be readily available to school administrators and personnel. When crisis situations arise, the appropriate emergency personnel should be contacted immediately, followed by communication to central office personnel in the school district. Also, it is important to have current emergency contact information for students and staff in a secure location, readily available to administrators and office staff. School staff must receive ongoing guidelines for handling emergency situations beyond routine safety drills, including how to respond to media inquiries. Basic recommendations for school crises and emergencies are

- Regular review and revision of crisis plans.
- Assignment of administrators to accessible locations.
- Creation of a school Incident Command Center (ICS).
- Maintenance of communication devices.
- Evacuation and reunification procedures.
- Parent and community debriefings following an incident. (United States Department of Education, 2006, pp. 3–5)

After an incident has occurred, review and discussion by crisis team members and administrators is essential, with any necessary revisions added to the school crisis plan. Parents and community members may ask for additional information regarding the events that took place, how the situation was handled, and explanation of future ways to address such incidents. School administrators may need to reassure those in the school community, listening to and addressing concerns while protecting the confidentiality of those who may have been involved. Office personnel may need guidelines from administrators regarding appropriate response to public inquiry that may occur within the school or by telephone. In some cases, written communication to parents is advisable to prevent fear and inaccurate speculation following a school incident. This communication may be quite simple in nature, such as a memo from school administrators indicating that *an incident occurred at or near school today; administrators and staff handled the incident involving other resources as appropriate; all involved are safe; and any additional information will be sent as needed.*

Above all, students, staff, parents, and community members want to know that there is a culture and climate of safety in the school. If parents are concerned that their children may be at risk of harm, they are likely to react with fear and anger after a school emergency (Cornell & Sheras, 1998). Effective school leaders are aware of the multiple sources of potential conflict and emergency within their school settings and are proactive in crisis planning. They involve other appropriate individuals and resources, communicate effectively, and strive to maintain a positive and safe school climate.

Key Research Findings

- Effective school leaders are proactive rather than reactive in establishing and using safety and crisis management plans (Cornell & Sheras, 1998; United States Department of Education, 2006).
- Parents and community members should be kept informed of school safety issues, understand how incidents are handled, and be reassured that their children are not at risk of harm in the school setting (Cornell & Sheras, 1998).

Related Resources: Cornell & Sheras, 1998; United States Department of Education, 2006.

School Climate and Shared Decision Making

Examination of the principal's role over the past century reveals an evolution from school manager to instructional leader. In practice, however, the multitude of managerial and leadership responsibilities required of principals makes balancing both roles difficult. Few principals, according to Fink and Resnick (2001), are able to act as true instructional leaders when their time is spent in multiple managerial tasks, crises, and the unique situations that arise in schools. The result is a trend toward shared decision making within the school, discarding the role of the omniscient leader and replacing it with one of the facilitative learner (Boris-Schacter & Merrifield, 2000). When leaders are able to delegate and distribute authority and develop a trusting relationship with staff members, a paradox of power results in which leaders become more powerful as they give power away (Kouzes & Posner, 2002).

Developing Shared Leadership

The topic of shared decision making has been described by others with a number of terms, including distributed leadership. In this relatively recent concept of leadership, traditional administrative functions are spread throughout the organization, thus creating multiple leaders within the school. The school, then, rather than the administrator, becomes the unit of analysis in developing leadership expertise (Spillane et al., 2001). In other words, leaders matter, but they are not all that matters.

Providing that leadership areas are effectively addressed, these functions may be distributed among many capable individuals within the school. In a study of 21 Chicago schools, seven critical areas of leadership were evident:

managerial, cultural, instructional, human resources, strategic, external development, and micropolitical (Portin et al., 2003). The leadership role of the principal was to ensure that these areas were performed; whether they were performed by the principal or shared among others was a secondary consideration.

When staff members collaborate and take ownership of tasks in these areas, ownership of problem solving and decision making resides with a team rather than remaining solely the responsibility of school leaders. Most significantly, development of multiple leaders promotes sustainability, allowing the established belief system and practices of the school to endure beyond the tenure of one leader. In the end, the success of the leader is determined not by student learning outcomes alone, but by the number of others who remain and can go beyond what has already been accomplished (Fullan et al., 2004).

There are likely as many examples of shared leadership as there are schools. The common factor, however, is acknowledgment that one leader—or administrative team—simply cannot do it all. In an effective model of shared leadership, a core part of the principal's work is to serve as a diagnostician and facilitator, identifying school issues and available resources (Portin et al., 2003). While not relinquishing responsibility, the school leader promotes others, builds relationships, and encourages group decision making. Cotton (2003) refers to this behavior as "shared leadership/decision-making and staff empowerment" (p. 69), whereas Marzano, Waters, and McNulty (2005) describe this principal responsibility as "input" (p. 82).

The effective school leader consistently promotes shared leadership in numerous ways (e.g., encouraging teachers to serve as staff development trainers, conducting team review of instructional data, and facilitating group decision making regarding students who are not meeting with academic success). Above all, shared leadership becomes a trust relationship in which leaders provide ongoing opportunities for staff input and allow flexibility in how tasks are accomplished. Providing choices is a powerful catalyst in enabling others to act. As Kouzes and Posner (2002) summarized: "People can't lead and make a difference unless they have a choice" (p. 290).

The need for shared or distributed leadership is evident in one study of Virginia principals that cited two highly significant organizational management problems as (1) working with parents (88 percent), and (2) handling nonacademic student behaviors (85 percent) (Tucker & Tschannen-Moran,

2002). In practice, these two areas alone could account for the majority of working hours spent by a school administrator, leaving minimal time for instructional matters. If, however, ownership for parent questions and concerns regarding instructional issues consistently begins with classroom teachers, administrators become more available to address issues beyond the classroom. Likewise, office staff may prove invaluable in routing phone calls and inquiries to the appropriate source, allowing greater availability of administrators to monitor instruction. When considering student placement, teachers are able to provide a wealth of information regarding student skills and can assist in developing class rolls as well as determining those in need of acceleration or additional instructional assistance. Because of their in-depth instructional expertise, teachers are also excellent sources of information when developing a school master schedule or when making decisions regarding standardized assessments. The development of these—and many more—forms of shared leadership enables the school to move from a traditional hierarchical form of leadership to one in which there is group responsibility for the success of all students.

Creating Professional Learning Communities

Ideally, the end result of shared leadership can enable educators to move beyond school management tasks and move toward professional collaboration focused on student learning—a professional learning community. Those in the professional learning community focus on shared values and commitments regarding responsibility for student learning rather than placing the sole focus on teaching (DuFour, 2004). The role of the school leader, then, is to facilitate and protect the school vision and values, challenging actions or behaviors that are inconsistent with those values (Eaker, DuFour, & DuFour, 2002). Because schools with a positive climate are collaborative by nature, staff may perceive that they are already functioning as a professional learning community. Collaboration and participation in shared decision making alone, however, do not necessarily equate to development of a true professional learning community. DuFour (2004) described three critical questions that must guide the work of those engaged in a professional learning community:

- What do we want each student to learn?
- How will we know when each student has learned it?
- How will we respond when a student experiences difficulty in learning? (p. 8)

A key element of the professional learning community—in comparison to a collaborative school environment—is emphasis on the word *we;* the success of students experiencing difficulty becomes the responsibility of the school community rather than the individual teacher (DuFour, 2004). School leaders and staff engage in regular dialogue regarding student learning, making changes as needed, to promote student achievement. As Reeves (2006) contends,

> . . . messy leadership—the practice of reviewing data, making midcourse corrections, and focusing decision making on the greatest points of leverage—is superior to "neat" leadership in which planning, processes, and procedures take precedence over achievement. (p. xi)

Key Research Findings

- Effective school leaders distribute administrative tasks and create multiple leaders within the school (Kouzes & Posner, 2002; Portin et al., 2003; Spillane et al., 2001).
- In an authentic model of shared leadership, the principal serves as diagnostician and facilitator, empowering staff to engage in group decision making (Cotton, 2003; Fullan et al., 2004; Marzano et al., 2005; Portin et al., 2003).
- Shared decision making ideally promotes sustainability (Fullan et al., 2004) and the development of a professional learning community (DuFour, 2004; Eaker et al., 2002).
- Collaborative and ongoing review of school progress, making changes as necessary ("messy leadership"), is preferable to "neat leadership," in which the process takes precedence over achievement (Reeves, 2006).

Related Resources: Boris-Schacter & Merrifield, 2000; DuFour, 2004; Eaker et al., 2002; Fink & Resnick, 2001; Fullan, 2002; Kouzes & Posner, 2002; Marzano et al., 2005; Portin et al., 2003; Leithwood & Riehl, 2003; Spillane et al., 2001; Tschannen-Moran, 2004.

A Final Word on the Role of the Principal in School Climate

Review of the literature over the past quarter century reveals that effective school leadership *does* matter. While the influence of leadership may be primarily indirect in nature, a statistically significant relationship

($p<.01$)[1] exists between "principal leadership and school climate variables" (Hallinger et al., 1996, p. 543). When the principal establishes a clear mission and facilitates a positive school climate, there is a positive impact on teaching and learning (Hallinger et al., 1996).

In an era of rapid change, the effective school leader recognizes the desirability of involving stakeholders in school decision making. This represents a new paradigm, in which the principal is no longer a larger-than-life figure, tackling the challenges of school leadership alone (Marks & Printy, 2003, Tschannen-Moran, 2004). As Reeves (2006) confirmed, "the prevailing leadership mythology that generally embraces the unitary 'heroic' leadership model is unsustainable, unsupportable, and dangerous to individual and organizational health" (p. xi). Instead, through shared decision making with those in the school community, a culture of mutual responsibility is established to ensure student success. The effective school leader helps create a shared vision and mission, cultivates a culture of trust, focuses on the right work, and develops other leaders within the school to promote sustainability.

While the needs of schools may vary, creating a need for differing types of leadership in different contexts, the importance of a safe and positive learning environment in all schools remains critical to school success. The school leader sets the tone for, nurtures, and sustains such an environment. In order to do so, the effective school leader must consistently model honesty, credibility, and trustworthiness to inspire the commitment of others. According to Fullan (2001), this requires that the leader demonstrate moral purpose, understanding of the change process, strength in relationship building, knowledge sharing, and the ability to provide coherence. In order to build effective professional learning communities within schools, it is necessary to move beyond traditional thoughts of the school leader's role and to acknowledge that the role is multifaceted and context-dependent. As Fullan (2002) concluded:

> We need leaders who can create a fundamental transformation in the learning cultures of schools and of the teaching profession itself. The role of the principal as instructional leader is too narrow a concept to carry the weight of the kinds of reforms that will create the schools that we need for the future. (p. 17)

---

[1]There is less than a 1 percent chance this finding is due to random error; thus, the finding is likely a real one.

Figure 2.1 Key References for School Climate

Reference	Principal's Role	Internal and External Dynamics	High Expectations and Respect	Conflict and Crisis Management	Shared Decision Making
Barth, 2002	•				
Boris-Schacter & Merrifield, 2000		•			•
Charlotte Advocates for Education, 2004					
Collins, 2001		•			
Cornell & Sheras, 1998	•			•	
Cotton, 2003	•	•	•		•
Council of Chief State School Officers, 2002	•				
Covey, 2006		•			
Deal & Kennedy, 1983	•				
DuFour, 2004					•
Eaker et al., 2002					•
Fink & Resnick, 2001	•				•
Fullan, 2001	•	•			
Fullan, 2002		•			•
Fullan, 2005		•			
Fullan et al., 2004		•			•
Hallinger et al., 1996	•		•		
Hallinger & Heck, 1996			•		
Harris & Lowery, 2002	•		•		
Johnson, 2005		•			
Kouzes & Posner, 2002		•			•
Kythreotis & Pashiardis, 1998b	•				
Leithwood & Riehl, 2003	•		•		•
Marks & Printy, 2003					

(continued)

Figure 2.1 **Key References for School Climate,** *cont.*

Reference	Principal's Role	Internal and External Dynamics	High Expectations and Respect	Conflict and Crisis Management	Shared Decision Making
Marzano et al., 2005	•	•			•
Mendel et al., 2002			•		
Mendro, 1998		•			
Piltch & Fredericks, 2005	•	•			
Portin et al., 2003		•			•
Reeves, 2006					•
Spillane et al., 2001		•			•
Tschannen-Moran, 2004		•			
Tucker & Tschannen-Moran, 2002					•
United States Department of Education, 2006	•			•	
Villani, 1997	•				

3

Human Resource Administration: Selecting, Supporting, and Retaining Quality Teachers and Staff

Curtis characterizes his role of elementary school principal as that of a CEO. Believing in forging a connection with students and staff, he strives to spend half of his time in the classrooms. To meet this goal, he uses an effective division of labor, so that each member of his administrative team has an impact on instruction and a presence in the classrooms while addressing school needs. Curtis delegates zones of responsibility to his assistant principals so they can focus their efforts on particular aspects of running a school. Then he follows up with regular meetings so they will be prepared to run their own schools in the future. When interviewing for new teachers, Curtis uses a team approach that always includes at least one teacher familiar with the position being filled, an assistant principal, and himself. Then he asks effective teachers to provide the new teacher orientation so professionals can talk teacher-to-teacher and begin forging connections. Curtis says that the golden rule of human resources in school is to remember that everyone is a member of the family. People need to care about each other. Accomplishments need to be celebrated and sometimes hard truths need to be spoken and plans made to address those concerns. He truly values his staff members, and they know that they can (and they do) come to him with professional and personal concerns and accomplishments. These are just some of the ways that his "people resources" attend to the needs of the school and the profession.

Human resource administration too frequently is thought of as a responsibility that is fulfilled by a department somewhere deep in the bowels of the school district's central office. And, yet, of all the job responsibilities that principals enact, the human resource administration functions may be among the most important and cast the longest shadow over the school community. There is little more important in the life of the school than the quality of teachers and other personnel that are hired, supported, and retained, and this is precisely what human resources administration at the building level entails.

The effective school principal or assistant principal recognizes that human resource administration is fundamental to the success of the school and, thus, attends to these functions in a proactive manner. Components of the principal's human resource responsibilities include the following:

- Selecting quality teachers and other employees
- Inducting and supporting new teachers
- Mentoring novice teachers
- Providing professional growth opportunities
- Retaining quality staff

Figure 3.1, at the end of this chapter, summarizes specific elements of effective human resource administration at the building level and links these elements to key references.

Selecting Quality Teachers and Other Employees

Of course, what principals do matters inordinately in the quality of life in their schools. The time they spend at work, the cumulative interactions they have on a day-to-day and even hour-to-hour basis, the professional relationships they foster, the budget and allocating resources, and a host of other responsibilities have a powerful and lasting effect on the success of their schools. However, it isn't only a principal's direct work and involvement in the life of the school that counts; rather, it is their *indirect* effect that may be even more influential in the long term.

Hallinger and Heck (1996) found in their study of the principal's role in school effectiveness that the effects of principal leadership are most likely to occur indirectly through the principal's efforts to influence those who come into direct contact with students in the instructional setting. In other words, hiring, supporting, and retaining the best teachers—as well as other employees who have direct instructional contact with students—is the foundation of the principal's legacy on teaching and learning. The issue of the principal's indirect influence on student achievement and school success is explored in more depth in Chapter 8.

Selecting the Right Employees

Having—and exercising—the ability to select quality teachers and others is paramount to success in the business of schooling. This point is aptly made by Collins (2001) in his study of American companies that successfully transformed themselves into what he termed "great" companies:

> We expected that good-to-great leaders would begin by setting a new vision and strategy. We found instead that they *first* got the right people on the bus, the wrong people off the bus, and the right people in the right seats—and *then* they figured out where to drive it. The old adage, "People are your most important asset" turns out to be wrong. People are *not* your most important asset. The *right* people are. (p. 13)

So how do effective principals make their schools more effective? As Marzano and colleagues (2005) surmised in their meta-analysis of principal effectiveness, principals improve teaching and learning (and, consequently, school effectiveness) by surrounding themselves with the right people to do the job. More specifically, Fink and Resnick (2001) noted in their review of principals as instructional leaders, "Above all, principals are responsible for selecting and cultivating a teaching staff that is able to teach effectively. . . . He or she must be able to judge the quality of teaching in order to select and maintain good teaching staff" (p. 6). In another study of the school principalship, the researchers found that "across the board, school leaders singled out the importance of hiring and inducting teachers for their schools. As the principal of a public middle school noted, 'Getting the right staff was the key' " (Portin et al., 2003, p. 25).

It isn't just teachers that make a difference. The principal's role in selecting the right people extends to both teaching (licensed educators) and support (nonlicensed employees) staff. In their study of the principalship, Portin and colleagues (2003) found that principals talked about how important the classified staff are to the climate of the school. Additionally, paying attention to the quality of nonteaching professional staff (e.g., counselors, library and media specialists, school psychologists, school nurses) is essential. These certified or licensed professional staff members account for upward of 25 percent of the professional employees who walk through the schoolhouse door (Stronge & Tucker, 1995).

Interviewing and Teacher Selection

Stronge and Hindman (2006) developed a teacher hiring protocol—the *Teacher Quality Index* (TQI)—based on a U.S. stratified random sample of principals designed to establish content and construct validation for the interview protocol. The TQI process recommends that teacher hiring decisions be based on a thorough analysis of all applicable evidence about the candidate, including review of the applicant's credentials and recommendations, screening and building-based interviews, and performance samples (i.e., teacher demonstration of a sample lesson). Additionally, the TQI was developed explicitly to focus the building-level interview of teachers on the following key characteristics:

- Standardized questions that reflect solid content validation for the practices of effective teachers (Stronge, 2002, 2007).
- Research-based quality indicators as a means to focus the interviewer on what the teacher interviewee could be expected to say in response to a given question (Stronge, 2002, 2007).
- Space for note taking to provide a record on important points made in the interview (Burnett, Fan, Motowidlo, & DeGroot, 1998).
- A four-level scoring rubric (unsatisfactory, developing, proficient, and exemplary) to help standardize scoring of interview answers, to reduce subjectivity in scoring, and to increase inter-rater reliability among interviewers (Taylor & Small, 2002).

Although the above-noted interviewing characteristics are solidly ensconced in existing research, particularly research drawn from business and industry, these practices aren't always reflected in actual practice in school settings. A national study of interviewer practices of principals from a stratified random sample found that of 141 U.S. principals, only 38 (27 percent) had ever received formal training in teacher selection or hiring (Hindman, 2004). Instead, principals established their interview practices as hand-me-down techniques from other administrators. Moreover, "according to respondents,

interviewing background and training have little influence on their interviewing practices" (Hindman, 2004, p. 11).

This finding poses various potential problems for hiring quality teachers
and other staff, including (1) well-intentioned principals "may unknowingly
perpetuate ineffective interview habits; and (2) administrators may not be
aware of EEOC [Equal Employment Opportunity Commission] guidelines"
(Stronge & Hindman, 2006, p. 49). Furthermore, one study found that principals did not ask the questions that solicited the information they wanted
and sometimes asked illegal hiring questions (Perkins, 1998).

A study in business and industry found that when employers provide
training to interviewers using standard protocols, the interview process proves
to be more reliable and valid (Williamson et al., 1997). In school settings,
Hindman found in her national study of principal hiring practices that those
with training were statistically ($p < .05$)[1] more likely to use multiple interviewers in teacher selection, use prepared questions, and use a scoring rubric
for interview responses—all of which are research-based good practices.

If principals are to maximize the opportunity they have to improve their
schools by hiring the best staff, they must have proper training in research-
based hiring practices. Additionally, if principals are well equipped to make
thoughtful, research-informed decisions—instead of gut-level, intuitive
decisions—they will be better positioned to distinguish quality employees
from those who are not. And they will be positioned to implement the sound
advice offered by Collins (2001) in his book, *Good to Great:* "When in doubt,
don't hire—keep looking" (p. 54).

Problems with Hiring

One study revealed that private and charter schools generally had more
control over hiring and the conditions of employment than did traditional
public schools. The primary impetus for hiring in public schools was found
to be a combination of centralized personnel departments and specific
practices defined by union contracts and state codes. "Principals in traditional public schools had to rely on their ability to 'work the system.' This
included timing posted openings to ensure access to a preferred post of

---

[1]There is less than a 5 percent chance this finding is due to random error; thus, the finding is
likely a real one.

candidates" (Portin et al., 2003, p. 26). The authors noted that in several instances, public school principals negotiated special provisions with their districts to provide them with greater latitude in staffing decisions.

Peterson (2002), in his ASCD book, *Effective Teacher Hiring*, identified several common teacher hiring mistakes that principals and others are prone to make. These include

- Hirers not being trained.
- Improper hiring criteria (e.g., important attributes ignored) or criteria unrelated to the job, or emphasis on a particular style.
- Failure to adequately assess applicant's work with students.
- Over-reliance on interviews.
- Disregard of candidate's demonstrated effect on student achievement.
- Hirer prejudices left unchecked.
- Inadequate check of candidate materials.
- Inadequate follow-up of recommendations.

Without proper training (as discussed in the previous section) and evaluation of actual hiring practices, illegal questioning, as well as illegal decision making, may be more prone to occur. To illustrate, two separate studies investigated the impact of age on principals' decisions to hire physical education and physics teachers, respectively (Young, Rinehart, & Baits, 1997). The physical education teacher study included 360 principals, and the physics teacher study included 495 principals; in both studies the response rate was higher than 60 percent. In each of the studies, principals were given information about two applicants whose qualifications were the same, with the exception of adjectives used to describe the two candidates: one age 29 and the other age 49. In the case of the physics teacher, there was no significant difference in the participating principals' hiring preferences. However, in the physical education teacher study, there was a statistically significant difference with principals preferring the younger teacher—a finding suggesting possible age discrimination.

Key Research Findings

Research findings related to the issue of teacher selection note the following elements:

- Effective principal leadership has the most influence on teaching and learning indirectly, rather than directly, through the principal's efforts to influence those who come into direct contact with students in the instructional setting (Hallinger & Heck, 1996).

• Selecting capable and committed teachers is the core of the principal's human resource responsibilities (Collins, 2001; Fink & Resnick, 2001; Marzano et al., 2005; Portin et al., 2003).

• In addition to teachers, it is fundamentally important to the well-being of the school to select capable and committed nonteaching staff members (Portin et al., 2003).

• Using research-based interviewing practices in order to gain adequate information to make an appropriate decision in hiring is key to the principal's responsibility in staffing schools with the most effective teachers from the hiring pool; moreover, effective school leaders seek out training to make justified, legal decisions in the hiring process (Perkins, 1998; Peterson, 2002; Stronge & Hindman, 2006; Young et al., 1997).

• Effective school leaders know the hiring system in their school district and use the information to position themselves to gain access to the best possible candidates (Peterson, 2002; Portin et al., 2003).

Related Resources: Collins, 2001; Fink & Resnick, 2001; Hallinger & Heck, 1996; Hindman, 2004; Marzano et al., 2005; Perkins, 1998; Peterson, 2002; Portin et al., 2003; Stronge, 2002, 2007; Stronge & Hindman, 2006; Stronge & Tucker, 1995; Young et al., 1997.

Inducting and Supporting New Employees

The recent state of teacher shortages and expected attrition rates are compelling reasons for school systems to make sure they not only employ talented teachers but also find ways to support and keep them. Research suggests that approximately one-third of new teachers leave the profession within five years (Ingersoll, 2002). Based on an analysis of data available from the National Center for Education Statistics (NCES), it is estimated that approximately one-third of new teachers leave the profession during their first three years of teaching, and almost half leave within five years (Luekens, Lyter, & Fox, 2004). Moreover, 39 percent of newly prepared teachers don't teach (Darling-Hammond, 2000a) because they receive better offers, feel a lack of respect, are asked to teach outside their certification area, feel unsafe, and lose interest (Henke, Chen, & Geis, 2000). Despite regional trends, the overall picture continues to suggest that there is a shortage in teaching candidates, particularly in specialized fields such as mathematics and science, in certain geographic regions, and in schools that serve high at-risk populations in both urban and rural districts (American Association for Employment in Education, 2000; American Association of State Colleges and Universities, 2005). Thus, it seems clear that enticing capable teacher candidates to select teaching and then retaining those new teachers is particularly important to the lifeblood of schools.

Teacher induction programs generally consist of the activities and processes necessary to successfully induct a novice teacher into the teaching profession (Sweeny, 2001). Such programs were nonexistent in the early years of public education, but they became widely accepted in the mid-1980s as teaching became more complex and efforts to build collaborative learning communities were increasing (Hargreaves & Fullan, 2000). Contemporary teacher induction programs include orientation, mentoring, staff development, observations of experienced teachers at work, and peer support groups, among other components (Sweeny, 2001). In all of these endeavors, principals play an essential role in fostering and sustaining quality induction programs.

What Is Induction and Why Is It Needed?

For anyone who has been a teacher, we merely need to recall those first days—and even the first few years—of teaching experiences to affirm the necessity for large-scale, high-quality induction programs. Teaching—more precisely, *teaching effectively*—is complex work and requires, in most cases, years to fully master (see, for example, Darling-Hammond, 2000b; Education Review Office, 1998; Nye, Konstantopoulos, & Hedges, 2004). Consequently, most new teachers experience a myriad of instruction-related problems. To illustrate the magnitude of the teacher readiness problem, a Public Agenda/Wallace Foundation survey reported that 95 percent of superintendents and 87 percent of principals stated that teaching certification guarantees at best a minimum of teaching skills (cited in Johnson, 2004).

A fundamental concern for new teachers and a key reason to deploy effective induction programs is the unacceptable rate of new teacher turnover. Consider the following findings:

• In an average five-year period, 2.2 million of 3.1 million teachers will leave the profession (Marshak & Klotz, 2002).

- Depending on the source, various studies indicate that teacher attrition ranges from about one fourth to one half of all new teachers nationally and in selected states leaving the field within five years (DeAngelis & Presley, 2007; Ingersoll, 2002; Luekens et al., 2004).
- The rate is even higher for teaching fields such as special education (Bergert & Burnette, 2001; Edgar & Pair, 2005), with approximately half of all new teachers leaving the field in the first five years.
- The teacher leaving pattern is higher in high-poverty than low-poverty schools, with comparable rates of 20 percent versus 13 percent in 2000–2001 (Association of Community Organizations for Reform Now, n.d.).
- In a survey of teacher turnover, the National Center for Education Statistics (Marvel et al., 2007) estimated that in the 2004–2005 school year, approximately 16 percent of public school teachers did not continue teaching at the same school; approximately 19 percent of private school teachers did not continue (including both those leaving the profession and those moving to other schools).

Teacher turnover not only disrupts the continuity in the school but also can be costly for the school district. Regardless of the reason for leaving a school, the annual estimated national cost of public school teacher attrition is over $7.3 billion a year (National Commission on Teaching and America's Future, 2007).

Generally, induction responsibilities for the principal entail implementing formal and informal procedures to support and assist all new employees. More specifically, induction is defined as an active, two- to three-year systematic training and supporting process that focuses on the following overarching objectives:

- Objective 1: Efforts to ease the transition into teaching
- Objective 2: Improving teaching effectiveness in classroom management and instructional delivery
- Objective 3: Promoting the district's culture
- Objective 4: Increasing the teacher retention rate (Marshak & Klotz, 2002)

Clearly, retaining highly qualified teachers and helping new teachers make the transition to becoming highly effective teachers takes a whole school of willing participants who are dedicated to improving teaching and learning. Furthermore, the principal plays a central role in cultivating collective teacher efficacy and must take every opportunity to recognize teacher accomplishments.

Creating a Culture of Support

Moore-Johnson (2004), in a study of first- and second-year teachers, found that this new generation of teachers wants to be well paid in their profession, seeks a variety of roles and opportunities for advancement, and desires to collaborate and find support within a professional community. Consequently, creating and sustaining a culture of support appears essential to attract and keep the best and brightest new teachers. Portin and colleagues (2003) found in their study of the school principalship that creating a positive school climate was an essential component for school effectiveness. In the study, they noted that both principals and teachers "talked about the importance of maintaining their school's sense of tradition and tone—of fortifying the school's sense of how things get done around here" (p. 24). We suggest these findings hold true particularly for new staff. Additionally, they noted the power of empowering teachers as part of a healthy, robust school climate:

> The "A" and "B" principals [those principals denoted as high performing], however, identified the importance of not only giving information to people or turning people loose to make decisions that affect their own practice, but of developing common agendas, developing a "work/play atmosphere," and addressing problems as a team. . . . The premise behind principal empowerment is that those closest to students know the context and needs of children in their schools and, consequently, should be meaningfully involved in decision making that impacts teaching and learning. A principal, as the leader of leaders within the school, is instrumental in creating a culture that enhances collegial efforts to do what is in the best interest educationally for the children attending the school. (Reed, McDonough, Ross, & Robichaux, 2001, p. 19)

Developing people involves building the capacity of those within the school and using their strengths to support the school's efforts (Marzano et al., 2005). Additionally, Leithwood and colleagues (2004) identified specific factors important in building teacher capacity, including offering intellectual stimulation, providing individualized support, and providing best practice models. Relating this concept of capacity building specifically to

Induction, Marshak and Klotz (2002) noted that the functional support provided to novice teachers during the induction period should include numerous knowledge and skill areas, including knowledge and skills related to instruction and to an understanding of the educational system at the building, district, state, and national levels. Specifically, new teachers need assistance in

- Becoming consumers and users of assessment data, including the collection of data through valid and reliable assessments.
- Modifying instruction based on assessed needs of individual students.
- Focusing on instruction that reaches higher levels of learning, not just recall and comprehension.
- Integrating technology seamlessly into instruction.
- Delivering high-quality instruction every day.

Additionally, new teachers need to have an understanding of the cultural norms of the school and the expectations that the local community has in educating the community's children and youth. New teachers must see the education system as a whole, including how building and district initiatives support state and national standards (Marshak & Klotz, 2002).

In this collaborative and supportive vein, Cotton (2003) noted that effective principals need to create opportunities for teachers to work, plan, and learn together around instructional issues. We contend that while the collaborative culture described in this section is important for all teachers and school staff, it is paramount for new teachers as they become acclimated to the life of the school.

Key Research Findings

Numerous studies summarize the importance of inducting and supporting new employees, including the following:

- A teaching certification does not automatically translate into effective teaching practices (Johnson, 2004).
- New teachers leave the profession at an alarming rate (Luekens et al., 2004; Marshak & Klotz, 2002).
- New teachers desire learning communities in which they can grow professionally and advance (Moore-Johnson, 2004).
- A positive school climate in which teachers make their own decisions in relation to common school goals is essential to helping new teachers

develop a sense of cultural norms and traditions at the school (Portin et al., 2003; Reed et al., 2001).

- Effective school leaders build the capacity of new teachers within their school by identifying their strengths, providing support in instruction and in an understanding of the education system, and providing collaborative opportunities (Cotton, 2003; Marshak & Klotz, 2002; Marzano et al., 2005).

Related Resources: Cotton, 2003; Darling-Hammond, 2000a; Hargreaves & Fullan, 2000; Henke et al., 2000; Ingersoll, 2002; Marshak & Klotz, 2002; Marzano et al., 2005; Moore-Johnson, 2004; Portin et al., 2003; Reed et al., 2001; Sweeny, 2001.

Mentoring Novice Teachers[2]

As defined by Sweeny (2001), mentoring is the complex developmental process used to support and guide new teachers through the transitions that are a necessary part of learning how to be an effective educator and career-long learner. The process takes time—a year at the least and up to three years in some successful programs. Learning—that is, teacher learning—*is* what it is all about. Mentors, typically veteran teachers, spend time with new teachers assisting them with instructional planning and delivery, classroom management, and generally learning the ropes. Often new teachers lack the focus to make such connections as they engage in tactical planning just to get through one day at a time. Moreover, studies indicate that new teachers feel isolated and need help with classroom management and discipline (Portner, 2003). The mentoring relationship involves the sharing of such frustrations and allows for the checking of perceptions in a safe environment. Teachers and their mentors informally think through problems as well as successes (Jonson, 2002), and typically it is the principal's duty to find the right fit for this relationship.

Assuming a principal knows her staff well, she is in an ideal position to match mentors with new teachers. The reality in many schools today is that

---

[2]A portion of the section regarding teacher mentoring was originally researched and written by Ellen Turner in an unpublished paper titled, "The Principal's Role in Supporting the Mentoring Process for Novice Teachers," December 7, 2005, submitted for a Human Resources Administration graduate course at the College of William and Mary. The aspects of her work included in this section are reprinted and revised with her permission.

while assigned mentors may know more about school procedures and classroom management than new teachers, many new teachers come to school
armed with cutting edge teaching strategies unfamiliar to the veteran teacher
(Hargreaves & Fullan, 2000). The challenge then becomes to match the needs
of the new teacher or "mentee" to the strengths of the mentor (Sweeny,
2001). Even the principal who knows her staff well must reflect on what is
meant by "highly qualified" before assigning mentors.

Accepting the Beginning Teacher

The principal must balance the need to make new teachers feel welcome
while communicating high expectations for student achievement. Boreen and
colleagues (2000) suggested that principals seize opportunities to involve new
teachers in staff development or school inservice training. For example, if a
new teacher demonstrates special knowledge in the field of technology, the
principal can invite the teacher to share information informally at a meeting
or present in a planned staff development session. The new teacher's participation may lead to an increased sense of belonging and community. Other
suggestions from Boreen and colleagues (2000) included frequently addressing the new teacher by his or her first name to show acceptance and asking
specific questions of the new teacher to show interest in his or her individual
experiences. Instead of asking the teacher how things are going, the principal can ask a direct question pertaining to the students.

Beginning teachers want principals to communicate student expectations
and the criteria for good teaching. They also want principals to visit their
classrooms often as they desire affirmation about their performance (Mullen
& Lick, 1999). Feedback enhances learning, and new teachers need feedback
just as students do.

Finally, mentoring pays dividends in terms of new teacher retention.
A review of 10 studies measuring the impact of mentoring programs
across the United States and Canada found that mentoring programs do
result in a new teacher staying in the field (Ingersoll & Kralik, 2004). From
this review, researchers concluded that there is hope in the use of induction
and mentoring as a means of reducing high teacher turnover rates (Ingersoll
& Kralik, 2004). Similarly, a Rochester, New York, mentoring program for
first-year teachers increased the return rate of teachers for a second year from
69 percent in 1987 to 86 percent in 1999 (Heller, 2004). A program in

Lafourche Parish, Louisiana, reduced the teacher dropout rate from 51 percent to 15 percent directly after implementation of the program (Wong, 2002). In summary, Boreen and colleagues (2000) noted that an effective mentoring program can reduce attrition of first-year teachers by one-half or more.

The Principal's Role in Supporting a Mentoring Program

While principals do not have time to serve as new teacher mentors themselves, they can develop and nurture schoolwide support for a mentoring program in numerous ways. First, principals must establish a school culture where the idea of a "village raising a child" translates into a "school mentoring a new teacher." Then they must clarify the vision of the mentoring program with the staff and "explicitly affirm the value of informal mentoring" (Sweeny, 2001, p. 14). The expectation should be that everyone is a learner. In an effort to foster such a collaborative environment, principals can publicly acknowledge contributions made by staff members other than the assigned or formal mentors. Support from the entire staff ultimately fosters the novice teacher's sense of belonging.

Fibkins (2002) suggested that principals become aware of their own individual strengths and weaknesses and teach themselves mentoring skills before publicly promoting a mentoring program. It is likely that principals will serve as role models—or even mentors—to the experienced teachers that have agreed to participate in the program. By identifying their own mentoring skills, principals will be involved not only as learners but also as participants and be more prepared to train the selected team of mentors.

Surely, leading by example is part of training mentors and advancing a collaborative school culture. The principal must display the same six qualities that Rowley (1999) considers basic to being a good mentor: "(1) commitment to the role of mentoring; (2) accepting the beginning teacher; (3) skilled at providing instructional support; (4) effective in different interpersonal contexts; (5) modeler of a continuous learner; and (6) communicator of hope and optimism" (p. 20).

In addition to training mentors and exemplifying good mentor qualities, the principal can take the following specific actions to support a mentor program: consider class size and teaching load when making teacher assignments (Darling-Hammond, 2003); provide release time for mentors to visit other

schools to gather instructional techniques; and provide release time for new
teachers for the purpose of staff development. Finally, Darling-Hammond
(2003) added that, overall, the administrator needs to be highly supportive of
the mentoring program to ensure its success.

Key Research Findings

The importance of mentoring new teachers is reflected in numerous
studies, including those summarized below:

- Experts in the field, principals, and new teachers themselves recognize
  that principals are a critical resource for new teachers as they work to
  improve instructional practice and student performance (Boreen et al.,
  2000; Mullen & Lick, 1999).
- Effective mentoring programs can reduce new teacher attrition
  (Boreen et al., 2000; Heller, 2004; Ingersoll & Kralik, 2004; Wong,
  2002).
- Effective principals create a culture in which new teachers are supported and mentored by others in the building and are not left to
  flounder alone in their classroom (Sweeny, 2001).
- Principals must support mentoring programs by knowing their own
  mentoring abilities, developing the necessary qualities that make an
  effective mentoring program, and providing the support structures
  for successful implementation (Darling-Hammond, 2003; Fibkins,
  2002; Rowley, 1999).

Related Resources: Boreen et al., 2000; Darling-Hammond, 2003; Fibkins, 2002; Heller,
2004; Ingersoll & Kralik, 2004; Jonson, 2002; Mullen & Lick, 1999; Portner, 2003; Rowley,
1999; Sweeny, 2001; Wong, 2002.

Providing Professional Development Opportunities

"Once in a great while, an outstanding teacher is born. But in most cases,
excellent teachers are made. People have to be encouraged and helped to
become good teachers" (Brody, 1977, p. 28). This quote epitomizes the
essence of the principal's role in fostering professional development. Principals
need not deliver or even directly plan, for that matter, the professional
development program in their schools. However, if principals want to create
a dynamic school community in which students and teachers thrive, then

it's incumbent upon them to make certain that teachers and other staff have every opportunity to grow and flourish.

In earlier sections of this chapter, we focused on the learning and support needs of new teachers. Here, we turn our attention to the entire school. All teachers and staff—from the least to the most experienced—can continue to learn and improve their practice. And learning and improving practice is precisely what professional development is about, whether it be organized at the school, district, state, or national level. In fact, we contend that regardless of the unit delivering the professional growth opportunities, they must be relevant and germane to each individual (i.e., highly localized) recipient. Thus, borrowing from well-known political catechism, we think it safe to say that "all professional development is local."

In this section of the chapter, we offer a review of relevant research and recommended practice related to the principal's role in coordinating and supporting professional learning opportunities for teachers and other staff members. The role of the principal in successful implementation of professional development is underscored by the National Staff Development Council (NSDC). As the ultimate goal of professional development is increased student learning, "quality teaching in all classrooms necessitates skillful leadership at the community, district, school, and classroom levels" (NSDC, 2001).

Supporting Professional Development Initiatives

Supporting professional development initiatives comes in many forms. One way in which principals support professional development is through articulation of their values. The NSDC's Standards for Professional Development state that the principals must "be clear about their own values and beliefs and the effects these values and beliefs have on others and on the achievement of organizational goals" (NSDC, 2001).

A study that analyzed the effectiveness of content-specific professional development found that the principal's support was essential. Indeed, the researchers found that those implementing the professional development "cited principal support as the most important factor in determining teacher participation in PD and in developing a supportive context for reform in schools" (Weiss & Pasley, 2006, p. 11). Similarly, a study examining the successful reform of schools cited principal support as an essential factor in successful implementation (Bodily, Keltner, Purnell, Reichardt, & Schuyler, 1998). In schools where implementation was not successful, teachers explained that the principal was not supportive, which resulted in internal conflicts in the school.

Coordinating Professional Learning Opportunities

One of the most important roles of an instructional leader is to coordinate the professional learning opportunities within their schools. Coordination can stem from teachers' perceived needs or the principal's perceived needs. Regardless of who initiates the professional development, the principal ensures that the activities meet teacher needs, that they are valued by teachers, and that they meet both teachers' goals and school goals (Blase & Blase, 2001). In their summation of what makes reform successful at the district level, Fullan and colleagues (2004) emphasized the importance of designing and delivering coordinated professional learning opportunities related to school and district goals. Referring to the Chicago Public Schools, they stated that "within each school, the principal and teacher leaders head teams that drive the school's coordinated professional learning and goals" (p. 43). Similarly, in a study involving 20 principals from Charlotte-Mecklenburg, North Carolina, schools using predetermined selection criteria, researchers found that effective principals provided specific opportunities within the school for teachers to learn continually (e.g. peer coaching, study groups) (Charlotte Advocates for Education, 2004).

Schools are in the business of student learning, and effective principals recognize the connection between the primary goal of student learning and staff development. Cotton (2003) stated in her content analysis of principals' impact on student achievement that

> the research attributes much of the principals' success to the professional development opportunities that they provide for their staff members, particularly the teaching staff. The successful principals offered not only more activities but also a wider range of them, both in terms of structure and content, than less successful ones did. Opportunities included in-school activities provided by principals or staff members, group learning sessions like those described in the learning organization literature, district sponsored events, off-site workshops and conferences, and college coursework. (pp. 35–36)

Portin and colleagues (2003) offered an excellent summation of the important role principals play in coordinating and supporting professional learning opportunities for teachers and other staff in their schools:

> Finally, the human resource function included professional development of staff. For teachers, school-based inservice training and development required a nimble principal who could both gain access to resources and match development activities to the school's strategic goals. (p. 26)

Indeed, by whatever the means at hand might be, principals make quality professional development happen—and count—in their schools.

Effective principals exhibit specific behaviors and take targeted action to ensure professional development opportunities are meaningful. School leaders provide the context for successful professional development. They must orchestrate multiple changes that provide quality learning opportunities for teachers to work in teams, to focus resources effectively on curriculum development and implementation, and to establish accountability for results (Ruebling et al., 2004). They also provide leadership opportunities for teachers to initiate, engage in, and provide professional development (Blase & Blase, 2001; Drago-Severson, 2004).

Consistent with the concept of principal-as-coordinator, Blase and Blase (1999) found several noteworthy leadership behaviors in their study of the role that instructional leaders play in providing professional development. These behaviors include collaborating, promoting coaching, using inquiry to drive staff development, providing resources to support growth and development, and applying the principles of adult development to staff development efforts. The purpose of their study, which was designed to broaden Bruce Joyce's approach to professional development, was to investigate the question "What characteristics (e.g., strategies, behaviors, attitudes, goals) of instructional leaders positively influence classroom teaching?" (p. 3). Among the key findings they derived from the investigation are a number of elements that are directly relevant to the fundamental role as instructional leader in the school:

- Effective instructional leaders frequently provided professional development opportunities that address emergent instructional needs that, in turn, had substantial effects on teachers.
- Teacher input into the design and content of professional development, optional attendance, and active participation of the instructional leader were important.

- Principals who were effective instructional leaders helped faculty members stay informed about current trends and issues.
- The multiple formal and informal opportunities principals provided for teacher collaboration yielded vast positive results for teachers.
- The effective leaders were described by teachers in the study as attempting to plan and operate staff development of a large-scale action research project, although they acknowledged the need to focus greater attention on action research related to student progress.
- The effective leaders helped to develop faculty by providing essential resources.
- The leaders recognized and supported different phases within teachers' life cycles and accommodated teachers' various roles.
- They focused professional development programs on curriculum, instruction, and technology, as these areas are more likely to have effects on student learning.
- They organized study groups and supported their activities.
- They developed peer coaching relationships and supported their activities.
- They provided time for collaboration for the study of teaching and learning.
- The principals encouraged a commitment to spend time studying outcomes, curriculum, and teaching practice rather than "administrivia" and technical or managerial matters. (Blase & Blase, 1999, pp. 13–14)

Marzano and colleagues (2005) described from their meta-analysis what they referred to as "intellectual stimulation"—the "extent to which the school leader ensures that faculty and staff are aware of the most current theories and practices regarding effective schooling and makes discussions of those theories and practices a regular aspect of the school's culture" (p. 52). Particular characteristics associated with the principal's intellectual stimulation responsibility include

- Keeping informed and continually exposing staff to the latest research and theory on effective schooling.
- Fostering systematic discussion of this research and theory.
- Understanding the research and theory regarding given innovations and promoting staff understanding through reading and discussion.

Cotton (2003) noted that "effective principals were creative in finding ways to secure the resources necessary to make professional development opportunities available. In fact, principals of high-achieving schools are adept at finding and providing resources—financial, human, time, materials, and facilities—for all kinds of instruction-related needs" (p. 36). Furthermore, effective principals "walk their talk," exemplifying the outlook and behavior they expect from staff and students (p. 72).

Key Research Findings

Many studies summarize these key elements related to the principal's role in professional development, including the following:

- Effective principals support professional development within their schools that meet both teacher needs and school goals (Blase & Blase, 2001; Cotton, 2003; Fullan et al., 2004).
- Effective principals recognize the teacher leadership within the building and involve teachers in the design and implementation of professional development opportunities (Blase & Blase, 2001; Cotton, 2003; Drago-Severson, 2004).
- Effective principals provide the time, resources, and structure for meaningful professional development (Blase & Blase, 1999; Drago-Severson, 2004; Ruebling et al., 2004).
- Effective principals are aware of the professional literature related to best practice and keep their staff informed as a part of professional development, developing a culture of learning (Blase & Blase, 2001; Marzano et al., 2005).

Related Resources: Blase & Blase, 1999, 2001; Charlotte Advocates for Education, 2004; Cotton, 2003; Drago-Severson, 2004; Fullan et al., 2004; Marzano et al., 2005; NSDC, 2001; Portin et al., 2003; Ruebling et al., 2004; Weiss & Pasley, 2006.

Retaining Quality Staff

Consider the following statistics concerned with teacher retention:

- The rate of teacher leaving or retiring is higher than the ability to hire (Ingersoll, 2001a, 2001b).

- There is a greater teacher turnover annually in educational communities with high-poverty families, by nearly a third, compared to other school communities (Ingersoll, 2001a, 2001b).
- The average teacher age in 1999 was 44 versus the national worker age of 30 (Hussar, 1999).
- The average annual teacher turnover rate is significantly higher for teachers compared to other occupations—13.2 percent in teaching compared to a national average of 11 percent for all workers (Ingersoll, 2001b, 2002).
- The cost of teacher turnover in Texas was estimated in 2002 to consume approximately 25 to 33 percent of the employee's salary once hiring, vacancy, training, and learning curve costs were factored in. One case study regarding turnover was conducted in three school districts, revealing a cost range of $355 to $5,166 to replace a teacher (Texas Center for Educational Research, 2002).
- The cost of teacher turnover is fairly consistent with business and industry costs. However, worker attrition patterns in business and industry denote primary reasons for leaving as other job opportunities (41 percent), better offers (36 percent), and relocation, none of which are mentioned in the teaching profession (Cheney, 2001).
- Common reasons for teacher leaving include early retirement, regular retirement, lack of support by administration, class size concerns, student enrollment issues, student behavior, school violence, unsatisfactory working conditions, and salaries (American Association for Employment in Education, 2000; Hanushek & Rivkin, 2004; Wollmer, 2000).
- Teachers who enter the field out of a sense of service are more likely to leave (Miech & Elder, 1996).
- In a study conducted by the National Commission on Teaching and America's Future (2003), the researchers stated "we have concluded that teacher shortages will never end and that quality teaching will not be achieved for every child until we change the conditions that are driving teachers out of too many of our schools" (p. 5).
- High rates of teacher turnover are negatively correlated with the school climate, affecting professional development initiatives, instruction, and student learning (Guin, 2004).

- Additional findings from the National Commission on Teaching and America's Future (2003) include the following:
  - The key problem is not teacher supply but rather a lack of retention, as teacher attrition decreases a teacher's career, increases school district costs, and hurts student learning.
  - Good teachers are "worn down" by heavy mentoring loads and dealing with students who had less effective teachers the previous year(s).
  - Frustrations for teachers in order of frustration level include lack of administrator support, lack of faculty influence, classroom intrusions, inadequate time, low pay, student behavior, student motivation, and class size.

Given these and similar findings, no wonder teacher retention is such a front-burner issue for school improvement and student achievement. Ultimately, keeping quality teachers and staff is as important (or perhaps more so, given the costs associated with turnover) as hiring the right people.

Opportunity Costs Associated with Teacher Turnover

Opportunity costs associated with teacher attrition can be high in terms of teaching effectiveness and student achievement. As Stronge (2007) noted in his analysis of existing research on the relationship between teacher experience and teacher effectiveness, experience does, indeed, matter:

> Experienced teachers differ from rookie teachers in that they have attained expertise through real-life experiences, classroom practice, and time. These teachers typically have a greater repertoire from which to incorporate and organize routines for monitoring students and creating flowing, meaningful lessons. Teachers who are both experienced and effective are experts who know the content and students they teach, use efficient planning strategies, practice interactive decision-making, and embody effective classroom management skills. These experienced and effective teachers are efficient; they can do more in less time than novice educators. (p. 11)

Research related to the effect of experience on teaching effectiveness indicates that teachers with more experience tend to show better planning skills (Borko & Livingston, 1989; Covino & Iwanicki, 1996; Jay, 2002; Yildirim, 2001); are better able to apply a range of teaching strategies, including depth and differentiation in learning activities (Covino & Iwanicki, 1996); understand students' learning needs, learning styles, prerequisite skills, and interests better (Borko & Livingston, 1989; Covino & Iwanicki, 1996; Jay, 2002); and are better organized and better able to handle problems (Covino & Iwanicki, 1996; Cruickshank & Haefele, 2001).

Various studies suggest that teacher maturation—that is, developing from novices to masters—takes time, ranging from five to eight years to master the art and science of teaching (Darling-Hammond, 2000b; Education Review Office, 1998). For instance, teachers with more than three years of experience are more effective than those with three years or fewer (Kaufman et al., 2002; Nye et al., 2004). A striking statistic is that teacher expertise as defined by experience (as well as education and scores on licensing exams) accounts for as much as 40 percent of the variation in students' achievement—more than race and social economic status (Ferguson, 1991; Virshup, 1997). Additionally, schools with more beginning teachers tend to have lower student achievement (Betts, Rueben, & Danenberg, 2000; Esch et al., 2005; Fetler, 1999; Goe, 2002). Again, it seems clear that teacher retention must be a vital concern for building administrators.

Creating a Culture of Retention: What Principals Can Do

Teacher attrition is going to occur; this is the natural course of events in the life of a school and in many ways is healthy and desirable. Thus, we're not advocating eliminating teacher loss; rather, our focus is eliminating undesired teacher turnover and its inherent negative consequences. There are numerous strategies—some within the grasp of the principal (administrative support) and some not (e.g., teacher pay)—that can be considered and enacted to protect the school from undue teacher turnover. But we focus our attention here on one key factor that consistently has been related to teacher attrition: imbuing the school with a positive and collaborative learning environment.

Although working conditions may not be a motivator for work, they most assuredly are necessary for maintaining staff (Herzberg, 1966, 1982). One essential element in fostering a learning environment in which teachers and others can thrive and desire to work is collaboration. "A large and growing volume of research repeatedly finds that, when principals empower their staffs through sharing leadership and decision-making authority with them, everyone benefits, including students" (Cotton, 2003, p. 21).

In a study of school leadership style in Cyprian elementary schools, the researchers emphasized in their findings that principals' practices need to promote behaviors that enhance collaborative working conditions, such as "creating one to one relationships between the principal and each teacher or between the principal and each student. For this reason, the principal's presence in every aspect of school life seems to be very important. Moreover, both principals and teachers should emphasize a strong, positive culture where commitment and responsibility, innovations, and a shared decision-making process are the main characteristics" (Kythreotis & Pashiardis, 1998a, p. 29).

In a case study concerned with integrating teachers and principals in leadership decision making, the authors noted that unlike conventional notions of instructional leadership, shared instructional leadership is an inclusive concept, compatible with competent and empowered teachers. "As teachers inquire together, they encourage each other toward answers for instructional problems. Leadership for instruction emerges from both the principal and the teachers. Principals contribute importantly to these communities when they promote teacher reflection and professional growth" (Marks & Printy, 2003, p. 374). Additionally, their findings suggest that strong transformational leadership (i.e., leadership that engages and empowers teachers in a collaborative decision process) by the principal is essential in supporting the commitment of teachers. Consistent with this line of collaborative leadership, Marzano and colleagues (2005) found in their meta-analysis that high-achieving school principals

- Provide opportunities for staff to be involved in developing school policies.
- Provide opportunities for staff input on all important decisions.
- Use leadership teams in decision making.

Further, they surmised that a "defining characteristic of a purposeful community is that it accomplishes goals that matter to all community members. The critical phrase here is 'all community members.' The driving force behind this concept is that all the members of the school staff believe that their day-to-day efforts serve common goals" (p. 102).

The Effect of Losing Good Teachers

One report that summarized the detrimental effect of losing good teachers found that high teacher turnover rates result in

- A deficiency of quality teachers for every classroom and thus lower quality of instruction.
- Loss of continuity within the school in that school reform requires sustained and shared commitment by a school's staff.
- Time, attention, and funds being devoted to attracting new teachers and not to the classrooms (Charlotte Advocates for Education, 2004, p. 1).

So how does the school principal achieve higher retention rates of highly able teachers? Although not a complete answer to this dilemma, a study by the Charlotte Advocates for Education (2004) did find that principals who have been more successful in retaining teachers have characteristics of successful entrepreneurs. Thus, creative problem solvers seem to have the advantage in keeping good staff.

A final implication related to teacher turnover that certainly is not trivial is the loss of promising candidates for the principalship. Fullan (2002) noted:

> We will not have a large pool of quality principals until we have a large pool of quality teachers because quality teachers form the ranks of the quality principal pipeline. Individualistic strategies—signing bonuses, pay hikes—will not work to boost the ranks of quality teachers; the conditions of teacher work must be conducive to continual development and proud accomplishment. And this is certainly not the case now. (p. 20)

Consequently, if we want quality school leaders, we first must attend to the matter of keeping quality teachers.

Key Research Findings

As demonstrated in the narrative above, numerous studies summarize concerns and potential solutions related to teacher retention, including the following:

- Teachers leave for a variety of reasons, one of which includes lack of administrative support (American Association for Employment in Education, 2000; Cheney, 2001; Hanushek & Rivkin, 2004; National Commission on Teaching and America's Future, 2003; Wollmer, 2000).
- More experienced teachers are more effective than novice teachers in terms of planning, instructional delivery, problem solving, and,

most important, student achievement (Betts et al., 2000; Borko & Livingston, 1989; Covino & Iwanicki, 1996; Fetler, 1999; Goe, 2002; Jay, 2002; Yildirim, 2001).

- Effective principals promote collaboration and shared leadership, which is associated with a positive culture in which teachers will want to stay (Cotton, 2003; Kythreotis & Pashiardis, 1998b; Marks & Printy, 2003; Marzano et al., 2005).
- Principals who are risk takers and who help in problem solving with their staff are more likely to empower teachers and thus retain them (Blase & Blase, 2001; Charlotte Advocates for Education, 2004).

Related Resources: American Association for Employment in Education, 2000; Betts et al., 2000; Borko & Livingston, 1989; Charlotte Advocates for Education, 2004; Cheney, 2001; Cotton, 2003; Covino & Iwanicki, 1996; Cruickshank & Haefele, 2001; Darling-Hammond, 2000b; Education Review Office, 1989; Esch et al., 2005; Ferguson, 1991; Fetler, 1999; Fullan, 2002; Goe, 2002; Guin, 2004; Hanushek & Rivkin, 2004; Herzberg, 1966, 1982; Hussar, 1999; Ingersoll, 2001a, 2001b, 2002; Jay, 2002; Kaufman et al., 2002; Kythreotis & Pashiardis, 1998a; Marks & Printy, 2003; Marzano et al., 2005; Miech & Elder, 1996; National Commission on Teaching and America's Future, 2003; Nye et al., 2004; Texas Center for Educational Research, 2002; Virshup, 1997; Wollmer, 2000; Yildirim, 2001.

A Final Word on the Importance of Human Resource Administration

Education is a people business with approximately 80 to 90 percent of a school's operational budget invested in its people. Ken Chenault, CEO of American Express, succinctly captured the essence of the importance and influence of capable people in a service industry such as AmEx or education: "given the times we're in—and the fact that we're in the service business—people are our greatest asset" (cited in Colvin, 2007, p. 102). When we understand that, among the factors within the school, the influence of principals is second only to teachers in affecting student achievement (Leithwood et al., 2004), we begin to understand the power of people—the right people—in educational success. The teachers and other staff in a building are far more important to success than the building itself. Thus, selecting, supporting, developing, and keeping the right people *is* the central tenet for success in our business.

Figure 3.1 **Key References for Human Resource Administration**

Reference	Selection	Induction and Support	Mentoring	Professional Development	Retaining
American Association for Employment in Education, 2000		•			•
American Association of State Colleges and Universities, 2005		•			
Association of Community Organizations for Reform Now, (n.d.)		•			
Bergert & Burnette, 2001		•			
Betts et al., 2000					•
Blase & Blase, 1999				•	•
Blase & Blase, 2001				•	•
Bodily et al., 1998				•	
Boreen et al., 2000			•		
Borko & Livingston, 1989					•
Brody, 1977				•	
Burnett et al., 1998	•				
Charlotte Advocates for Education, 2004				•	•
Cheney, 2001					•
Collins, 2001	•				
Cotton, 2003		•		•	•
Covino & Iwanicki, 1996					•
Cruickshank & Haefele, 2001					•
Darling-Hammond, 2000a		•			
Darling-Hammond, 2000b		•			•
Darling-Hammond, 2003			•		

(continued)

Figure 3.1 Key References for Human Resource Administration, *cont.*

Reference	Selection	Induction and Support	Mentoring	Professional Development	Retaining
Drago-Severson, 2004				•	
Edgar & Pair, 2005		•			
Education Review Office, 1998		•			•
Esch et al., 2005					•
Ferguson, 1991					•
Fetler, 1999					•
Fibkins, 2002			•		
Fink & Resnick, 2001	•				
Fullan, 2002					•
Fullan et al., 2004				•	
Goe, 2002					•
Guin, 2004					•
Hallinger & Heck, 1996	•				
Hanushek & Rivkin, 2004					•
Hargreaves & Fullan, 2000		•	•		
Heller, 2004			•		
Henke et al., 2000		•			
Herzberg, 1966					•
Herzberg, 1982					•
Hindman, 2004	•				
Hussar, 1999					•
Ingersoll, 2001a					•
Ingersoll, 2001b					•
Ingersoll, 2002		•			
Ingersoll & Kralick, 2004			•		
Jay, 2002					•

Reference	Selection	Induction and Support	Mentoring	Professional Development	Retaining
Johnson, 2004		●			
Jonson, 2002			●		●
Kaufman et al., 2002					●
Kythreotis & Pashiardis, 1998b					●
Leithwood et al., 2004		●			
Luekens et al., 2004		●			
Marks & Printy, 2003					●
Marshak & Klotz, 2002		●			
Marvel et al., 2007		●			
Marzano et al., 2005	●	●		●	●
Miech & Elder, 1996					●
Moore-Johnson, 2004		●			
Mullen & Lick, 1999			●		
National Commission on Teaching and America's Future, 2003					●
National Commission on Teaching and America's Future, 2007					●
National Staff Development Council, 2001				●	
Nye et al., 2004		●			●
Perkins, 1998	●				
Peterson, 2002	●				
Portin et al., 2003	●	●		●	
Portner, 2003			●		
Reed et al., 2001		●			

Figure 3.1 **Key References for Human Resource Administration,** *cont.*

(continued)

Figure 3.1 **Key References for Human Resource Administration, *cont.***

Reference	Selection	Induction and Support	Mentoring	Professional Development	Retaining
Rowley, 1999			•		
Ruebling et al., 2004				•	
Stronge, 2002	•				
Stronge, 2007	•				•
Stronge & Hindman, 2006	•				
Stronge & Tucker, 1995	•				
Sweeny, 2001		•	•		
Taylor & Small, 2002	•				
Texas Center for Educational Research, 2002					•
Virshup, 1997					•
Weiss & Pasley, 2006				•	
Williamson et al., 1997	•				
Wollmer, 2000					•
Wong, 2002			•		
Yildirim, 2001					•
Young et al., 1997	•				

4

Teacher Evaluation: Assessing Instructional Quality

Felisha has worked in several districts as her military husband was trans-ferred to various bases. In the last 12 years as an assistant principal, depending on the district, she has evaluated teachers using observations, portfolios, 360-degree feedback information, checklists, and a combination of these methods. Felisha was asked by the director of instruction for her current school district to serve on the evaluation design team for develop-ing a new teacher performance appraisal system. Over the course of sev-eral months, Felisha and the rest of the team, consisting of teachers, building administrators, and central office supervisors, worked with a consultant to design a system that worked for their setting. She was intro-duced to the concept of academic goal setting in which teachers set goals based on learner needs and developed a growth plan to address those needs. Felisha liked this tool and began using it informally with some of the teachers with whom she was working. When the pilot year for the revised system started, some of her teachers provided sample student learn-ing goals to their colleagues, and Felisha helped her fellow administrators make the paradigm shift from an inspector model to a growth-oriented, value-added evaluation process.

The importance of teacher effectiveness in providing quality learning experiences for students of all ages is absolutely clear. In fact, there is ample evidence to support the claim that, of all the vari-ables within the control of schools, the quality of the teacher's teaching has one of the most powerful effects on student learning (Mendro, 1998; Nye et al., 2004; Rivkin, Hanushek, & Kain, 2001; Wright, Horn, & Sanders, 1997). To illustrate, in one study, Nye and colleagues (2004) found that teacher effects explained 12 to 14 percent of the variance in mathematics achievement gains and approximately 7 percent of the variance in reading. Thus, "the variance in student achievement gains attributable to teachers was two to three times as great as that of the schools students attended, suggesting that policies addressing teacher effectiveness would yield greater gains than those addressing school improvement efforts" (Tucker & Stronge, 2006, p. 154).

"So why does teacher evaluation matter? Because teaching matters" (Stronge, 2006, p. 1). Given that teacher evaluation, essentially, is the ability to judge and develop teacher effectiveness, it seems paramount that we get teacher evaluation right. Traditionally, the teacher evaluation process was informal and based on general satisfaction of the community, but over recent decades, evaluation has evolved into a highly structured and formalized process used in most school systems today (Stronge & Tucker, 2003). In this chapter, we provide a summary of research and practice on key issues related to the principal's role in performance evaluation. Specifically, we address the following questions:

- Why evaluate?
- What are good practices for teacher evaluation?
- How should teacher performance be documented?
- What are legal guidelines for teacher evaluation?

Figure 4.3, at the end of this chapter, provides key references for effective performance evaluation.

Why Evaluate?

Teacher evaluation should never be just a required form that must be filled out every year or so. If this is all that evaluation amounts to, then both the principal and teacher are wasting their time—however limited that time might be. Rather, if implemented properly, teacher evaluation can be a catalyst for school improvement, especially if we accept the claim stated at the beginning of the chapter that teacher quality has a powerful effect on student learning. In order to move teacher evaluation away from being merely a prescribed procedure and to the point of making a difference in school success, we offer two complementary purposes for teacher evaluation: teacher improvement and teacher accountability.

The evaluation purpose of performance improvement relates to the teacher's professional growth and improvement and involves helping teachers learn about, reflect on, and improve their practice (Duke, 1997; Howard & McColsky, 2001). Thus, it is growth oriented (or formative) (Iwanicki, 1990) and implies that the principal should be assisting the teacher with improving his or her practice systematically over time. The accountability purpose of teacher evaluation "reflects a commitment to the important professional goals of competence and quality performance" (Stronge & Tucker, 2003, p. 4). Thus, it is perceived typically as final (or summative) and concerned with determining effectiveness (McGahie, 1991).

These two major purposes of teacher evaluation—professional growth and performance accountability—often are viewed as mutually exclusive. We argue, however, that for teacher evaluation to be most beneficial, this artificial dichotomy must be eliminated. "There is room in [teacher] evaluation systems for both accountability and performance improvement purposes. Indeed, evaluation systems that reflect both accountability and personal growth dimensions are not only desirable but also necessary for evaluation to productively serve the needs of individual [teachers] and the community at large" (Stronge, 1995, p. 131). As Fullan (1991) noted, "combining individual and institutional development has its tensions, but the message . . . should be abundantly clear. You cannot have one without the other" (p. 349).

For both improvement and accountability purposes in teacher evaluation systems to be feasible, there must be a concerted effort on the part of the principal to logically link them. McGreal (1988) aptly summarized that multiple purposes of evaluation can be successfully met within a single evaluation system when the system is viewed as one component of a larger mission—furthering the goals for the organization. As principals exercise their responsibility to evaluate their staff, it is imperative that they keep uppermost in their thinking that they are responsible to help their teachers grow and flourish (formative evaluation purposes) and, ultimately, to exercise their responsibility for ensuring results of performance (summative evaluation purposes).

Key Research Findings

Research findings related to the purposes of teacher evaluation highlight the following elements:

- Teacher supervision and evaluation are fundamental responsibilities of the principal. Yet principals and teachers find their supervisory interactions to be difficult and unsatisfying experiences (Cooper, Ehrensal, & Bromme, 2005).
- The number of incompetent teachers is well above the number of teachers who were actually documented as incompetent, leading to a serious disconnect recognized by both administrators and teachers between the ideal purposes of an evaluation system and reality (Menuey, 2005; Tucker, 1997).
- Over the past two decades, teacher evaluation systems have been recognized as integral to teacher improvement and to overall school improvement (Ellett & Teddlie, 2003) and improvement in the classroom (Duke, 1997; Howard & McColsky, 2001).
- Teacher evaluation systems of the past have failed to fulfill both purposes of accountability and improvement because of poor implementation and a negative atmosphere in which the evaluation takes place (Danielson, 2001).

Related Resources: Cooper et al., 2005; Danielson, 2001; Duke, 1997; Ellett & Teddlie, 2003; Howard & McColsky, 2001; Iwanicki, 1990; McGahie, 1991; McGreal, 1988; Menuey, 2005; Stronge, 1995; Stronge & Tucker, 2003; Tucker, 1997.

What Are Good Practices in Teacher Evaluation?

Although we strongly advocated in the previous section for quality teacher evaluation with the clear purposes of professional growth and accountability, too many teacher evaluation systems accomplish neither (Stronge & Tucker, 2003). If quality teacher evaluation is to lead to better-quality teaching, then we must inject quality characteristics into our daily practice. In particular, we recommend that teacher evaluation be designed to include four essential characteristics: (1) a positive climate for evaluation, (2) good communication between the principal and teacher throughout the evaluation process, (3) a commitment to teacher evaluation, and (4) technically sound practices.

Providing a Positive Climate for Teacher Evaluation

Teacher evaluation that is conducted in an environment that fosters mutual trust between the teacher and principal offers the greatest potential for benefiting the school and, ultimately, the students. Although teacher evaluation as a process has too often generated suspicion if not conflict, "trust between evaluator and evaluate . . . can . . . prevail in an effective personnel evaluation system" (Stronge, 1995, p. 137). As Tschannen-Moran (2004) found in her study of trust in schools, "Trustworthy leadership is likely to lead to more active and constructive supervision that contributes to improved instruction in the school" (p. 181). Going back more than 28 years, Redfern (1980) suggested that a cooperative atmosphere created in the evaluation process enhances the opportunities for satisfying the concerns of everyone involved.

The Importance of Good Communication in Teacher Evaluation

"Teacher evaluation systems should reflect the importance that effective communication plays in every aspect of the evaluation process" (Stronge, 2006b, p. 7). Unless teachers and evaluators communicate early and often about what is learned through evaluation, its value will be lost and opportunities for growth will be missed. In an effort to establish clear understanding about the evaluation system and a productive dialogue throughout the evaluation process, we recommend giving attention to both public and confidential aspects of principal-teacher communication.

One important feature of clear communication in teacher evaluation relates to public disclosure of elements about which teachers have a right to be informed. Elements for which public disclosure is vital include

- Establishing clear goals for school improvement.
- Determining how teacher evaluation relates to those goals (e.g., teacher improvement, student achievement).
- Developing clear performance standards upon which teacher evaluation will be based.
- Identifying acceptable standards of performance.
- Building clear and consistent procedural guidelines and safeguards for all evaluation procedures.
- Establishing a reasonable evaluation timeline and sticking to it (Stronge, 1995, 2006b).

"A second vital aspect of effective communication in teacher evaluation is its personal and private side—ongoing two-way communication between the evaluator and teacher" (Stronge & Tucker, 2003, p. 7). Good communication between the principal and the teacher includes

- Cooperatively developing evaluation protocols and procedures (e.g., timelines, feedback process following classroom visits).
- Focusing on opportunities for teacher development and performance improvement throughout the process—not just at the end of the evaluation cycle.
- Identifying ways and means to reach higher standards and correct any subtle or significant discrepancies in performance (Stronge, 1995, 2006b).

Of particular importance on the private side of communication in evaluation is the conferencing between the principal and teacher. The evaluation conference serves multiple purposes, such as documenting performance for use in decision making, informing teachers about their performance, and motivating teachers to higher levels of performance (Helm & St. Maurice, 2006). The authors identified various features of effective principal-teacher conferences concerned with the teacher's evaluation:

- *Two-Way Communication:* Principals who listen more than they talk will obtain more useful information about teachers' performance.
- *Balanced Review of Past Performance and Future Goals:* While reviewing performance is essential, setting performance goals or developing professional growth plans as part of the evaluation conference can be a very constructive way to promote the teacher's professional growth.
- *Recognition of Teacher Strengths and Successes:* It is important to understand that the more specific teacher commendations or recommendations for improvement, the more meaningful they are.
- *Identification and Analysis of Problems Affecting the Teacher's Performance:* When teacher performance doesn't meet reasonable standards or expectations, it is important to understand the context for these failures and then to move immediately toward identifying solutions to the problems.

Demonstrating a Commitment to Teacher Evaluation

Establishing teacher evaluation as a priority is essential if the evaluation system is to contribute substantially to school and teacher improvement. Teacher evaluation systems that lack strong support from the school administration are superficial at best (Stronge, 1991). As Conley (1987) noted, one of the critical attributes of an evaluation system is that it be elevated to a priority in the school district.

To become a reality, the principal must be clear about his or her commitment in tangible ways. In fact, the principal's daily practices related to teacher quality and teacher evaluation are far more influential than any teacher evaluation policy or manual (i.e., the walk is more powerful than the talk). Of particular importance for demonstrating a commitment to teacher evaluation as a means to school improvement are

- Establishing teaching excellence as a priority in everything that occurs in the school.
- Allocating time—adequate time—and attention to implementing effective evaluation procedures.
- Devoting available resources (e.g., professional development funds) to support the evaluation process and teacher improvement (Bridges, 1992; Conley, 1987; Duke, 1990; Poston & Manatt, 1993, Stronge & Tucker, 2003).

Technically Sound Teacher Evaluation Practices

"While a conceptually sound and technically correct teacher evaluation system will not guarantee effective evaluation, one that is technically flawed and irrational most assuredly *will* guarantee failure" (Stronge, 2006b, p. 9). The basic building blocks for technically sound evaluation systems are the standards developed by the Joint Committee on Standards for Educational Evaluation in 1988 and revised in 2007: propriety, utility, feasibility, and accuracy. The standards can be summarized as depicted in Figure 4.1:

- Effective principals do not "wing it" in their assessments of teaching. Rather, they participate in extensive training programs to increase their own skills in performance evaluation (Cotton, 2003).

Figure 4.1 **Personnel Evaluation Standards Applied to Teacher Evaluation**		
Standards	**Description of the Standards**	**Application to Teacher Evaluation**
Propriety Standards	Evaluations should be legal, ethical, and conducted with concern for both the welfare of the teachers and their clients. (Joint Committee on Standards for Educational Evaluation, 1988, p. 11)	• Written policy inclusive of criteria and procedures. • Job-related evaluation criteria. • Prior notification before evaluation begins. • Legal compatibility with statutory mandates. • Equitable treatment of all teachers.
Utility Standards	Evaluations should be offered in a timely manner, useful format, and with information that the teacher can use to improve performance. (Joint Committee on Standards for Educational Evaluation, 1988, p. 45)	• Detailed and focused feedback that enhances instruction for children. • Constructive suggestions that allow sufficient time for improvement. • Process promotes growth.
Feasibility Standards	Evaluation systems must be reasonable to use in terms of the time and resources required to conduct the evaluation, in addition to providing valuable feedback (Joint Committee on Standards for Educational Evaluation, 1988, p. 71)	• Practical procedures for both teachers and administrators. • Perception of meaningful evaluation as a priority for the school system, with adequate support.
Accuracy Standards	Information collected during the evaluation must be valid and precise in order to draw conclusions about job performance (Joint Committee on Standards for Educational Evaluation, 1988, p. 83)	• Written documentation of all communications regarding performance. • Recommendations based on patterns of behavior. • Substantiation for personnel recommendations that are made.

Source: From *Handbook on teacher evaluation: Assessing and improving performance* (p. 20), by J. H. Stronge and P. D. Tucker, 2002, Larchmont, NY: Eye on Education. Reprinted with permission.

- The more "an employee (i.e., the teacher) participates in the evaluation conference, the more satisfied he or she will be with the conference and the supervisor." A principal's "encouraging substantial contributions by the teacher also ensures greater commitment of the teacher to the process" (Helm & St. Maurice, 2006, p. 244).

- A productive evaluation conference can help with problem-solving, strategy-developing, and goal-setting functions. Additionally, conferences need not be only formal events that occur at the end of the evaluation cycle. Rather, informal conferencing can (and should) occur early and often. Simply talking about both strengths and areas for improvement can provide help and encouragement for the teacher when they can do the most good (Helm, 1997).

- The availability of resources to respond to individual needs serves teacher accountability that is rooted in professional norms and values (McLaughlin, 1990).

- Principal-teacher collaboration is a means of maintaining trust and mutual respect in the evaluation process and is key to developing a sense of ownership by all participants (Duke, 1990; McConney, Schalock, & Schalock, 1997; Poston & Manatt, 1993).

- Principals who balance both caring and high expectations of teacher performance develop more trustworthy relationships than principals who focus on caring without high expectations or high expectations without caring (Tschannen-Moran, 2004).

- Involving teachers at every level in the evaluation process is an irreducible requirement for effective teacher evaluation. Conversely, the exclusion of teachers from the evaluation process perpetuates a "them and us" schism between principals and teachers. This divide is fatal to teacher evaluation and reinforces a view of teacher evaluation as indifferent to teachers' professional expertise and classroom realities (McLaughlin, 1990).

- Principals' perceptions of their own competence in evaluating teachers affect successful implementation of teacher evaluation policies that focus on removing incompetent teachers from the classroom (Painter, 2000).

- As a result of a review of almost 8,000 studies, Hattie concluded that the most powerful single modification that enhances achievement is feedback (as cited in Marzano et al., 2005).

Related Resources: Bridges, 1992; Conley, 1987; Cotton, 2003; Duke, 1990; Helm, 1997; Helm & St. Maurice, 2006; Joint Committee on Standards for Educational Evaluation, 1988; Marzano et al., 2005; McConney et al., 1997; McLaughlin, 1990; Painter, 2000; Poston & Manatt, 1993; Stronge, 1991, 1995, 2006b; Stronge & Tucker, 2003; Tschannen-Moran, 2004.

How Should Teacher Performance Be Documented?

Teacher evaluation historically has relied heavily—and often solely—on direct observation. For decades, teacher evaluation consisted of an untrained supervisor (principal or department head) dropping in on a teacher's class once a year (at best) and writing a few words about the teacher's enthusiasm or organization. The written "evaluation" was then filed and probably never read or used again.

Later, the clinical supervision model came to dominate the evaluation procedure. The supervisor usually was trained and met with the teacher in a pre-observation conference as well as a post-observation conference in which the supervisor highlighted strengths and weaknesses of the teacher. Yet the sole basis for performance evaluation was still the supervisor's observation. In fact, under this system, being observed was synonymous with being evaluated. Observation can be a helpful mode of data collection for classroom teachers, but as a sole source it is too limiting and doesn't allow for a full and fair picture of the teacher's performance. Thus, we need to consider the use of multiple data sources in evaluating teaching performance.

In summarizing some of the problems facing teacher evaluation practice, Peterson (2000b) noted:

> Seventy years of empirical research on teacher evaluation shows that current practices do not improve teachers or accurately tell what happens in classrooms. . . .
> Teacher evaluation as presently practiced does not identify innovative teaching so that it can be adopted by other teachers and used in teacher education programs.
> Finally, current procedures do not reward exemplary teachers. (p. 18)

Given the existing ineffectiveness too frequently found in contemporary teacher evaluation, it seems essential that we improve—and improve dramatically in some cases—our practices.

What Is Wrong with Using Only Observation in Teacher Evaluation?

If used productively, nothing is wrong with including observation in teacher evaluation. What *is* wrong is relying solely on teacher observation as it is insufficient to fairly and fully document teacher performance as a single source. Furthermore, as traditionally practiced, principal reports based on teacher observations "do not increase good teachers' confidence or reassure the public about teacher quality" (Peterson, 2000b, p. 18). Consider the following concerns:

- Classroom observation visits typically represent less than one-half of one percent of actual teaching performance in a given year. Thus, observations alone are far too unreliable to give an accurate picture of teacher work.
- Classroom observations are prone to being artificial, especially when special lessons are prepared for a planned classroom observation visit. Although a pre-conference, observation, post-conference sequence can be helpful for teacher development, it also can lead to an inaccurate view of what happens in the classroom on a day-to-day basis.
- Observation is useful for documenting only part of the important work that teachers do. Class visits can yield useful information about selected processes of teaching, such as instructional delivery and classroom management, but only a glimpse at teacher planning, student assessment, communication with parents and others, and professional development of the teacher. Perhaps most important, observations yield little or no information about the outcomes of teacher-student achievement.
- No matter how it is viewed, observation is a form of inspection, and inspection can be viewed as de-professionalizing (Stronge & Tucker, 2003).

Why Use Multiple Data Sources in Teacher Evaluation?

The primary purpose of gathering information in teacher evaluation is to obtain factual descriptions of the teacher's behavior or performance to the fullest extent possible. Documentation is merely the process of recording sufficient information about the teacher's performance to support ongoing evaluation and to justify improvement and personnel decisions based on the evaluation. Thus, the basic question to ask regarding documenting performance is: *How will the teacher demonstrate the required professional responsibilities that he or she is required to fulfill?*

The use of multiple data sources is beneficial because it provides for a more flexible approach to capturing a broad range of responsibilities and increases the validity of the evaluation process. Multiple data sources are used in teacher evaluation because teaching is too complex for any one source to sufficiently capture the role or performance (Peterson, 2004). Also, no single data source is valid or feasible for all teachers in all school districts (Peterson, 2006). Consequently, we need to consider using appropriate data sources as part of a full and fair documentation of the teachers' work.

Classroom Observation

Although classroom observation should not be the sole source of information used for a teacher's performance evaluation, it can serve as an essential building block of a more comprehensive data collection system. Observation can be categorized into two basic types: formal and informal. In performing a formal observation, the principal conducts a structured, planned, 40-minute observation of a teacher who is presenting a classroom lesson. Informal observation is shorter and often more extemporaneous. It might include, for example, the principal's walk-through visit or even a planned, 10- to 15-minute visit. Both formal and informal observations can play an important role in collecting meaningful data about a teacher's performance—as long as they comprise only one source for documenting teacher performance.

Teacher Portfolios

Another important source for obtaining documentation of a teacher's performance is a professional portfolio (i.e., a purposeful collection of written records and documents produced by the teacher as a part of his or her job responsibilities) or a set of artifacts about performance (e.g., lesson plans, newsletters to parents). Portfolios, typically, are more prescribed and comprehensive. They might include, for example, copies of lesson plans, syllabi developed or adapted for a given class, representative samples of student work, correspondence sent to and received from parents, and evidence of student performance. Most important, portfolios or less formal artifact analysis can

serve a valuable self-evaluation function when the teacher includes thoughtful, reflective comments about his or her teaching.

Student Surveys

Asking questions of those with whom a teacher works most closely—
the students—about their perceptions of the teacher's performance can constitute an important source of documentation. After all, "students are the only
ones of the teacher's clients who have direct knowledge about classroom practices on a regular basis" (Stronge, & Ostrander, 2006, pp. 135, 137). Additionally, various studies have found that students throughout the school-age
range can accurately assess teacher performance (Driscoll et al., 1990;
Ebmeier, Jenkins, & Crawford, 1991; Peterson & Kauchak, 1982). Perhaps
most convincing, in a study of the validity of student ratings of teacher performance, Wilkerson and colleagues (2000) found that student ratings of
teachers were better predictors of student achievement than ratings by principals and the teachers themselves.

Despite the encouraging evidence related to the use of student surveys,
they should be employed with a degree of caution. For instance, student ratings might be restricted to descriptions of life in the classroom or discrete
and visible behaviors in an effort to increase the reliability of the ratings
(Peterson & Kauchak, 1982). Although there are exceptions, most public
schools that currently require student surveys in their teacher evaluation systems do so on a "for your eyes only" basis—that is, the teacher only views the
student feedback and uses the information for his or her own formative
improvement.

Student Performance Measures

There are various concerns with including student performance in
teacher evaluation, including

- The collective nature of accountability and input into student performance (i.e., student learning is the product of teachers' influence and
  student learning over time).
- The fact that many variables both within a classroom and beyond the
  control of the teacher affect student learning and that, thus, all learning (or the absence thereof) cannot be attributed to the teacher.

- The technical challenges of adequately measuring student learning (e.g., absence of meaningful pre- and post-test achievement data for all teachers, nature of single point-in-time tests as indicators of student progress, alignment of achievement tests with the curriculum) (Tucker & Stronge, 2005).

Nonetheless, there are numerous compelling reasons for including student achievement data in the teacher evaluation process, including the following:

- There is abundant research substantiating the claim that teacher quality is the most important school-related factor influencing student achievement (Nye et al., 2004; Rivkin et al., 2001).
- There is growing evidence and recognition that value-added approaches to teacher evaluation offer convincing evidence and defensible methodologies regarding the influence of the classroom teacher on student learning (Stronge & Tucker, 2000; Tucker & Stronge, 2005, 2006; Wenglinsky, 2002).
- Measures of student learning provide the ultimate accountability for teacher evaluation (Tucker & Stronge, 2006).

Regardless of one's personal perspective on the issue of connecting student performance to teacher performance (for teacher evaluation purposes or otherwise), public policy and educational practice have begun to broadly embrace various methodologies for doing so. As of this writing, states such as Arizona, Florida, Ohio, Pennsylvania, Tennessee, and Virginia, among others, have various statewide requirements for either including substantial measures of student achievement in teacher evaluation or using value-added methodologies for assessment of school and teacher performance. For example, recent legal decisions regarding teacher dismissal in Florida have mandated that student achievement be used as a primary factor in teacher dismissal cases (*Sherrod v. Palm Beach County School Board,* 2006; *Young v. Palm Beach County School Board,* 2006).

Figure 4.2 offers a summary of selected data sources that might be used to provide a more comprehensive picture of teacher performance than any single source might do on its own. Although good teaching and student learning are inextricably connected, we have attempted to denote the primary focus of the given data sources.

Figure 4.2 **Data Sources for Documenting Teacher Performance**					
Teacher Evaluation Information Sources					
Evidence of:	Formal Observation	Informal Observation	Teaching Portfolio or Performance Artifacts	Student Surveys	Student Achievement
Good Teaching	✔	✔	✔	✔	
Student Learning			✔		✔

Source: Adapted from a model created by C. Gareis and J. Stronge.

Key Research Findings

Research findings related to using multiple data sources in teacher evaluation highlight the following elements:

- Effective principals visit classrooms with a purpose—to support and provide feedback regarding instructional practices. Research supports the link between classroom observation practices, feedback regarding teaching, and student performance (Cotton, 2003).
- Effective principals are available through being visible. Their presence in the classroom and outside the classroom sends a message to students, parents, teachers, and others that educating students is a team effort, not the work of one or two individuals (Marzano et al., 2005).
- Feedback through surveys of client groups such as students, parents, and peers included along with classroom observation reduces the reliance on one data source (Stronge & Ostrander, 2006) and "has a more powerful impact on people than information from a single source, such as a principal" (Manatt & Benway, 1998, p. 23).
- In a study of the relationship between feedback from students, teachers, and parents and student academic achievement, researchers found that feedback from students regarding teacher performance and student achievement showed the strongest significant relationship, indicating that student feedback can be a useful tool in performance evaluations (Wilkerson et al., 2000) and can be a valid and reliable tool in evaluation (Peterson, Wahlquist, & Bone, 2000).

- The use of portfolios actively engages teachers in the evaluation process and encourages reflective practice by the teacher (Danielson, 2001; Wolf, 2006) which is a quality of an effective teacher (Stronge, 2007).
- Student performance measures focus on the value that teachers add to the academic performance of students and should be included as *one* data source in an evaluation system (Tucker & Stronge, 2006).

Related Resources: Cotton, 2003; Danielson, 2001; Driscoll et al., 1990; Ebmeier et al., 1991; Manatt & Benway, 1998; Marzano et al., 2005; Nye et al., 2004; Peterson, 2000b, 2004, 2006; Peterson & Kauchak, 1982; Peterson et al., 2000; Rivkin et al., 2001; Stronge & Ostrander, 2006; Stronge & Tucker, 2003; Tucker & Stronge, 2005, 2006; Wenglinsky, 2002; Wilkerson et al., 2000; Wolf, 2006.

What Are the Legal Guidelines for Teacher Evaluation?

Despite our best efforts to implement fair and sound evaluation systems, teacher evaluation frequently falls well short of the mark, due to ineffective, irrelevant, and in some cases legally indefensible evaluation systems. Fundamentally, the rights of individual teachers to due process "must be weighed against the obligation of the school board to ensure the quality of instruction that students receive" (Tucker & DeSander, 2006, p. 69). Thus, in all of our teacher evaluation policies and practices, it is imperative to keep this balancing act in mind: individual rights versus institutional commitment to quality educational delivery.

Although there is a solid record of support from state and federal courts involving proper due process, principals and other school administrators often are "leery of the legal ramifications of teacher evaluation" (Tucker & DeSander, 2006, p. 69). This section of the chapter is devoted to a review of legally sound practices that must accompany any teacher evaluation practices in the school. Specifically, we offer the following guidelines to help make the principal's evaluation practices fundamentally sound and legally defensible:[1]

1. *Principal/evaluators must inform teachers of all standards, criteria, and procedures for evaluation before implementation.* This step is required

---

[1] The list provided here offers general guidelines for legally sound teacher evaluation practices. Consult with your school board attorney or other appropriate individuals for guidance in specific situations.

because one component of due process is "notice," the concept of which has been expanded by the courts to include notification of expected or prohibited behavior prior to holding someone accountable for the behavior. Clearly, a person evaluated by criteria and procedures about which he or she has not been previously informed has been deprived of the "notice" component of due process.

2. *Principal/evaluators must follow any and all state and local procedural requirements.* Failure to follow prescribed statutory or administrative procedural requirements or to follow district policies and procedures is among the most frequent reasons for judicial rejections of evaluations. It would be erroneous to generalize that such failure to follow prescribed procedures always results in reversal of district or organizational decisions; courts sometimes tolerate variances, but usually only when it is clear that even strict compliance with prescribed procedures would not have changed the outcome of the action.

3. *Principal/evaluators must be objective and must ensure an objective evaluation process.* Evidence of objectivity, or absence of bias, in implementing the evaluation process helps defend evaluators against charges of political or personal motives indicative of "bad faith" or arbitrary and capricious behavior. An objective evaluation process is one that is designed and implemented with fairness and applied consistently to all employees.

4. *Principal/evaluators should document patterns and effects of behavior.* Case law is replete with lessons about the importance of frequent rather than single or even sporadic evaluations. How else can evaluators establish patterns of behavior? It is, after all, a pattern of behavior rather than an isolated incident (barring something like sexual involvement or crime of moral turpitude) that the courts require as convincing evidence that a major personnel decision is warranted. Increasingly, the courts expect the administration to prove that the educator's unacceptable behaviors have an adverse impact on students or staff.

5. *Principal/evaluators must determine whether the educator's behavior is remediable or irremediable.* Irremediable behavior has been defined in case law as behavior that has a seriously damaging effect on students or others in the school environment or behavior that could not

have been corrected even with prior warning. Most behavior connected with job performance, however, is considered potentially remediable. Thus, remediation, whether required by state statute, local board policy, or applicable case law, almost always will need to be provided to the individual prior to dismissal for cause. However, there are at least two circumstances in which on-the-job behavior may be considered potentially irremediable: (1) when the behavior is repeated over a period of time, especially when the employee has been notified that the behavior is unacceptable; and (2) when there are many deficiencies or unacceptable behaviors, any of which as single behaviors might be remediable but which taken in the aggregate may become irremediable.

6. *Where remediable deficiencies exist, provide clear descriptions of the deficiencies and clear, specific descriptions of the expected corrections or improvements in performance behaviors.* The principal/evaluators must prescribe the specific behaviors that will indicate improved performance.

7. *Where serious performance deficiencies have been cited, the principal/evaluators must allow reasonable time to improve, and reasonable assistance in improving should be provided by the staff of the school or school district.* Resources and assistance needed to improve, a specific timeline for improvement, and performance measures that will be used to ascertain adequate improvement must be provided and then adequately monitored. Ideally, an evaluator's primary goal in working with an employee having performance difficulties should be to help that person improve his or her performance. (Adapted from Stronge & Helm, 1991)

Key Research Findings

Research findings related to legal aspects of teacher evaluation are highlighted in the following elements:

- In studying high-trust cultures in Chicago, these cultures are more—not less—likely to take action against persistently uncaring or incompetent teachers. "Failure to act can poison the whole atmosphere. Students, parents, and colleagues know when bad teaching is being tolerated" (Fullan et al., 2004, p. 45).

- In a study from the Dallas Independent School District concerning the discernable elements of high-performing schools (i.e., schools that consistently experienced higher-than-expected student gain scores), the researchers found that using the results of teacher assessment was one of three discernable characteristics. Specifically, "the principals of effective schools did not tolerate ineffective teachers" (Mendro, 1998, p. 264).

- The responsibility to remediate low-performing teachers or remove them falls on the shoulders of school principals (Painter, 2000).

- Factors that affect principals' ability to move for dismissal of incompetent teachers include legal, political, and social considerations as well as principals' own abilities in evaluation (Painter, 2000) and participation in evaluator training (Tucker, 1997).

- Nationally, over two-thirds of principals say they need more autonomy in removing ineffective teachers from the classroom and rewarding outstanding teachers and staff (Tucker & Tschannen-Moran, 2002).

- Effective principals work with teachers who are struggling to improve performance while also documenting deficiencies in order to provide evidence of incompetence if a move for dismissal is necessary (McGrath, 2006).

- Effective principals follow district and state guidelines in ensuring due process (DiPaola & Hoy, 2008), including informing the teachers of their strengths and weaknesses and working with them to remediate the problem (Tucker & DeSander, 2006).

Related Resources: DiPaola & Hoy, 2008; Fullan et al., 2004; McGrath, 2006; Mendro, 1998; Painter, 2000; Stronge & Helm, 1991; Tucker, 1997; Tucker & DeSander, 2006; Tucker & Tschannen-Moran, 2002.

A Final Word on Making Evaluation Meaningful

Some of the most powerful tools for school improvement and effectiveness that the principal has at his or her fingertips are program and personnel evaluations. Strategic plans, mission statements, and school improvement plans are important documents for defining current priorities and future goals, but they are not sufficient alone. There must be quality people to implement those plans and programs, make improvements, and work toward fulfilling the school's mission. No school or program is better than the people who deliver its services. And related to the delivery of quality services, both programs and the people responsible for implementing them must be assessed on a regular basis to maintain and improve performance. Evaluation, therefore, is an essential activity for the principal of a successful school.

Despite the fact that proper evaluation of personnel is fundamental, this part of the personnel process often fails to receive the attention it deserves due to the many competing demands on the principal's time. In most schools, principals are responsible for evaluating at least 30 to 40 teachers and a variety of specialists who support the educational program. The latter group of specialists, with diverse responsibilities, are particularly difficult to evaluate because they do not fit easily into the categories of teacher or administrator for which evaluation procedures usually exist.

Reference	Purposes	Good Practices	Documentation	Legal Guidelines
Bridges, 1992		•		
Conley, 1987		•		
Cooper et al., 2005	•			
Cotton, 2003		•	•	
Danielson, 2001	•		•	
DiPaola & Hoy, 2008				•
Driscoll et al., 1990			•	
Duke, 1990		•		
Duke, 1997	•			
Ebmeier et al., 1991			•	
Ellett & Teddlie, 2003	•			
Fullan, 1991	•			
Fullan et al., 2004				•
Helm, 1997		•		
Helm & St. Maurice, 2006		•		
Howard & McColsky, 2001	•			
Iwanicki, 1990	•			
Joint Committee on Standards for Educational Evaluation, 1998		•		
Manatt & Benway, 1998			•	
Marzano et al., 2005		•	•	
McConney et al., 1997		•		
McGahie, 1991	•			
McGrath, 2006				•

Figure 4.3 Key References for Teacher Evaluation

(continued)

Figure 4.3 **Key References for Teacher Evaluation,** *cont.*

Reference	Purposes	Good Practices	Documentation	Legal Guidelines
McGreal, 1988	•			
McLaughlin, 1990		•		
Mendro, 1998				•
Menuey, 2005	•			
Nye et al., 2004			•	
Painter, 2000		•		•
Peterson, 2000b			•	
Peterson, 2004			•	
Peterson, 2006			•	
Peterson et al., 2000			•	
Peterson & Kauchak, 1982			•	
Poston & Manatt, 1993		•		
Redfern, 1980		•		
Rivkin et al., 2001			•	
Stronge, 1991		•		
Stronge, 1995	•	•		
Stronge, 2006b		•		
Stronge, 2007			•	
Stronge & Helm, 1991				•
Stronge & Ostrander, 2006			•	
Stronge & Tucker, 2000			•	
Stronge & Tucker, 2003	•	•	•	
Tschannen-Moran, 2004		•		
Tucker, 1997	•			•

Figure 4.3 Key References for Teacher Evaluation, cont.

Reference	Purposes	Good Practices	Documentation	Legal Guidelines
Tucker & DeSander, 2006				•
Tucker & Stronge, 2005			•	
Tucker & Stronge, 2006			•	
Tucker & Tschannen-Moran, 2002				•
Wenglinsky, 2002			•	
Wilkerson et al., 2000			•	
Wolf, 2006			•	
Wright et al., 1997	•			

5

Organizational Management: Building a Foundation for Teaching and Learning

Being an effective building manager used to be good enough. For the past century, principals were expected to comply with district level edicts, address personnel issues, order supplies, balance program budgets, keep hallways and playgrounds safe, put out fires that threatened public relations, and make sure that busing and meal services were operating smoothly. And principals still need to do all those things. But now they must do more. (Institute for Educational Leadership, 2000, p. 2)

Organizational management is a crucial role of the principal. After all, a school must first and foremost be a safe and positive learning environment for students and staff. Effective management is a necessary component in high-quality schools, and principals with strong managerial skills are more likely to create a culture of continual instructional improvement (Shellard, 2003).

Historically, organizational management of the school was the primary role of the principal. Despite the significant social, economic, and cultural changes in the past quarter century, this focus on managerial duties persisted until recent years (Cuban, 1984, 1988; Tyack & Hansot, 1982). As the emphasis on instructional leadership became more prominent, however, the importance of the principal's role in managing school operations has been questioned. School reform challenges necessitate that school leaders serve as change agents, while the managerial aspects of the job have lost centrality (Marks & Printy, 2003). Classroom instruction and student learning are, in fact, the central functions of schooling and must take priority, yet a multitude of vital management tasks continue to place inevitable time demands on principals (Lashway, 2002b). Given the importance of instructional leadership, how does the school leader prioritize and balance these roles?

The effective principal recognizes the importance of the myriad managerial responsibilities in the school while continuing to prioritize student learning. Nonetheless, balancing competing priorities is a daily reality for principals. A survey of principals in Charlotte, North Carolina, confirms the dilemma. While most principals surveyed acknowledged the central office guideline of spending the majority of their day engaged in instructional leadership tasks, half of the principals reported spending 50 percent or less of their time in this role while spending the remainder of their time in managerial tasks (Charlotte Advocates for Education, 2004). Manasse (1985) captured the time constraints faced by principals in handling multiple managerial tasks over two decades ago, stating:

> We must look beyond the activity patterns to begin to identify those factors that distinguish effective principals. What we find, in general, is that effective principals have learned to be proactive within a reactive work environment. (p. 443)

In some instances, these organizational management tasks are made more complex by the number of other departments and personnel involved. Important school operations such as technology, transportation, building maintenance, custodial duties, and administration of the school cafeteria may be administered from a central level, thus increasing the number of interactions necessary to ensure smooth functioning on a daily basis. Regardless, the principal is ultimately held accountable for overall school operations, both instructional and noninstructional. Because neglecting these areas may ultimately result in lost instructional time, safety issues, or a decline in school climate, the principal must continually work to balance instructional leadership duties with those required for efficient organizational management. Establishing a safe and orderly school environment is, therefore, a primary responsibility of school leaders (Cotton, 2003; Marzano et al., 2005), and one that may affect teaching and learning as well as the school's capacity to meet required standards (Lashway, 2001).

Key components of the principal's organizational management responsibilities include

- Coordinating safety, daily operations, and maintenance of the facility.
- Using data in organizational management.

- Seeking and allocating fiscal resources.
- Organizing and managing technology resources.

Each of these areas will be addressed, in turn. Figure 5.1, at the end of the chapter, summarizes the key references for these organizational management duties of the effective principal.

Coordinating Safety, Daily Operations, and Maintenance of the Facility

School Safety

There is no more important responsibility assigned to the school principal than the safety of those within the school; until this is established, it is at best difficult to create an effective learning atmosphere. To ensure school safety, school leaders provide procedures and routines to create an orderly school environment. Marzano and colleagues (2005) recognized order as one of 21 research-based responsibilities of leaders. In their meta-analysis, the following specific leadership behaviors are evident:

- Establishing routines for the smooth running of the school that staff understand and follow.
- Providing and reinforcing clear structures, rules, and procedures for staff.
- Providing and reinforcing clear structures, rules, and procedures for students. (p. 57)

The maintenance of a safe and orderly school environment is confirmed by Cotton's (2003) research findings on effective principal behaviors. Expectations for student behavior are clear, discipline is fair and consistently enforced, input is obtained from students and staff regarding behavior policies, and authority is delegated to teachers to maintain these policies. Additionally, the availability of a trained school crisis team ensures that when crises or emergencies arise that may affect the well-being of those within the school, procedures and personnel are in place to manage such situations effectively. Clearly, creating a safe and effective learning environment is the result of purposeful actions on the part of administrators as well as involvement of staff, students, and other stakeholder groups. It is fair to say that the safety of students and staff is Job One.

Safety Threats

School leaders face innumerable daily situations that may result in safety risks to students, staff, visitors, or themselves. Data provided from the National Schools and Staffing Survey (SASS) lead to a general conclusion that challenges to discipline and safety exist regardless of the type of school — traditional public, charter, or private (Christensen, 2007). SASS divides these issues into two broad categories:

1. Threats to persons or property, including bullying, physical conflicts, robbery or theft, vandalism, gang activities, weapons possession, and physical abuse of teachers.
2. Behavioral problems, including disrespect and verbal abuse of teachers, widespread classroom disorder, use of illegal drugs and alcohol, and student racial tension. (Christensen, 2007, p. 6)

In addition to these issues, school administrators may find themselves faced with potential safety concerns involving building and grounds security, such as access to the building by others, student check-out procedures, and the risk of injury from hazards on school grounds. For instance, the use of modular classrooms and access to the school building may present heightened challenges as students move between the building and classroom spaces located outside the building. Weather-related challenges such as storms, icy conditions, high wind, and lightning compound the risk of possible injury, particularly for those in modular instructional spaces. While the nature and severity of safety issues may vary depending on the level and type of school as well as community factors, the school leader's failure to address these may, in fact, create interruptions to the school's instructional program when unanticipated issues arise. Effective school leaders not only enlist the help of others to address potential safety issues but also provide clear direction and details regarding how to handle the wide range of possible safety risks. Equally important, procedures and policies must be flexible enough to be adapted as new situations evolve over time.

Principal Liability for School Safety

In the past decade, school safety has been highly publicized as increasing reports of school violence have warranted careful planning and monitoring on the part of school administrators. Although the resources available to schools to address these concerns may vary, the responsibilities remain. In legal terms, school personnel in most circumstances serve *in loco parentis;* they have an obligation to act in place of parents to ensure student safety. Since the vast majority of K–12 students are under the age of 18 years, a duty of care is placed on staff and administrators to adequately supervise student safety. Additionally, the principal is also charged with the safety of others on school grounds, including staff and visitors (Barrios, Jones, & Gallagher, 2007; Bosher, Kaminski, & Vacca, 2004; Standler, 1999–2000; Zirkel, 2001).

The prevention of school-related injuries is both an ethical and legal obligation for school leaders (Barrios et al., 2007). Maintaining a safe learning environment free from hazards and distractions has implications beyond that of a positive school climate; when injuries occur, school districts may be held legally responsible and face costly litigation. Because 10 to 25 percent of injuries to children and adolescents occur at school (Barrios et al., 2007), the proactive principal must address and monitor safety issues on an ongoing basis. Most school injuries (83 percent) are unintentional, with the greatest number involving falls (21.9 percent), followed by injuries sustained during recess, physical education, and while riding in school vehicles. Notably, among cases with student injuries, 58 percent cited lack of proper supervision as a contributing factor (Barrios et al., 2007, pp. 275, 278).

The implications for principals are significant. Even unintentional student injury may result in subsequent legal action, claiming negligence and resulting in time diverted from other school concerns. In a study of Virginia principals, 88 percent rated legal issues as a highly significant organizational management problem (Tucker & Tschannen-Moran, 2002). Legal issues involving student injury faced by school administrators include not only cases of accidental injury, but also those in which students are injured by others in the school setting.

Although a far lesser concern than actual injuries to students, public perception and concerns for safety remain a reality. Findings suggest that the odds of violence toward children at school are one in a million (Brooks, Schiraldi, & Zeidenberg, 2000). Nonetheless, media coverage of student injury and death in places such as Littleton, Colorado, and Jonesboro, Arkansas reinforces parental concerns regarding the safety of children while at school, and rightfully so.

Principals nationwide tend to feel a heightened urgency regarding safety. Despite concerns of possible litigation, however, there have not been significant changes by federal and state courts concerning legal liability against public school officials in cases of student injury (Brooks et al., 2000). Likewise, federal and state courts have consistently rejected civil liability actions against school officials for student injury, absent extenuating circumstances (Brooks et al., 2000). School employees are generally shielded against civil negligence actions by governmental immunity, provided that their actions are

- Within the scope of the job
- Not a result of malicious intent
- Not considered reckless in performance of their duties
- Not grossly negligent (Bosher et al., 2004, p. 180).

Daily Operations

School administrators are responsible for a wide variety of tasks on any given day, many of which may appear to be unrelated to student learning. However, Lashway (2003) pointed out that even basic managerial tasks may have instructional impact. The effective school leader recognizes the importance of the conditions in which students and staff work and ensures that the school maintains a positive learning environment. Overseeing routine maintenance is essential so that school buildings and classrooms are safe and healthy places of learning. Factors including adequate light, heating and air conditioning, furnishings, and clinic facilities are critical in daily school operation. For example, facilities as mundane as fully functional intercom systems are important in that they provide immediate communication between the school office and classrooms. Bells and alarms provide time signals such as the start and end of classes as well as potential emergency situations, including fire and weather alerts. Sprinkler systems must be operational to ensure that if a fire erupts in the building, it can be quickly extinguished with minimal damage and safety risk. Classrooms, restrooms, and cafeteria facilities must be thoroughly cleaned on a daily basis to reduce the risk of illness. Although these tasks may be the responsibility of other departments in the school district, they are nonetheless monitored by school leaders (Lashway, 2002b).

Certain areas of the school provide administrators with both logistical and safety challenges, including the playground, bus and car loops, parking lots, cafeteria, and hallways. Although these are noninstructional areas, they are areas of potential risk due to high-volume student use, the reduced level of adult supervision, and the vehicular traffic in some outside areas. As a result, safety and discipline situations are more likely to occur and create unanticipated loss of instructional time. The proactive principal organizes, maintains, and addresses effective procedures for high-volume and high-risk areas in order to ensure the smooth operation of the entire school program, including the instructional schedule.

Master Schedules

Development of the school master schedule is typically another school-level administrative task. The master schedule reflects state and school district requirements for the length of time spent in core subject areas and elective or resource classes as well as noninstructional periods, such as lunch periods. As Danielson (2002) confirmed, master scheduling is a task of significant importance as it affects the nature and depth of instruction. Thoughtful and deliberate planning can increase instructional time by reducing time lost in transition. It can also minimize overcrowding in key areas of the school, such as hallways, playing fields, and the cafeteria.

Likewise, a strategically planned master schedule assists special education and support personnel in effective service delivery for students with disabilities or other learning challenges. When school personnel are able to work collaboratively within the classroom, the need for "resource room" instruction outside the general education class is decreased. According to Friend (2007), coteaching should ideally become standard practice in order to meet the learning needs of all students. However, participation in the general education classroom or least restrictive environment is not just a desirable instructional practice; rather, it is required by law under the Individuals with Disabilities Education Act (Dunklee & Shoop, 2002; Hehir, 2007).

To enable special education resource teachers or other school personnel to serve students in multiple subject areas and grade levels requires that school leaders consider all aspects of scheduling well in advance of the start of the school year. They must consider the input of classroom teachers, special education teachers, resource teachers, and support staff. Early collaborative planning is essential to reduce the common logistical problems of shared planning time, scheduling, and the classroom grouping of students. Above all, the master schedule must reflect a consistent emphasis on student learning (Danielson, 2002). By coordinating the school schedule with key personnel, including teachers of students with gifted or special education identification, students with a range of learning needs can be more effectively served (Friend, 2007). Combining strategic student grouping and an effective, collaboratively planned master schedule is the responsibility of school leaders, one that proactively promotes teaching and learning.

Key Research Findings

- Despite an increased emphasis on the principal's responsibility for instructional leadership, school management duties have not decreased and remain a time-consuming responsibility (Charlotte Advocates for Education, 2004; Lashway, 2002b; Marks & Printy, 2003).
- Maintaining a safe and orderly environment is likely to affect teaching and learning and is therefore a fundamental responsibility of school leaders (Cotton, 2003; Lashway, 2001; Marzano et al., 2005; Shellard, 2003).
- School leaders are responsible for the safety of those on school grounds and may be held liable if injury results due to negligence of school personnel (Barrios et al., 2007; Bosher et al., 2004).
- Collaborative planning of student grouping and development of the school master schedule has significant implications for teaching and learning (Danielson, 2002; Friend, 2007).

Related Resources: Barrios et al., 2007; Bosher et al., 2004; Brooks et al., 2000; Charlotte Advocates for Education, 2004; Christensen, 2007; Cotton, 2003; Cuban, 1984, 1988; Danielson, 2002; Dunklee & Shoop, 2002; Friend, 2007; Hehir, 2007; Institute for Educational Leadership, 2000; Lashway, 2002b; Manasse, 1985; Marks & Printy, 2003; Marzano et al., 2005; Reeves, 2006; Shellard, 2003; Standler, 1999–2000; Tucker & Tschannen-Moran, 2002.

Using Data in Organizational Management

Of the myriad of organizational management responsibilities required of school leaders, making use of student data to plan and improve student learning is clearly a priority. In an era of accountability, the effective school leader must demonstrate the ability to gather, analyze, and monitor school data on an ongoing basis with teachers and staff. The use of assessment data is invaluable in analysis of student progress toward instructional standards and is considered a quality of successful schools (Cotton, 2003; Marzano et al., 2005; Shellard, 2005). It is no longer sufficient, however, for the principal to single-handedly review student assessment data after instruction has taken place and suggest remediation strategies when students are unsuccessful.

Collaborating in Data Collection and Use

In order to proactively address potential student learning concerns, school personnel must collaboratively and regularly review multiple forms of data and develop workable strategies to address learning needs as they arise. In addition to summative assessment, including school district and state testing, use of more frequent formative assessment while learning is taking place provides ongoing evidence of student achievement (DuFour, 2004; Reeves, 2006; Shellard, 2005). Formative assessments may include curriculum benchmark tests or other teacher-made assessments, and may be both qualitative and quantitative (Shellard, 2005). Regardless, the emphasis is ongoing and is placed on the essential learning expected of students in given subject areas, and there is regular dialogue regarding student progress. When staff members engage in joint responsibility for instructional results, a professional learning community is established—and immediate interventions occur when students do not achieve at satisfactory levels (DuFour, 2004). Proactive learning communities have a timely action plan for response to learning challenges, eliminating excuses for lack of student success such as, "I taught it—they just didn't learn it" (Reeves, 2006, p. 91).

Such collaboration does not occur by accident; rather, it is the responsibility of school leaders to instill it and sustain it. By creating regular opportunities for staff to engage in team planning, discussion, and data analysis, school leaders lay the groundwork for true collaboration focused squarely on the success of all students. The likelihood of authentic instructional collaboration will diminish if such opportunities are not incorporated into the daily schedule and school calendar prior to the start of the school year. When teachers are confronted with having to find time on their own for instructional discussion and teamwork, leaders are more likely to hear the refrain, "We don't have time to collaborate."

School Improvement Planning

The use of school data for instructional planning and collaboration is, of course, critical to the development and implementation of the school improvement planning process. A school-specific strategic plan includes both student achievement data as well as the demographic data of the school community. Statistical information such as socioeconomic, discipline, and school climate survey data should be reviewed to assess the strengths, weaknesses, opportunities, and challenges of the particular school. Student achievement results are examined both as a whole (e.g., school and grade-level "pass rates" on state assessments) and in disaggregated form, including review of minority, special education, and other student subgroup results. Not only is data disaggregation necessary to make effective instructional decisions at the school level, but it is also required to determine the school's status under the federal No Child Left Behind (NCLB) Act and in decision making regarding Adequate Yearly Progress (AYP) status of the school (Zavadsky, 2006).

Effective data analysis, however, must not be limited to comparison of yearly summative testing. Review of successful schools that have overcome achievement challenges indicates that these successful schools use multiple forms of data, specifically cohort data comparing the same student over time (Reeves, 2004). According to Reeves, rather than comparing the previous year's class to the current class, the following questions should be asked:

- "What percentage of a group of students is proficient now compared to a year ago?"
- "What percentage of our students has gained one or more grade levels in reading when we compare their scores today to their scores a year ago?"
- "Of those students who were not proficient a year ago, what percentage are now proficient?"
- "Of those students who were proficient a year ago, what percentage are now advanced?" (Reeves, 2004, p. 70)

Following the thorough review of all relevant school data and in accordance with state requirements, the school improvement plan is then developed, implemented, and monitored based on the needs, vision, and mission of the individual school as well as the vision and mission of the school district. This review process promotes an ethic of continual improvement at the school level, another hallmark of successful school leaders (Boris-Schacter & Merrifield, 2000). Marzano and colleagues (2005) noted the practice of monitoring and evaluating the results of school strategies on student achievement as one of the 21 critical responsibilities of school leaders. Additional confirmation is evident in the Planning, Implementation, and Monitoring (PIM) research in the large Clark County, Nevada, school district, where frequent monitoring of data was found to be a significant variable in student achievement and closing the equity gap (Reeves, 2006).

Clearly, the effective principal regularly uses data to analyze the needs of the school and collaboratively develop, implement, and monitor a school improvement plan. The plan should serve as a guide to focus efforts and resources toward the mutual goals of the school community. Despite the temptation to develop elaborate school improvement documents, however, there is little evidence that this practice, alone, is associated with improvement in student achievement (Reeves, 2006). According to Reeves:

> Several new research studies . . . provide clear evidence that when it comes to achievement and equity, planning and process are less important than implementation, execution, and monitoring. (p. 62)

In fact, examination of eight high-performing, high-poverty Kentucky schools revealed that although these schools performed well on a state-conducted audit, they didn't perform as well on the state planning process itself (Kannapel et al., 2005). Others concur that the "pretty" plan is not necessarily the best plan (Reeves, 2006). Fullan (1996) warned of the fragmentation and overload of such efforts, while Elmore (2000) noted that "schools are almost always aboil with 'change,' but they are rarely involved in any deliberate process of improvement" (p. 3).

In the case of school improvement planning, as in other types of strategic planning, it appears that less is more; the simple plan is preferable (Collins, 2001; Schmoker, 2006). The effective school leader focuses on doing the right work (Marzano et al., 2005), with a focus on those factors within the school that affect student achievement. According to Marzano (2003), factors to consider at the school level are

- Guaranteed and viable curriculum
- Challenging and effective feedback
- Parent and community involvement
- Safe and orderly environment
- Collegiality and professionalism (p. 15)

Factors to consider at the teacher level include

- Instructional strategies
- Classroom management
- Classroom curriculum design (p. 76)

In designing the school improvement plan, therefore, it is the responsibility of the school leader to work collaboratively with those in the school community to develop a realistic, flexible school plan based on a variety of data relevant to student achievement. According to Kelly and Lezotte (2003), the ability to monitor and adjust throughout the implementation of the school improvement plan is "the central principle of continuous school improvement" (p. 6). Reeves (2006) confirmed that "the final characteristic of schools that are making dramatic strides in improving educational achievement and equity is the constructive use of data" (p. 89). More significant, the school leader ensures that school data are used to focus on the right work for the schoolwork that is research based, sustainable, and directly related to the continual improvement of teaching and learning. Sustainable school change is comprised of five key factors, creating school improvement that

- Sustains learning
- Endures over time
- Does not negatively affect the environment or surrounding schools
- Promotes ecological diversity and capacity in the school community (Hargreaves & Fink, 2003, pp. 4–5)

Key Research Findings

- The effective school leader uses multiple forms of data to inform school planning (Cotton, 2003; Marzano et al., 2005; Shellard, 2005).
- School leaders are instrumental in developing professional learning communities focused on student learning (DuFour, 2004; Reeves, 2006; Shellard, 2005).
- Successful school improvement plans are developed collaboratively, are monitored continually, and are flexible in design, allowing adjustments to changing circumstances (Kelly & Lezotte, 2003).

Related Resources: Boris-Schacter & Merrifield, 2000; Collins, 2001; Elmore, 2000; Hargreaves & Fink, 2003; Kannapel et al., 2005; Kelly & Lezotte, 2003; Reeves, 2004; Reeves, 2006.

Seeking and Allocating Fiscal Resources

Instructional leaders make creative use of all resources—people, time, and money—to support school improvement. To make time for teachers to work together, instructional leaders come up with strategies to add to, borrow from, or rearrange the daily schedule. Their focus on teaching and learning drives every conversation about budget development and every decision about how to use existing resources. (King, 2002, p. 63)

The leadership responsibility for the resources of a school refers to those materials and opportunities necessary for teaching and learning (Marzano et al., 2005). This includes the managerial and financial responsibility for items such as books and equipment as well as professional opportunities for staff development and professional collaboration (Cotton, 2003). In addition to state and local school fiscal policies, the Interstate Leaders Licensure Consortium (ISLLC) provides standards that have been adopted in the majority of states to provide uniform guidelines for school leaders. Standard 3 includes the responsibility for fiscal management and allocation of resources, stating:

A school administrator is an educational leader who promotes the success of all students by ensuring management of the organization, operations, and resources for a safe, efficient, and effective learning environment. (Council of Chief State School Officers, 2002, p. 16; see also Wilmore, 2002)

In traditional school financial planning, only a fraction of total school expenses is directly controlled by the principal, but school finance remains a critical responsibility, requiring a thorough understanding of local school board and state policy. This responsibility requires that the effective principal establish an ongoing cycle of actions to plan and oversee the school budget. A typical cycle might involve the following steps:

- *Review previous school budgets:* Examine projected and actual costs over a multiyear period in order to discern patterns of expenditure and price fluctuations.
- *Develop the budget for the next fiscal year:* Involve other school administrators and staff, and consider sources of school income and expenditures that come from other school district budgets (e.g., textbooks and school furnishings) or outside sources.
- *Plan and prioritize expenses:* Particularly in the case of items involving large expenditures that may be distributed over a multiyear period,

long-range planning is essential. Use school district budget categories and codes, providing any necessary breakdown of expenses (e.g., team or departmental budgets within the overall category of instruction).

- *Communicate distribution procedures and timing:* Ensure staff understanding of departmental or individual budgets, while maintaining awareness of possible budget freezes and deadlines.
- *Create and adhere to procedures for reimbursement:* School district audit procedures are likely to require original receipts, description of the item purchased, and principal (or designee) signature to reimburse for school items purchased by staff. Likewise, policies and procedures for expenditures are often specific to the school district. For example, it may be perfectly acceptable for administrators to purchase refreshments for staff meetings in one school district, but it may be forbidden in a neighboring district.
- *Monitor and adjust:* Be prepared for cost increases of consumable items and unanticipated necessities that were not included in the original budget. Follow school district procedures for budget changes to move funds from one category to another when necessary.
- *Follow school board policy for bids and vendors:* In many cases, school districts have contracted with numerous vendors in order to obtain the lowest cost on certain items, particularly those that are used in bulk, are consumable, or are costly. When purchasing expensive items such as computers or copying machines, adhere to the number of bids and documentation required. This process also applies to school-sponsored trips, which are likely to require use of particular transportation companies due to both cost and risk management factors.
- *Re-evaluate the budget:* Prior to beginning the next fiscal year budget, review the previous year's budget to determine any necessary revisions.
- *Determine the rotation for school capital expenses:* Prior to allocating school funds for costly expenses, investigate which expenses are absorbed in the school board budget. Items involving replacement or major maintenance—such as repaving the school basketball court or replacing carpeting—are generally anticipated in the school district capital improvement plan on a rotating basis.
- *Develop partnerships:* Often community organizations are willing to partner with schools in philanthropic efforts or in exchange for use of the facilities. By working with those in parent-teacher organizations;

the faith community; athletic, service, or parks and recreational groups, resources may be affordable when finances are shared. Likewise, grants may be available to provide additional funding for school projects.

Although school finances are the responsibility of administrators, the school budgeting and decision-making processes should be understood by school staff as well as other stakeholders (Danielson, 2002). Budgeting can be a time-consuming process but is essential to protect school funds and ensure that funds and resources are equitably distributed and used appropriately. As technological systems become available to assist in school financial responsibilities, centralized systems and a school database can support staff understanding and involvement in school budget procedures and save time in the process (Buck, 2007). The effective school leader seeks and monitors financial and other available resources that will benefit the school community. When necessary, leaders redesign school structures and allocate resources as necessary (within established guidelines) in order to achieve goals, working with all stakeholders toward accomplishment of the school vision (Leithwood & Riehl, 2003).

Key Research Findings

- Effective school leaders make creative use of all resources—people, time, and money—to improve teaching and learning (Cotton, 2003; King, 2002; Marzano et al., 2005).
- The principal's responsibility for school resources—including budget and purchasing—is recognized in local, state, and national standards for school leaders and should involve stakeholders (Danielson, 2002; Wilmore, 2002).

Related Resources: Buck, 2007; Cotton, 2003; Danielson, 2002; King, 2002; Leithwood & Riehl, 2003; Marzano et al., 2005; Wilmore, 2002.

Organizing and Managing Technology Resources

Acquiring and monitoring the use of school technological resources has become an increasing responsibility of school leaders—one that has changed rapidly in the past decade. Consider that in the 1990s

- Student-to-computer ratios were approximately 20 to 1.
- Computers were more often located in central labs than in classrooms.

- Student technology skills consisted primarily of learning basic computer skills rather than integrating technology with the curriculum. (Wenglinsky, 2005–2006, p. 29)

Within a decade, however, profound changes had occurred:

- Almost all schools in the United States had faster and more powerful computers with Internet access.
- The student-to-computer ratio was reduced to 5 to 1.
- Greater numbers of computers were located in classrooms.
- Teachers were demonstrating greater confidence in classroom computer use as a result of training. (Wenglinsky, 2005–2006, p. 30)

Intuitively, school leaders recognize the importance of making technology resources available throughout the school to facilitate student learning and staff productivity. The majority of teachers confirm the effect of technology, with 86 percent indicating that it affects their teaching to some extent, and 55.6 percent stating that it affects their teaching a great deal (Ascione, 2005). Likewise, student computer use in schools is increasing—from preschool through high school. The following percentages of students in the United States used computers in school in 2003:

- 97 percent of high school students
- 95 percent of middle school students
- 91 percent of first- through fifth-grade students
- 80 percent of kindergarten students
- 67 percent of preschool students (DeBell, 2006)

Given the proliferation of information technology resources available within schools, the effective principal is responsible for ensuring equitable and instructionally appropriate allocation and use of technology, including

- Making computer hardware and software available to all students and staff members.
- Providing technology staff development on an ongoing basis.
- Modeling the effective use of technology for group communication (e.g., parent-teacher meetings and presentations).
- Monitoring the use of technology within the school by students and staff.

- Following school district technology requirements and policies, including use of technology for daily record keeping, budgeting and financial applications, attendance, student assessment, and student grading and reporting purposes.
- Using technology as an administrative tool to analyze data, reduce the use of paper communication, reduce unnecessary staff meeting time, and communicate within school district departments to accomplish other school managerial tasks (e.g., online work orders and purchase of school-related supplies).
- Maintaining effective school-community communication through Internet-based resources, including the school Web site, electronic newsletters, and teacher- or grade-level Web sites.

Despite the rapid increase in the availability of computers, however, until recently there has been little research linking classroom computer use to student achievement (Wenglinsky, 2005–2006). Similarly, because the nature and use of information technology available to schools have changed rapidly in a short period of time, the use of previous research is unlikely to provide answers to current issues (Protheroe, 2005).

Evidence is emerging, however, to guide educators in the effective use of information technology for a range of student age groups and populations. Early analyses conducted in 1996 by the National Assessment of Educational Progress (NAEP) provided information regarding student progress in core subject areas as well as survey data, including computer access and use. Results in the areas of mathematics, science, and reading for 4th and 8th graders revealed that the amount of student benefit derived depended to a large degree on how individual teachers used technology. Due to lack of teacher technology training at that time, it is not surprising to find that computers were more often used in simpler ways rather than to encourage higher-order thinking skills (Wenglinsky, 2005–2006).

The potential for the positive effect of information technology on student learning was described in a review of over 200 landmark studies on computer technology and student learning. These studies were conducted by the U.S. Army Research Institute for Behavioral and Social Sciences, the Consortium Research Fellows Program, and the Boise State University College of Education (Stratham & Torell, 1996). According to this research summary:

- The use of properly implemented computer technology in education has a "significant positive impact on student achievement as measured by test scores across subject areas and with all levels of students" (p. 2).
- Appropriate use of computer technology increases student-teacher interaction, problem-solving, and cooperative learning.
- Students who learn in computer-rich classroom settings demonstrate improved behavior and lower absentee and dropout rates, have a higher rate of college attendance, and earn more college scholarships than those from non-computer classrooms.
- Computer-based instruction is particularly effective among students in at-risk populations. (Stratham & Torell, 1996)

More recent NAEP research confirms what educators might expect— that the role of technology differs for high school students and younger students. Mixed results are evident regarding the amount of time students use computer technology and whether this takes place at school or in the home. Review of NAEP U.S. History scores revealed a negative effect for the amount of computer time at school and a positive effect for the amount of computer time for schoolwork outside school (Wenglinsky, 2005–2006). It is evident from the research, however, that the relationship between student learning and computer technology is a complex one with numerous variables (Protheroe, 2005). Waddoups (2004, cited in Protheroe, 2005) provided several research themes from existing research, combined in four principles:

1. Teacher training, knowledge of, and attitude toward technology are critical for successful technology integration.
2. Coordination with curriculum design, teaching methodology, and the needs of learners must be considered to make effective use of technology.
3. Technology design determines the effect on student achievement to a large degree and must therefore be flexible, provide timely and appropriate feedback, and create multiple opportunities for students to be engaged in content.
4. Continued improvement in technology integration requires ongoing formative evaluation.

The school leader, therefore, promotes the availability and use of technology resources and ensures that training needs are met in order to facilitate successful technology integration. Although traditional instructional planning by teachers will still be necessary, research has found that effective technology integration may encourage teachers to move from traditional to more modern teaching models (Protheroe, 2005). In an era of rapid change and technological advances, the school leader's management of technology resources at the school level has become a necessity to develop the skills needed by learners of the twenty-first century.

Key Research Findings

- The use of computer technology in schools has increased rapidly in the past decade, requiring that school leaders make concurrent teacher training available for effective implementation (Prensky, 2005; Protheroe, 2005; Wenglinsky, 2005–2006).
- Although difficult to measure, there is emerging evidence that effective computer instruction is positively related to student achievement, particularly in at-risk populations (Protheroe, 2005; Stratham & Torell, 1996; Wenglinsky, 2005–2006).
- Many administrative and organizational management tasks can be completed more efficiently through effective use of technology, allowing more available time for instructional leadership responsibilities (Buck, 2007).

Related Resources: Buck, 2007; DeBell, 2006; Leithwood & Riehl, 2003; Prensky, 2005; Protheroe, 2005; Stratham & Torell, 1996; Wenglinsky, 2005–2006; Wilmore, 2002.

A Final Word on School Organizational Management

In the past quarter century, the responsibilities of school administrators have changed dramatically, from building manager to instructional leader—and more. Although the expectations have shifted to encompass the leadership role, however, the managerial tasks required of school leaders have not diminished—and may also affect student learning. Today's principalship requires a dynamic combination of management, leadership, technical, and interpersonal skills. The effective school leader is a master diagnostician, facilitator, and collaborator who works with those in the school community to obtain resources, monitor progress, and continually improve teaching and learning.

The principal's role is rapidly evolving, requiring skills that may bear little resemblance to those learned in school leadership preparation programs. It is a job that requires lifelong learning, the ability to manage change, and tolerance of ambiguity—a job that is never finished. More than ever it is evident that one person cannot do it all: the effective principal must share the many responsibilities of the role with those in the school community. To understate the complexity of these multiple and often competing responsibilities, today's principalship is no easy task.

Figure 5.1 **Key References for Organizational Management**[1]

Reference	Safety, Daily Operations, and Maintenance	Data and School Improvement	Fiscal Resources	Technology Resources	Leadership Role in Organizational Management
Ascione, 2005				•	
Barrios et al., 2007	•				•
Boris-Schacter & Merrifield, 2000	•	•			•
Bosher et al., 2004	•				•
Brooks et al., 2000	•				
Buck, 2007			•	•	•
Charlotte Advocates for Education, 2004	•				•
Christensen, 2007	•				
Collins, 2001		•			•
Cotton, 2003	•	•	•		•
Council of Chief State School Officers, 2002			•		•
Cuban, 1984	•				
Cuban, 1988	•				
Danielson, 2002	•		•		•
DeBell, 2006				•	
DuFour, 2004		•			•
Dunklee & Shoop, 2002	•				•
Elmore, 1999–2000					•
Friend, 2007	•				•
Fullan, 1996		•			
Hargreaves & Fink, 2003		•			
Hehir, 2007	•				
Institute for Educational Leadership, 2000	•				•
Kannapel et al., 2005					•

Figure 5.1 **Key References for Organizational Management, cont.**

Reference	Safety, Daily Operations, and Maintenance	Data and School Improvement	Fiscal Resources	Technology Resources	Leadership Role in Organizational Management
Kelly & Lezotte, 2003		•			
King, 2002			•		•
Lashway, 2001	•				
Lashway, 2002b	•				•
Lashway, 2003	•				
Leithwood & Riehl, 2003			•	•	•
Manasse, 1985	•				
Marks & Printy, 2003	•				•
Marzano, 2003		•			
Marzano et al., 2005	•	•	•		•
Prensky, 2005				•	
Protheroe, 2005				•	
Reeves, 2004		•			
Reeves, 2006		•			•
Schmoker, 2006		•			
Shellard, 2003	•				•
Shellard, 2005		•			
Standler, 1999–2000	•				
Stratham & Torell, 1996				•	
Tucker & Tschannen-Moran, 2002	•				•
Tyack & Hansot, 1982					•
Wenglinsky, 2005–2006				•	
Wilmore, 2002			•	•	•
Zavadsky, 2006		•			
Zirkel, 2001	•				

[1]The column "Leadership Role in Organizational Management" does not correspond with a specific section in Chapter 5. However, we believe the information provided may be of value to our readers.

6

Communication and Community Relations: Working with Internal and External Constituencies

Patricia is principal of a middle school located within a culturally, linguistically, and economically diverse community. Her school has worked hard to meet the needs of all of its students. The staff has found that working with various local businesses, agencies, and churches has helped to strengthen relationships with community and parent groups and, as a bonus, brings much-needed resources into the school. For instance, students and parents recently interacted with members of the school staff at a local bookstore event featuring their school. Also, the school has held curriculum evenings where parents and teachers participated in learning activities with students. Patricia also serves as a member of a community outreach organization that works with local church groups to provide educational workshops to parents who are seeking a better understanding of the current demands of K–12 education. Additionally, she meets monthly with the school's PTA Board to provide updates regarding school progress and events. Collaboration with the PTA provides additional opportunities for Patricia to communicate with parents through the PTA's monthly newsletter. Internally, she uses staff meetings, team meetings, e-mail, a weekly newsletter, and face-to-face interaction to encourage two-way communication on an ongoing basis with school staff.

Schools exist within dynamic, changing social systems. In order to adapt to constant and increasing global change, it is necessary to involve stakeholders to make necessary improvements. Strong community relations consist of staff members' personal relations with colleagues, students, parents, and the larger community. Each of these entities can significantly influence perceptions of a school. Additionally, effective schools provide planned activities that intentionally communicate programs, needs, and purposes, both internally and externally. Stakeholders' hopes and ideas are considered, and opportunities for their active involvement are created. This exchange of information and ideas promotes common understanding, thus allowing for critical improvements and sound decisions regarding educational programs (Gallagher, Bagin, & Kindred, 1997).

Today's principals function within environments that require constant attention to the needs of internal and external constituents. Public and private schools have experienced increased scrutiny from many stakeholders. On a day-to-day basis, practicing school principals interact with supervisors, teachers, parents, and students within an organizational structure loosely tied together. This ongoing and ever-evolving communication process requires principals to respond to problems and needs of multiple constituencies that are unpredictable. And, beyond the day-to-day communication channels, principals need to develop relationships with media and forge community partnerships if they are to be successful (Catano & Stronge, 2006).

Parents, corporate leaders, and community leaders are becoming increasingly more involved in education. Their involvement makes it necessary for principals to build even stronger relationships with families and the larger community than previously expected. They need to respond to political, social, economic, legal, and cultural contexts effectively and efficiently. Consequently, principals find themselves accountable to policymakers, parents, and business leaders alike for results related to local, state, and national assessments (Catano & Stronge, 2007).

Effective principals must possess the leadership skills and knowledge to unite all stakeholders around a commonly held goal of raising student performance (Lashway, 2003). Additionally, they understand the importance of involving staff and community members in making decisions about the school. A capacity for developing positive interpersonal relationships supports their efforts to recruit others to focus on school goals, monitor instruction and provide feedback, and promote communication within the school community. On a continual basis, these effective principals reach out to their stakeholders (Cotton, 2003). Moreover, they understand that the foundation of their work and their school's success is the ability to communicate effectively.

This chapter summarizes existing research that shows how principals employ communication and community relations in the best interests of their schools and community. In particular, we focus on the following key issues:

- The principal and effective communication
- Communicating with parents and families
- Communicating with the larger communit

Figure 6.1, at the end of the chapter, lists key references for communication and community relations.

The Principal and Effective Communication

Good communication involves the development of shared decision-making processes that incorporate the views of stakeholders—both internally and externally. Many forms are used to communicate and are embedded in the day-to-day work of a school. These multiple modes of effective communication are present in mission statements, belief statements, or slogans. By fostering effective communications on an ongoing basis, people understand what an effective principal stands for (Catano & Stronge, 2006; Cotton, 2003; Leithwood & Riehl, 2003).

Good Communication Requires Good Listening

Effective principals are good listeners. They apply stakeholder suggestions and share that information. Wisdom tells them that they do not have all the answers. Successful principals use communication to build strong relationships, and they strive to improve their own communication and listening skills because they value the feedback and ideas they receive (Cotton, 2003; Kythreotis & Pashiardis, 1998a; Leithwood & Riehl, 2003).

Although leadership effects on school goals are often indirect (as discussed in previous chapters), the multilayered and distributed leadership nature of schools and school districts makes it necessary for principals to exercise clear and consistent communication skills when interacting with multiple constituencies. Effective principals actively provide direction through persuasive leadership that articulates their expectations for high performance of staff. Skill in framing issues and focusing attention on primary purposes and goals in a meaningful and convincing manner is crucial to school effectiveness. This focus on school goals requires open and dem ocratic dialogue with multiple stakeholders (Kythreotis & Pashiardis, 1998b; Leithwood & Riehl, 2003).

Communicating with Teachers and Students

Effective communication connects a principal to teachers and students, and good communication is crucial to meeting school goals. In order to communicate effectively, however, principals (1) need to develop the means for teachers to communicate with each other, (2) need to be accessible to teachers, and (3) need to keep the lines of communication open to all staff. School leaders are effective when they create opportunities for teachers to discuss concerns or when they distribute newsletters highlighting significant decisions under consideration (Kythreotis & Pashiardis, 1998b; Leithwood & Riehl, 2003; Marzano et al., 2005).

When schools embark on changes that dramatically depart from the expected, stakeholders often feel that responsibilities related to culture, communication, order, and input decline. In order to address these views, effective principals distribute leadership across these areas of responsibility. Sharing leadership tasks helps to communicate the positive benefits of changes and the negative effect of maintaining the status quo (Waters & Grubb, 2004). Additionally, it is vital to harness the skills of multiple leaders to ensure effective communication to all stakeholders.

Key Research Findings

Research related to the power and importance of the principal as an effective communicator indicates the following:

- Effective principals incorporate stakeholder views in shared decision-making processes. Additionally, they are good listeners (Cotton, 2003).
- It is important for principals to engage in open and democratic dialogue with multiple stakeholders (Leithwood & Riehl, 2003).
- Good communication is crucial to meeting school goals (Marzano et al., 2005).
- Distributing leadership improves communication about the change process (Waters & Grubb, 2004).

Related Resources: Catano & Stronge, 2007; Million, 2002, 2004; Sorensen, 2005.

Communicating with Parents and Families

High levels of parent involvement have a positive effect on principal effectiveness; in other words, principals who reach out to parents and community members are more successful than principals who do not (Catano & Stronge, 2006, 2007; Cotton, 2003; Fullan et al., 2004). For one thing, these principals interact with parents to communicate the school's vision. A study investigating principal leadership, school context, and student reading achievement found that student socioeconomic status and parent involvement positively influenced principal leadership and the expectations that teachers had for student learning (Hallinger et al., 1996).

Outreach to All Families

Outreach efforts may take many forms, such as working with parent volunteers, taking meetings to neighborhoods, or encouraging parents to work with the children on academic activities at home. Highly effective principals make it a habit to gather input from parents and community members to aid in decision making. Interestingly, principals of high-achieving schools spend more of their work time—in one form or another—working on parent and community relationships compared to principals in average schools (Cotton, 2003; Mazzeo, 2003; Tucker & Tschannen-Moran, 2002). In addition, the staffs of the high-achieving schools personified an attitude of collaboration marked by respect, warmth, care, and sensitivity for all parents (Cotton, 2003).

Cotton and Wikelund (1989) reviewed existing literature and found that certain types of parent involvement are directly beneficial to schools. These types of involvement included attending conferences and school events, volunteering in classrooms, and helping students on academic tasks at home. And directly germane to our discussion of the roles and responsibilities of effective school leaders, schools can take a variety of actions to encourage positive parent involvement, including

- Telling parents that their involvement and support greatly enhances their children's school progress.
- Fostering parent involvement from the time that students first enter school.
- Teaching parents that they are role models for reading behavior.

- Developing parent programs that are focused on instruction
- Working to engage parents of disadvantaged students.
- Emphasizing that parents are partners of the school and that the school values their involvement.

Building Positive Parent Relationships

The nature of the relationships between the school and parents is very important. Specifically, building a positive relationship helps to support the mission of a school, while a negative relationship can inversely affect— indeed, impede—a school's mission. Principals who actively seek to build these relationships find they are better able to function effectively in their jobs. Principals invite parents to visit the school to help them develop an awareness regarding the way that parents can positively or negatively affect school effectiveness. This close collaboration with parents has beneficial outcomes on student achievement and school climate (Kythreotis & Pashiardis, 1998b).

Myriad challenges face school principals on a day-to-day basis, including matters related to parent communication. For instance, principals must deal with disruptions resulting from parents advocating on behalf of their children. Negative interactions with parents can deplete a principal's energy and detract from other important duties. To illustrate, high school principals nationally spend up to 20 hours per week working on parent issues, discipline, and community relations (Tucker & Tschannen-Moran, 2002).

Involving Minority Parents

Chavkin and Williams (1993) described an exploratory study seeking to identify attitudes and practices of minority parents regarding parent involvement. The study suggested that Hispanic parents desired greater information about their children's school progress; they also wanted students themselves to understand the importance of their parents' involvement, and they wanted to feel more welcome in the school. African American parents wanted greater access to school events for working parents; an increase in activities that involved parents, children, and teachers; and more information about their children's progress. African American and Hispanic parents desired more information about activities that they could do at home with their students in comparison to white parents.

A meta-analysis undertaken by Jeynes (2003) found that parent involvement has a positive effect on student achievement for adolescent minority students. Specifically, the benefits of parent involvement positively influenced standardized test scores. In addition, the benefits were greater for African Americans and Latinos than for Asian students.

As we discussed earlier, parent and community involvement is essential to school effectiveness, and principals who practice consistent two-way communication with parents and the community foster support for their schools. These practices become more central when parents, for various reasons, have been less engaged in school-home collaboration. Additionally, providing opportunities for parents and community members to participate in daily school functions and to provide input to school governance procedures strengthens school-community relationships (Marzano et al., 2005).

Key Research Findings

The research related to effective communication with parents suggests the following:

- Principals spend a great deal of time working with parents (Cotton, 2003; Tucker & Tschannen-Moran, 2002).
- Positive relationships with parents helps to support the mission of the schools (Kythreotis & Pashiardis, 1998b).
- High school principals spend 50 percent of their time with parent issues, discipline, and community relations (Tucker & Tschannen-Moran, 2002).
- Student socioeconomic status positively influences principals' leadership and teachers' expectations (Hallinger et al., 1996).
- Parent and community relationships are strengthened by effective two-way communication (Marzano et al., 2005).
- African American and Hispanic parents desire more information about their children's school progress (Chavkin & Williams, 1993).
- African American and Hispanic parents' views of parent involvement differ from those of Anglo parents (Jeynes, 2003).

Related Resources: Blank et al., 2004; Melaville & Blank, 2000; Million, 2002; Sobel & Kugler, 2007; Wherry, 2002.

Communicating with the Larger Community

School principals are frequently recruited based on stakeholder perceptions of the district's images of effective principals. As such, parents, teachers, central office administrators, and other principals look earnestly at how a prospective principal exhibits the attributes deemed important to the community (Manasse, 1985). And these perceptions for prospective principals are important barometers of principal effectiveness. Additionally, working with a participatory community is a changing role for school principals (Simkins, 2005). It is necessary for principals to take a big-picture view of the role their schools play in society (Usdan, McCloud, & Podmostko, 2000). Successful school leaders who actively pursue positive relationships with external constituents that focus on shared understanding are better able to secure necessary resources and support, and establish formal relationships across organizations. Additionally, school visions are strengthened when principals reach out to their communities to develop mutual support and shared purpose (Leithwood & Riehl, 2003).

Communicating with Local Agencies

A school does not exist in isolation; rather, it exists within an intricate context that influences its effectiveness. As such, a school principal is a school's best advocate and spokesperson internally as well as externally. Audiences that encompass the larger community—local community agencies, police and fire departments, newspapers, civic groups, and local government—all hold a stake in the effectiveness of schools. Consequently, principals are responsible for communicating district policy and serving as an advocate of the school to parents, central office, and community members (Marzano et al., 2005; Portin et al., 2003).

Public support builds successful schools, so there is a significant need to increase public confidence in schools. Unfortunately, too often the media portrays principals as authoritarian, bureaucratic, or comical. Additionally, many principals feel that public support can wax or wane with student test scores. As a result, it is important for principals to work to communicate a positive image of their schools. Mass media support is vital to this mission, and it behooves principals to develop positive relationships with the media (Portin et al., 2003; Riggens-Newby & Hayden, 2004).

Marketing Schools

Whether a school is private, public, or charter, it is beneficial for school principals to market their schools. Cultivating partnerships with outside organizations can help to garner resources and support for schools and promote a positive image to the public (Jacobsen & Gladstone, 1999; Portin et al., 2003). It is also important for school principals to market reform efforts to stakeholders within their school. Change is never easy, and communicating the need for change and its potential benefits can go a long way to implement those desired changes more smoothly. Marketing their school for recruitment purposes also helps principals attract staff that will support the mission and vision of their schools (Portin et al., 2003).

In one large-scale study in England, efforts were made to build capacity across all schools. As part of this ongoing effort, principals worked with each other to improve student learning. Benefits included a concern of principals in the success of other schools, and they gained new insights and ideas through their collaboration with school teams. Interestingly, school districts that showed improvements all had active external partners that included businesses, foundations, universities, and other community organizations. Moreover, effective external support can also come from neighboring school districts (Fullan et al., 2004).

Community and Business Partnerships

Community and business partnerships with schools help to improve existing programs, develop specific projects, or foster school reform (Ritter & Gottfried, 2002). Cultivating partnerships with businesses and educational organizations can reap benefits for both students and teachers. These partnerships can take many forms depending upon the needs they are designed to meet (Jacobsen & Gladstone, 1999; Leithwood & Riehl, 2003; Madison, Marson, & Reese, 1999; Ritter & Gottfried, 2002). Furthermore, positive pressure from external partners that is combined with internal energy within a school can be a catalyst that brings about success in meeting challenging school goals (Fullan et al., 2004).

Partnerships may be formed to benefit specific student populations. For example, in one collaborative endeavor involving several organizations, including a university partnership with a local school district, the dropout rate of at-risk special education students was substantially reduced.

Additionally, more than half of those who had already dropped out of school obtained employment (Madison et al., 1999).

Teachers and students both may become beneficiaries of partnership efforts. Sometimes partnerships are designed to encourage teachers to develop, collaborate on, and share innovative practices. For instance, a combined university and business partnership used technology to enhance instruction for elementary school students. Several technology firms provided teachers with staff development to help them effectively use the technology. With the additional donation of hardware and software to the schools, ultimately, student learning and performance improved as a result of these partnership efforts (Jacobsen & Gladstone, 1999).

Key Research Findings

Research shows the following:

- The current role of the principal is being redefined and often requires principals to network with individuals and groups in other organizations to build partnerships for pursuing shared goals (Simkins, 2005).
- Marketing their schools helps principals attract high-quality teaching staff (Portin et al., 2003).
- Community leadership is an important role for contemporary school principals to exercise. Understanding the role that a school has in society necessitates the inclusion of educators, community members, and parents in shared leadership (Usdan et al., 2000).
- Professional and state standards for school leaders have expectations for principals to form relationships with families and the larger community (Catano & Stronge, 2007).
- External partners can exert targeted pressure that leads to school improvement. School districts that demonstrated improved performance had external partners (Fullan et al., 2004).
- The type of community that a school serves influences how principals approach their jobs (Hallinger et al., 1996).
- Successful school leaders must be able to work effectively with parent, community, business, and government representatives (Leithwood & Riehl, 2003).
- A widely shared sense of community is an important support for families and children living in an unstable and insecure world (Leithwood et al., 2004).

- Public support creates more effective schools (Riggens-Newby & Hayden, 2004).
- Contemporary public school principals are often found raising supplementary funds from parents, businesses, and other organizations (Portin et al., 2003).
- Networking with people and groups in other organizations to solve common problems and pursue shared purposes is an emerging role for school principals (Simkins, 2005).
- Aspiring principals need to be aware of the school's role in society and developing community relationships (Usdan et al., 2000).
- Complex changes that conflict with current values and norms and break with past practice influence stakeholder perceptions of a principal's responsibilities. Stakeholders tend to view a principal's responsibilities as declining during periods of such change (Waters & Grubb, 2004).

Related Resources: Blank et al., 2004; Gallagher et al., 1997; Lashway, 2003; Leinau, 1997; Melaville & Blank, 2000; Million, 2004; Wherry, 2002.

A Final Word on the Importance of Effective Communication

Good communication is the foundation for building positive relationships with parents, families, and the larger community. This statement seems self-evident; unfortunately, the importance of effective communication can be taken for granted or even neglected. When a breakdown in communication occurs with any constituency, it is always to the detriment of the school and its students. Thus, it is critical for principals to communicate effectively to both internal and external constituents. The world outside schools is changing rapidly; consequently, it takes positive, effective, and ongoing communication to meet the challenges associated with preparing students to enter this changing world.

Reference	Effective Communication	Parents and Families	The Larger Community
Blank et al., 2004		•	•
Catano & Stronge, 2006	•	•	•
Catano & Stronge, 2007	•	•	•
Chavkin & Williams, 1993		•	
Cotton, 2003	•	•	
Cotton & Wikelund, 1989		•	
Fullan et al., 2004		•	•
Gallagher et al., 1997			•
Hallinger et al., 1996		•	•
Jacobsen & Gladstone, 1999			•
Jeynes, 2003		•	
Kythreotis & Pashiardis, 1998a	•		
Kythreotis & Pashiardis, 1998b	•	•	
Lashway, 2003			•
Leinau, 1997			•
Leithwood et al., 2004			•
Leithwood & Riehl, 2003	•		•
Madison et al., 1999			•
Manasse, 1985			•
Marzano et al., 2005	•	•	•
Mazzeo, 2003		•	•
Melaville & Blank, 2000		•	•
Million, 2002	•	•	
Million, 2004	•		
Portin et al., 2003			•
Riggins-Newby & Hayden, 2004			•

Figure 6.1 **Key References for Communication and Community Relations**

(continued)

Reference	Effective Communication	Parents and Families	The Larger Community
Figure 6.1 **Key References for Communication and Community Relations,** *cont.*			
Ritter & Gottfried, 2002			•
Simkins, 2005			•
Sobel & Kugler, 2007	•	•	
Sorenson, 2005	•		
Tucker & Tschannen-Moran, 2002		•	
Usdan et al., 2000			•
Waters & Grubb, 2004	•		•
Wherry, 2002		•	•

7

Professionalism and the Principal: Making a Contribution to the Educational Community

_____

When asked about himself, Fernando says that he is just doing what is right for students and teachers. Yet, his track record, service to the profession, and observations by others would suggest much more is occurring. As part of a school district initiative and Fernando's professional growth, he asked colleagues, teachers, and parents to complete an online survey about his leadership. When the outside consultants who analyzed the survey told Fernando the results, he politely listened. The consultants finally told him that he did not understand the significance of the survey; they had never seen such a positive, affirming, and outstanding set of findings and comments in all the years they had been administering the survey.

Fernando has a reputation as a hardworking high school principal. His leadership is a hands-on, no-holds-barred approach to education where what makes sense is done; what doesn't pass muster is sidelined. Slackers are not tolerated; they are transformed. Teachers want to work for him, parents and community members respect him, and students love him because he truly is invested in them. His leadership extends beyond his school's doors through conference presentations, committee service, and visits to other schools. Teams from other school districts are regularly welcomed into his school to observe the magic of learning that happens daily. He constantly has people and data on the brain. Fernando could work 24 hours a day, but he doesn't. At the end of a long workday, he does what many parents do: he picks up his children from after-school care, helps with homework, and kisses his daughters good night.

How should principals proceed with their work in terms of the competing demands for their time and attention? Contemporary principals find themselves managing competing tasks on a day to day basis. This challenge is, for the most part, the result of efforts to satisfy the many complex demands from both internal and external stakeholders of the school community (Catano & Stronge, 2006). From the national level to the local community, administrators, teachers, parents, and community members scrutinize the performance of schools and, subsequently, principals (Langer & Boris-Schacter, 2003; Thomas, Grigsby, Miller, & Scully, 2003; Tyack & Cuban, 1995). If all stakeholders were to demand the same outcomes, with the same methods, at the same time, then the job of a school principal would be dramatically simplified. However, more often than not, the demands are different and may even be at odds with one another. For example, state departments of education demand that schools and principals meet accountability standards that are developed at the state level and are focused primarily on instructional effectiveness in order to achieve predetermined benchmarks for academic standards (Glidden, 1999). On the other hand, public messages, illuminated by the media, indicate that schools should pay attention to violence prevention, bullies, and the emotional needs of their students (Garsten & Buckley, 1999; Price, 1999). Additionally, the increased scrutiny for improved academic performance applies pressure on schools to focus on the cognitive aspect of schooling, conflicting with the additional demand to focus on students' emotional needs (Shortt, Moffett, & Williams, 2001).

The principal's job, indeed, is comprehensive, increasingly complex, and often conflicting; in a word, it is challenging (and this description constitutes a major understatement). Although most of *Qualities of Effective Principals* focuses on the research related to what good principals do, it is essential that we also focus our attention on how they do their work. This chapter on the professionalism of the principal does precisely that, with particular attention given to research related to the following issues:

- Professional standards for the principalship
- The principal and ethical behavior
- The principal as a role model
- Professional development for the principal

Each of these components of professionalism will be explored, culminating with a summary of key findings and references. Figure 7.3, at the end of the chapter, provides a matrix of selected research associated with each of these issues.

Principal Performance Standards

In recent years, standards of performance for the principal have evolved to reflect the complexity of the job, with multiple sets of guiding principles and performance standards emanating from national, state, and local governing bodies. To illustrate, the Interstate School Leaders Licensure Consortium (ISLLC) developed national standards for school leaders (Murphy, 2003). Most states establish licensure standards for principals at the state level, and localities follow with attempts to standardize the work of principals through the development of job descriptions and evaluation instruments. Unfortunately, these various accrediting and governing bodies that are promulgating principal performance standards don't always agree, which often results in competing or confusing standards for the principal's licensure, evaluation, and work (Catano, 2002). Nonetheless, in an age of standards-based practices at all levels of schooling, it is essential that we consider the nature and contents of leading performance standards for the principalship.

ISLLC developed standards that support a multifaceted view of the role of school principals (ISLLC, 1996). As a consortium of educational organizations, it began work in 1994 to redefine school leadership. From the beginning of the project, the developers believed that the ISLLC standards would be strengthened if designed around a set of overarching principles. Following are the principles around which the ISLLC standards were designed and promulgated:

- Standards should reflect the centrality of student learning.
- Standards should acknowledge the changing role of the school leader.
- Standards should recognize the collaborative nature of school leadership.
- Standards should be high, upgrading the quality of the profession.
- Standards should inform performance-based systems of assessment and evaluation for school leaders.

- Standards should be integrated and coherent.
- Standards should be predicated on the concepts of access, opportunity, and empowerment for all members of the school community (Council of Chief State School Officers, 2002, p. 7).[1]

Ultimately, six standards emerged from the work of the Council of Chief State School Officers indicating that a school administrator is an educational leader who promotes the success of all students by (1) facilitating a shared vision, (2) promoting a school culture and instructional program focused on growth for staff and students, (3) attending to management and day-to-day operations, (4) building relationships with families and the larger community, (5) acting in a fair and ethical manner, and (6) responding to and influencing the larger political, social, economic, legal, and cultural context. Figure 7.1 provides the language of the standards.

Although these standards have been criticized in recent years (see, for example, Anderson, 2001, and English, 2006), they, nonetheless, have been quite influential in principal licensure and practice.

The Principal and Ethical Behavior

Lashway (2003), in his review of the role of the school principal, emphasized the importance of acting with integrity and fairness in an ethical manner. Ultimately, this description is the epitome of how principals are expected—or, more accurately, required—to behave in fulfilling their professional role and responsibilities. Principals can get all other aspects of their job right, but a failing here will render them unable to do the job well or, in some instances, even to continue in the job. Thus, we offer that the quality of ethical behavior is paramount to success in the principalship or any other profession, for that matter. In particular, we focus on the principal's behavior in relation to moral purpose, trust, and ethical standards in the following sections of the chapter.

Moral Purpose and the Principalship

Fullan (2002) defined moral purpose as "social responsibility to others and the environment" (p. 15). Further, he stated:

---

[1] Revisions to the ISLLC standards began in 2005 and were ongoing as of this writing.

Figure 7.1 **Interstate School Leadership Licensure Consortium Standards**

Standard	Description
Standard 1	A school administrator is an educational leader who promotes the success of all students by facilitating the development, articulation, implementation, and stewardship of a vision of learning that is shared and supported by the school community.
Standard 2	A school administrator is an educational leader who promotes the success of all students by advocating, nurturing, and sustaining a school culture and instructional program conducive to student learning and staff professional growth.
Standard 3	A school administrator is an educational leader who promotes the success of all students by ensuring management of the organization, operations, and resources for a safe, efficient, and effective learning environment.
Standard 4	A school administrator is an educational leader who promotes the success of all students by collaborating with families and community members, responding to diverse community interests and needs, and mobilizing community resources.
Standard 5	A school administrator is an educational leader who promotes the success of all students by acting with integrity, fairness, and in an ethical manner.
Standard 6	A school administrator is an educational leader who promotes the success of all students by understanding, responding to, and influencing the larger political, social, economic, legal, and cultural context.

Source: From *Interstate School Leaders Licensure Consortium (ISLLC) Standards for School Leaders,* 1996, Washington, DC: Author. Retrieved June 14, 2007, from http://www.castleton.edu/woodruffinstitute/isllcstd.pdf. Reprinted with permission.

School leaders with moral purpose seek to make a difference in the lives of students. They are concerned about closing the gap between high-performing and lower-performing schools and raising the achievement of—and closing the gap between—high-performing and lower-performing students. They act with the intention of making a positive difference in their own schools as well as improving the environment in other district schools. (p. 17)

The intended outcome of moral purpose is to make "explicit the goal of raising the bar and closing the gap for all individuals and schools" (Fullan et al., 2004, p. 3). As they commit themselves to helping all students succeed, however, school leaders cannot afford to seek success at the expense of ethical behavior. In other words, the ends do not justify the means—that is, if those means fall short of fair and ethical treatment of everyone concerned. In their review of districtwide reform, Fullan and colleagues (2004) noted that "many passionate, morally driven superintendents have failed because they blindly, even courageously, committed themselves to students, running roughshod over any adults who got in the way" (p. 3). Clearly, the same expectations for treatment of others apply to principals.

Principals provide the moral center to the school. Although personal ethical behavior is assumed in the principalship, one essential role of the principal is creating schools that serve moral purposes (Lashway, 2003). The concept—and, more important, practice—of moral leadership (see, for example, Sergiovanni, 1992) is the heart and soul of the school. Although it may occur only infrequently, we all are aware of moral failures in schools in the name of academic progress. Specifically, there are continuing accounts of principals and teachers cheating on high-stakes tests. When this occurs, the individuals involved are failures, regardless of any other results. Indeed, success by any measure must account for moral success.

This concept of the principal's obligation for moral behavior and moral leadership leads to the need for balance regarding *what* principals are expected to do with *how* they do their work. For instance, one study documented principal behaviors that sought to balance legal obligations with concern for people. Specifically, the researchers found that leadership behaviors can assist teachers in balancing the demands of accountability while simultaneously demonstrating respect and care for teacher concerns (Gross & Shapiro, 2000, as cited in Lashway, 2003).

Trust and the Principalship[2]

In a study of school culture in the Chicago Public Schools, Bryk and Schneider (2002) noted that in high-trust school cultures principals are more likely to initiate a personnel action against uncaring or incompetent teachers than leaders in low-trust schools. Thus, it appears that—for trust to exist—all school constituents (including teachers, parents, and students) must know that teaching and learning are central to the success of the school, and everyone must be able to trust that poor teaching simply will not be allowed.

---

[2] The issue of establishing a climate of trust is addressed in Chapter 2, "School Climate."

In one study of reasons why principals lose their jobs, it was found that principals who fail to maintain positive relationships with other people, or who fail to develop the trust and support of school constituents, are more likely to lose their jobs for that reason than for any other (Davis, 1998). "This isn't to suggest that principals must capitulate to the various whims, fancies, or pressure tactics of school constituents; rather, they must present themselves as caring, open, honest, forthright, and balanced in their efforts to address the needs and concerns of others" (Davis & Hensley, 1999, p. 401).

Trust involves relationships between people and must be cultivated (Tschannen-Moran, 2004). It doesn't just happen. As the principal is the one who has authority, it is the responsibility of the principal to begin building a trusting relationship with the faculty. In a study of one school with a high level of trust and two schools with low levels of trust, Tschannen-Moran (2004) found that five components of trust played an important role in the lack of or presence of trust. These factors include benevolence, honesty, openness, reliability, and competence. Indeed, "the principal sets the tone for a school. The principal's behavior has a significant influence on the culture of the school" (Tschannen-Moran, 2004, p. 175).

Ethical Standards for Educational Leaders

The American Association of School Administrators (AASA) (2007) issued a set of ethical standards to guide the practice of educational leaders that stipulates that "professional conduct must conform to an ethical code of behavior, and the code must set high standards for all educational leaders" (para. 1). Furthermore, the standards state that an educational leader's responsibility to the greater school community "requires the leader to maintain standards of exemplary professional conduct while recognizing that his or her actions will be viewed and appraised by the community, professional associates, and students" (AASA, 2007, para. 2).

Although educational leaders serve their schools and community by providing equal educational opportunities to each and every child, the work of the leader must emphasize accountability and results, increased student achievement, and high expectations for each and every student. Figure 7.2 depicts the AASA ethical standards.

To lead according to ethical standards, principals must have a strong understanding of their own beliefs, values, and moral code (Marzano et al.,

Figure 7.2 AASA Ethical Standards for Educational Leaders

Standard	Description
Standard 1	The educational leader makes the education and well-being of students the fundamental value of all decision making.
Standard 2	The educational leader fulfills all professional duties with honesty and integrity and always acts in a trustworthy and responsible manner.
Standard 3	The educational leader supports the principle of due process and protects the civil and human rights of all individuals.
Standard 4	The educational leader implements local, state, and national laws.
Standard 5	The educational leader advises the school board and implements the board's policies and administrative rules and regulations. *Note: This standard is applicable more directly to the superintendent.*
Standard 6	The educational leader pursues appropriate measures to correct those laws, policies, and regulations that are not consistent with sound educational goals or that are not in the best interest of children.
Standard 7	The educational leader avoids using his or her position for personal gain through political, social, religious, economic, or other influences.
Standard 8	The educational leader accepts academic degrees of professional certification only from accredited institutions.
Standard 9	The educational leader maintains the standards and seeks to improve the effectiveness of the profession through research and continuing professional development.
Standard 10	The educational leader honors all contracts until fulfillment, release, or dissolution mutually agreed upon by all parties.
Standard 11	The educational leader accepts responsibilities and accountability for one's own actions and behaviors.
Standard 12	The educational leader commits to serving others above self.

Source: From *Code of ethics: AASA's statement,* 2007, Arlington, VA: Author. Retrieved July 15, 2007, from http://www.aasa.org/about/content.cfm?ItemNumber=2157. Reprinted with permission.

2005). Indeed, Sergiovanni (1992) likens moral leadership to that of a steward or servant. He states, "Servant leadership is practiced by serving others, but its ultimate purpose is to place oneself, and others for whom one has responsibility, in the service of ideals" (p. 138). However, the principal must have a clear sense of the ideals in order to serve them.

It is not enough to have a sense of one's own beliefs, values, and moral codes; one must also communicate these to others through both words and action. Principals can communicate their beliefs to the faculty both verbally and in written form. Then, any decision is measured according to those beliefs. Principals more loudly communicate their ideals by taking action consistent with their ideals (Marzano et al., 2005). The old saying here certainly applies—actions do speak louder than words. Actions are then held up to the scrutiny of previously stated beliefs. A moral compass forms the basis for decision making and problem solving (Beck & Murphy, 1994).

Key Research Findings

Research findings on professional standards and ethical behavior consistently outline the following elements:

- Effective principals are honest and fair, possess a high degree of integrity, and hold themselves to a high standard of ethics (Lashway, 2003; Marzano et al., 2005).
- Effective principals are morally centered, communicating their beliefs and values to the faculty, staff, parents, and students (Beck & Murphy, 1994; Fullan et al., 2004; Sergiovanni, 1992).
- Effective principals balance responsibilities associated with educating young people with the needs of teachers (Gross & Shapiro, 2000 as cited in Lashway, 2003; Tschannen-Moran, 2004).
- Principals who fail to perform their duties with competence and integrity and fail to cultivate relationships have low levels of trust in their schools (Bryk & Schneider, 2002; Tschannen-Moran, 2004), and many lose their jobs for this reason (Davis, 1998).

Related Resources: Beck & Murphy, 1994; Bryk & Schneider, 2002; Davis, 1998; Davis & Hensley, 1999; Fullan, 2002; Fullan et al., 2004; Lashway, 2003; Marzano et al., 2005; Sergiovanni, 1992; Tschannen-Moran, 2004.

The Principal as a Role Model

An excellent review of the principal's influence as a role model is provided by Cotton (2003) in her analysis of the effect of principals on student achievement. In the review, she notes numerous aspects of the importance of principals serving as role models, including the following:

- In high-achieving schools, teacher surveys revealed that teachers' admiration for the principals' leadership is emphasized. Thus, principal esteem by teachers appears to be a factor related to principal effectiveness.
- The ability of principals to "walk their talk" was noted as one of the most valued attributes by teachers.
- The effect of principals on their schools' culture is strongly influenced by what they do, in that other staff and students tend to interpret their actions as what is valued in the school.
- Effective principals demonstrate core values in their daily routines.

Leithwood and colleagues (2004), in their review of the influence of leadership on student learning, stated that principals exert leadership by setting examples for their staff to follow that are consistent with the organization's values. These leadership practices are aimed at enhancing staff members' beliefs about their own capacities. Consistent with this finding, Marzano and colleagues (2005) found that "influence is characterized by modeling behavior through exemplary personal achievements, character, and behavior" (p. 14).

A qualitative study that examined teachers' perceptions of principal characteristics that contributed to feelings of empowerment underscored the importance of the principal as role model (Blase & Blase, 2001). Teachers in schools that were charter members of the League of Professional Schools were given a survey in which teachers were asked to describe these characteristics. Among other findings, the researchers concluded that principals who held and modeled the following five characteristics—optimism, caring, honesty, friendliness, and enthusiasm—were most influential in contributing to teacher empowerment.

Principals, by virtue of their roles as instructional leaders and moral agents in their schools, serve as models for respect, understanding, sensitivity, and appreciation of others. This point isn't negotiable: Principals are role models.

Key Research Findings

Research findings on the principal as role model consistently outline the following elements:

- Effective principals communicate and model core values through their interactions with students and teachers (Cotton, 2003).
- Effective principals increase the efficacy of staff by modeling (Leithwood et al., 2004; Marzano et al., 2005).
- Of the most important behaviors and attitudes to model, the effective principals model that they care for and have a genuine concern for children (Cotton, 2003).
- Principals who model positive characteristics contribute to the empowerment of teachers (Blase & Blase, 2001).

Related Resources: Blase & Blase, 2001; Cotton, 2003; Leithwood et al., 2004; Marzano et al., 2005.

Professional Development for the Principal

So, how do effective principals become effective in the first place? And how do principals maintain their cutting edge of effectiveness? Although they must be skilled practitioners who are committed to giving to others (see, for example, Sergiovanni, 1992, for a discussion of servant leadership), ultimately, principals must give back to themselves. School leaders, as noted throughout this book, serve in a highly skilled profession, and they require continual renewal in order to become and remain an expert. Thus, professional development for the principal is not optional.

In a study of the principalship in Cyprus, the researchers found that although the principals had diverse backgrounds, they did have a particular mentality associated with their careers in common—a degree of risk taking. "They all had varied, diverse, and very strong experiences and took chances with their careers. They all made strong efforts to further their education in order to enhance their options for advancement in the educational system" (Kythreotis & Pashiardis, 1998a, p. 7).

In another study—this time concerned with reasons why good principals don't leave the profession—the researchers found that continuing professional development plays a fundamental role. They noted that "there's so much to know, educators must keep on learning and growing. Professional development is an ethic . . . the administrators with whom we spoke did not see themselves as managers so much as educators and learners" (Boris-Schacter & Merrifield, 2000, p. 90). Professional development opportunities noted by the principals in the study ranged from formal conference attendance and journal reading to informal "just going to work every day."

One team of researchers straightforwardly noted that effective principals focus on their own professional growth in order to become and remain effective. A team of researchers from Stanford University's School of Education conducted a nationwide study of both the pre- and inservice professional development of school principals. Among their findings, they noted "the best principals attended professional development seminars and founded a support network. This encouraged them to provide similar opportunities to teachers in their schools" (LaPointe & Davis, 2006, p. 8).

One particular school district in New York City contributes its success at school improvement to the attention given to professional development for principals (Fink & Resnick, 2001). The school district deliberately developed and implemented a professional development system for principals. Professional development occurred in many different venues and within various contexts. The model for professional development was that of the apprentice. Therefore, principals discussed school needs and school successes, and participated in support groups for intense mentoring as well as study groups for instructional leadership. Principals learned from their peers and received intensive, individualized coaching from a more seasoned professional. Indeed, the researchers explained, "the centrality of professional development in District 2 stems from the assumption that increased student achievement will come only through continuous improvement of practice at every level in the system" (Fink & Resnick, 2001, p. 605). This process includes the principal level.

LaPointe and Davis (2006) noted the following about principal preparation (preservice development) programs:

> First, a growing consensus on the attributes of effective school principals shows that successful school leaders influence student achievement through two important pathways—the support and development of effective teachers and the implementation of effective organizational processes. Second, evidence indicates that effective programs are research-based, have curricular coherence,

provide experience in authentic contexts, use cohort groupings and mentors, and are structured to enable collaborative activity between the program and area schools. Despite anecdotal consensus, supporting empirical evidence is minimal (p 18)

Regarding postservice professional development, LaPointe and Davis (2006) also found that for effective principals:

> [they] not only attended more professional development activities than comparison principals, but found these activities to be more helpful. For example, program principals were nearly twice as likely to visit other schools, to participate in a network of principals, to be mentored by another principal, and to observe and critique the practice of other principals. They were also somewhat more likely to participate in professional development activities along with teachers from their schools. (p. 34)

Unfortunately, professional development for principals tends to focus on surface issues such as the roles and responsibilities of the principal and how to fulfill those roles and responsibilities (Waters & Grubb, 2004). However, just as important is a focus on contextual and foundational issues in fulfilling these roles. In other words, the *when* and *why* are just as critical as the *what* and *how*. So not only is it important that principals receive professional development, but the type of professional development is just as crucial.

As stated previously, the types of professional development for principals are varied. A small study of principal renewal sought to examine the types of professional development in which principals engaged (Drago-Severson, 2004). These activities included reading professional literature, both individually and in groups, participating in retreats, going to or presenting at professional conferences, becoming involved in professional organizations, and mentoring new principals. The researcher concluded, "Just as it is important to provide contexts for teachers to engage in collegial inquiry, so too is it important for principals" (Drago-Severson, 2004, p. 162).

Key Research Findings

Research findings on professional development and the principal consistently outline the following elements:

- Effective principals recognize the importance of their own professional development (Boris-Schacter & Merrifield, 2000; Kythreotis & Pashiardis, 1998a).

- Effective principals participate in various types of professional development, including attending conferences, networking, mentoring, and observing peers (Drago-Severson, 2004; Fink & Resnick, 2001; LaPointe & Davis, 2006).
- Effective principals receive professional development that focuses on their roles and responsibilities as well as the nuances of context that affect their decisions (Waters & Grubb, 2004).

Related Resources: Boris-Schacter & Merrifield, 2000; Drago-Severson, 2004; Fink & Resnick, 2001; Kythreotis & Pashiardis, 1998a; LaPointe & Davis, 2006; Waters & Grubb, 2004.

A Final Word on Why Professionalism Matters

So, how should principals proceed with their work in terms of the competing demands for their time and attention? In brief, the answer is consistent with professional standards and ethical behavior. Another way to summarize the essence of this chapter on professionalism is to say that how principals do their work is vitally important; results count, but so does the manner in which principals work. In order to be successful, principals must understand they are the public image of their schools and, as such, are role models to their students, their staff, and their community. Thus, professionalism is paramount to being a principal.

Figure 7.3 **Key References for Professionalism and the Principal**

Reference	Performance Standards	Ethical Behavior	Role Model	Professional Development
AASA, 2007		•		
Beck & Murphy, 1994		•		
Blase & Blase, 2001			•	
Boris-Schacter & Merrifield, 2000				•
Bryk & Schneider, 2002		•		
Cotton, 2003			•	
Davis, 1998		•		
Davis & Hensley, 1999		•		
Drago-Severson, 2004				•
Fink & Resnick, 2001				•
Fullan, 2002		•		
Fullan et al., 2004		•		
Kythreotis & Pashiardis, 1998b				•
LaPointe & Davis, 2006				•
Lashway, 2003		•		
Leithwood et al., 2004			•	
Marzano et al., 2005		•	•	
Sergiovanni, 1992		•		
Tschannen-Moran, 2004		•		
Waters & Grubb, 2004				•

8

The Ultimate Challenge:
The Principal's Role in
Student Achievement

"Nothing, absolutely nothing has happened in education until it has happened to a student" (Carroll, 1994, p. 87).

So, why does the enterprise of schooling exist? And why do we have school principals, teachers, counselors, and other important staff members? The answer, most simply, is the students. Our mission—from beginning to end—is about students. If this claim is true, then it is imperative that the principal makes a difference in the quality of teaching and learning in the school and, ultimately, in the quality of life of students.

In this final chapter, we focus on the principal's influence on student learning. Specifically, we discuss three key issues:

• The principal's indirect influence on student learning
• The role that school goal setting plays in student achievement
• The importance of using data to guide decision making

The chapter concludes with a brief review of the influence and importance of effective principals. As with the previous chapters, we also provide a matrix (see Figure 8.1) that links the evidence regarding the principal's influence on student achievement with key references.

The Principal's Indirect
Influence on Student Achievement

Evidence accumulated over the past few decades makes it abundantly clear: there is a relationship between the quality of the principal and student achievement, albeit an indirect one. Hallinger and Heck (1996) noted this influence in their synthesis on the role of the principal in student learning: "The effects of principal leadership will occur indirectly through the principal's efforts to influence those who come into more frequent direct contact with students" (p. 24). Reporting on initiatives concerned with the importance of recruiting and training better principals, Mazzeo (2003) found that "what these efforts share is a recognition that school leaders exert a powerful, if indirect, influence on teaching quality and student learning" (p. 1).

In actuality, it appears that many of the principal's duties and responsibilities may play a role in forming the basis for high-quality instructional programs and, ultimately, enhancing student achievement. There have been multiple efforts to define the principal's role in terms of what is important to his or her—and his or her school's—success, including national standards from groups such as the Interstate School Leaders Licensure Consortium (ISLLC) (1996). Even in these efforts, it appears that the ISLLC may underestimate the importance of many of the principal's duties in relation to student achievement:

> A meta-analysis of research that examined the features of leadership associated with student achievement suggests that the ISLLC standards may underemphasize some features of effective leadership practices. These include the ways in which leaders directly participate in curriculum design and implementation; support and promote effective instructional and student assessment practices; recognize individual and school accomplishments; and adapt their leadership to address the context-specific needs of teachers, students, and other stakeholders. (Davis, Darling-Hammond, LaPointe, & Meyerson, 2005, p. 6)

Cotton (2003), in describing the role of effective principals in student achievement, provided a useful example of how principals indirectly influence student achievement in their schools. In her review of existing research, she emphasized the importance of providing teachers with autonomy. "Principals of effective schools respect their teachers' skills and judgment, and allow them considerable autonomy in organizing and managing their classrooms.

They also protect staff members from excessive intrusion by forces outside the school" (Cotton, 2003, p. 70). Thus, it seems clear that the coordinating, facilitating, and encouraging roles—all of which are indirect in terms of students—are essential to successful schools and student achievement.

Actually, the cumulative effects of the principal's work results in a direct impact on school success. One study conducted with the Dallas Independent School District found "that the quickest way to change the effectiveness of a school, for better or worse, is to change the principal" (Mendro, 1998, pp. 263–264). By hiring quality teachers and other staff members, supporting them in their work, fostering a robust climate for student achievement, providing resources for instruction, keeping the focus on teaching and learning, and a host of other important accomplishments, the principal does affect student achievement. Thus, for the principal, "achieving results through others is the essence of leadership" (p. 39).

Key Research Findings

Research findings related to the principal's indirect influence on student achievement are highlighted in the following elements:

- The effects of principal leadership are most apparent through the principal's efforts to influence teachers and others who interact directly with students in instructional settings. Therefore, the principal's influence on student achievement is an indirect but nonetheless powerful one (Hallinger & Heck, 1996).
- Principals who work in schools characterized by high student achievement empower teachers to make their own decisions within the classroom and focus on student achievement (Cotton, 2003).
- School turnaround is significantly affected by principal turnaround (Mendro, 1998).
- Schools with high at-risk populations that exceed expectations for student achievement share a common element—a strong leader committed to education (Cawelti, 1999).
- Principals exert influence on student achievement through their influence on school climate (Hallinger et al. 1996; Mendro, 1998) and through their leadership style (Kythreotis & Pashiardis, 1998a).

Related Resources: Cawelti, 1999; Cotton, 2003; Hallinger et al., 1996; Hallinger & Heck, 1996; Kythreotis & Pashiardis, 1998a; Mazzeo, 2003; Mendro, 1998.

Focus on School Goals and Student Achievement

One way in which principals affect student success in their schools is by setting, supporting, and sustaining a focus on school goals and schoolwide student achievement. "Interestingly, when the studies that report positive findings are reviewed, only one mediating variable shows up with consistency as a significant factor interacting with principal leadership: school goals. . . . This function of the principal—sustaining a schoolwide purpose focusing on student learning—does receive empirical support" (Hallinger & Heck, 1996, p. 38).

A specific study that illustrates the power of focusing on school achievement goals comes from the Dallas Independent School District. For many years, the Dallas Independent School District used value-added student assessment indices to identify characteristics of effective and ineffective schools. Using these data, researchers investigated factors that were associated with high student achievement in whole schools. The results of one of these studies revealed the following:

> Effective and ineffective schools were sampled, and evaluators identified three consistent characteristics of effective schools. First, effective schools had achievement as a major focus. Second, the staff in effective schools expected students to achieve. (This is different from believing all students can learn but not expecting it.) Finally, the principals of effective schools did not tolerate ineffective teachers. Ineffective teachers were expected to change, or they were removed. Outside of these principles and a few others noted that were less prominent, the effective schools all differed in terms of atmosphere, management styles, and other dimensions. (Mendro, 1998, p. 264)

Of the three factors identified by Mendro, two (achievement as a schoolwide focus and expecting all students to learn) are focused explicitly on setting high achievement expectations and sticking to them. The third (not tolerating ineffective teachers) is a logical and powerful way in which principals of high-achieving schools hold themselves and their teachers accountable for student performance. Similarly, in a study of benchmark schools, Cawelti (1999) found that these schools focused on raising student achievement by setting goals. In fact, "in four of the six schools, the principals stated unabashedly that their main goal is to improve results on state assessments or other standardized tests" (p. 63).

Related to the matter of establishing high expectations through school goals, principals influence student achievement by shaping the school's instructional climate and instructional organization. This influence is a result of the principal's on-the-job direct actions as the school's leader and the ability to create and sustain school policies and norms (Bossert, Dwyer, Rowan, & Lee, 1982).

Holding high student expectations, however, is not synonymous with a focus on high-stakes test results to the exclusion of other worthy school goals. Also, it doesn't mean discarding the principal's leadership practices and starting over. Rather, a keen focus on student achievement more likely means a sharpening of the focus on robust, desirable school achievement goals. In interviews with principals concerning their practices regarding high-stakes tests, Reed and colleagues (2001) found that "principals in lower performing schools are more likely to modify their leadership focus to place a greater emphasis on improving test scores. Principals in higher performing schools seemed to focus on educating the whole child rather than simply concentrating on raising test scores" (p. 12).

Sergiovanni (1984) considered leadership to be less about managing and more about norms, beliefs, and principles, which are components of goal setting. Moreover, most definitions of instructional leadership include behaviors focused on the goal of influencing and improving student achievement (Copland, 2002; McEwan, 2003; Reeves, 2003; Supovitz & Poglinco, 2001; Waters, Marzano, & McNulty, 2003). Similarly, Lashway (2002a) described important behaviors for developing effective instructional leaders to include "making student and adult learning a priority, setting high expectations, and aligning instruction to standards" (p. 2). Each of these leadership behaviors relate directly to the principal's focus on setting robust learning goals.

Key Research Findings

Research findings related to the principal's influence through goal setting are summarized in the following elements:

- There is a relationship between principal leadership and school-level instructional processes. Additionally, selected school effectiveness factors have an effect on student achievement, and the principal's leadership plays an important role in the selection, support, and success of those school processes (Hallinger & Heck, 1996).

- "Just as leaders can have a positive impact on achievement, they also can have a marginal, or worse, a negative impact on achievement" (Waters et al., 2003, p. 5).
- Effective school leaders focus on student achievement through the use of goal setting based on curriculum standards (Cawelti, 1999; Hallinger & Heck, 1996; Leithwood et al., 2004).

Related Resources: Bossert, et al., 1982; Cawelti, 1999; Copland, 2002; Hallinger & Heck, 1996; Lashway, 2002a; Leithwood et al., 2004; McEwan, 2003; Mendro, 1998; Reed et al., 2001; Reeves, 2003; Sergiovanni, 1984; Supovitz & Poglinco, 2001; Usdan et al., 2000; Waters et al., 2003.

The Principal's Use of Data to Guide School Success

There is a fundamental link that connects school goals and attaining those goals, and that connecting thread is using data to make informed decisions. Success doesn't just occur through happenstance. Rather, it takes a commitment to data-informed decision making in order to assess

- What is the starting point in any worthy endeavor?
- What realistic, yet rigorous, achievement goals should be set?
- Where is the school in accomplishing various benchmarks along the way?
- What midcourse corrective action is needed in order to accomplish desired outcomes?
- Did the school achieve its goals?
- Why or why not? And what's next?

In summarizing the crucial role that principals play in improving teaching and learning, Usdan and colleagues (2000) reported that principals

> . . . must know academic content and pedagogical techniques. They must work with teachers to strengthen skills. *They must collect, analyze, and use data in ways that fuel excellence.* They must rally students, teachers, parents, local health and social service agencies, youth development groups, local businesses, and other community residents and partners around the common goal of raising student performance (emphasis added). (p. 2)

Supporting this claim regarding the efficacy of data-driven decision making in the school, Leithwood and colleagues (2004) found that "effective leaders are able to identify clearly how well the school organization is performing along multiple indicators and to use that information as goals are developed and refined. This requires astute skills for gathering information and turning it into useful knowledge" (p. 18). Additionally, effective school leaders encourage teachers to make decisions based on student achievement or progress data, rather than merely on instinct. They also ensure that teachers are provided training in how to use data to guide instruction (Snipes, Doolittle, & Herlihy, 2002, Togneri & Anderson, 2003). In fact, one of the standards from the National Staff Development Council (NSDC) states, "Staff development that improves the learning of all students uses disaggregated student data to determine adult learning priorities, monitor progress, and help sustain continuous improvement" (para. 1). They further state that both teachers and administrators must receive professional development in how to use data to address student needs (NSDC, 2001). Focusing on data keeps the focus on school and student improvement (Fink & Resnick, 2001; Schmoker, 2006).

Key Research Findings

Research findings related to the principal's influence through focusing on using data are summarized in the following elements:

- Principals in high-performing schools place less pressure on their teachers to perform well on standardized tests, even though high-stakes testing is still a concern. Modifications to the curriculum and teaching practices are more likely to occur in low-performing schools (Reed et al., 2001).
- High-performing schools focus on using varying types of data such as standardized scores as well as progress monitoring in order to guide school programs and instruction (Snipes et al., 2002; Togneri & Anderson, 2003).
- Effective school leaders provide professional development in using data to modify instruction as well as seek professional development themselves in how to use data for schoolwide decision making (NSDC, 2001).
- Effective school leaders keep the focus on school improvement through analyzing and using data (Fink & Resnick, 2001; Schmoker, 2006).

Related Resources: Fink & Resnick, 2001; Leithwood, et al., 2004; NSDC, 2001; Schmoker, 2006; Snipes et al., 2002; Togneri & Anderson, 2003; Usdan et al., 2000.

A Final Word on Why We Need Good Principals

In the final analysis, does it matter whether effective principals influence student achievement directly or indirectly, as long as they have a positive effect on student learning? The important point, both for research and practice, is understanding the ways and means by which principals do influence their schools' educational programs (Hallinger & Heck, 1996). For effective principals—all funds they receive and spend, all resources they allocate, every employee they hire, indeed, everything they do—is about the students. If what principals do doesn't positively touch the lives of students, then they probably shouldn't be doing it. The best measure of principals' success is that, at the end of the day, students should be better off for having spent time in their schools. And that's why good principals are important.

Figure 8.1 **Key References for Student Achievement**

Reference	Influence on Student Achievement	Focus on School Goals	Use of Data for Schoolwide Decision Making
Bossert et al., 1982		•	
Cawelti, 1999	•	•	
Copland, 2002		•	
Cotton, 2003	•		
Davis et al., 2005	•		
Fink & Resnick, 2001			•
Hallinger et al., 1996	•		
Hallinger & Heck, 1996	•	•	
Interstate School Leaders Licensure Consortium, 1996	•		
Kythreotis & Pashiardis, 1998a	•		
Lashway, 2002a		•	
Leithwood et al., 2004		•	•
Mazzeo, 2003	•		
McEwan, 2003		•	
Mendro, 1998	•	•	
National Staff Development Council, 2001			•
Reed et al., 2001		•	•
Reeves, 2003		•	
Schmoker, 2006			•
Sergiovanni, 1984		•	
Snipes et al., 2002			•
Supovitz & Poglinco, 2001		•	
Togneri & Anderson, 2003			•
Usdan et al., 2000		•	•
Waters et al., 2003		•	

Part 2

Principal Effectiveness: Tools You Can Use

Part 2 of *Qualities of Effective Principals* contains resources that can be used to apply the content and concepts presented in the chapters included in Part 1. Divided into three major sections, Part 2 provides skills checklists, detailed lists of principal quality indicators and red flags, and an annotated bibliography.[1]

• • •

Section I: Principal Skills Assessment Checklists

The Principal Skills Assessment Checklists are based on a synthesis of the research presented throughout *Qualities of Effective Principals*. The checklists are designed to help identify key indicators of effectiveness in a principal's leadership. Each effectiveness quality identified in a checklist includes multiple indicators of success. The checklists also provide a continuum for rating relative strengths and weaknesses, ranging from ineffective to master.

---

[1] Readers familiar with the ASCD book *Qualities of Effective Teachers* will recognize the format used in this section to present principal skills checklists, quality indicators and red flags, and an annotated bibliography.

The checklists can be used for self-assessment by the principal to review and reflect on the components identified as important for effective leadership. Additionally, supervisors and peers can use the skills checklists as part of their assessment of another principal's ability. The checklists are intended to support identification of strengths and weaknesses so that professional growth can be stimulated and professional development opportunities can be tailored to specific principal needs.

Section II: Principal Quality Indicators and Red Flags

The information in this section is designed primarily to assist building administrators and their supervisors in identifying key components of effectiveness as they view the practices of the administrator. In essence, Section II focuses on behaviors that principals exhibit in their daily work.

The quality indicators and red flags should not be applied indiscriminately; rather, the building administrator and his or her supervisor should carefully consider the actual roles and responsibilities fulfilled by the administrator. For instance, some assistant principals may not have a primary responsibility in the area of fiscal responsibility; thus, these individuals, logically, would not find the indicators related to finance appropriate. In all cases, we do trust that feedback from supervisors or self-reflection on the principal qualities can be the impetus to refine building administrator skills and practices.

Section III: Annotated Bibliography

Section III contains an annotated bibliography of selected sources drawn from existing research for the reader who would like to know more about specific aspects of the principal effectiveness research. Where possible, we selected publications that reflect empirical evidence related to principal research. In some instances, we chose to include annotations that are issue or policy oriented rather than empirically based.

The short annotations are presented in a straightforward, compact, and uniform format for ease in referencing and using the information. The matrix preceding the annotated bibliography is intended as a resource to connect the annotations with the book's chapters. Additionally, a complete list of references used in *Qualities of Effective Principals* is provided at the end of the text.

Principal Skills
Assessment Checklists

Key to the Principal Skills Checklists

Master: The principal exhibits the quality such that others would be able to use the principal as an expert for how to lead a school. The principal not only has a sense of the quality but demonstrates an understanding of the essence of the quality.

Professional: The principal exhibits the quality most of the time.

Apprentice: The principal demonstrates the quality to the degree necessary to make the school function. The principal may lack fluidness of use, but the result is still effective.

Ineffective: The principal's performance is less than acceptable, and he or she would benefit from a focused effort to improve performance.

Not Observed: The observer has not seen evidence, through either demonstration or observation, of the quality.

Checklist 1—Principal Skills Checklist

Instructional Leadership

Quality	Indicators	Not Observed	Ineffective	Apprentice	Professional	Master
School Vision	Develops a clear vision for the school.					
	Develops clear goals for the school.					
	Is confident about ability to accomplish vision and mission.					
	Protects instructional time in the school.					
	Focuses on school improvement.					
	Communicates the most important mission—learning.					
Shared Leadership	Works to attain goals through individual and collective efforts.					
	Uses expertise of teacher leaders in the school.					
	Creates opportunities for collaboration among teachers.					
	Distributes leadership roles and responsibilities to others.					
Learning Community	Makes student learning the centerpiece of any work.					
	Fosters a learning community among all stakeholders.					
	Learns along with faculty.					
	Provides staff development that focuses on improving teaching and learning.					
	Uses teacher experts to further teaching and learning.					

Checklist 1—Principal Skills Checklist

Instructional Leadership, *cont.*

Quality	Indicators	Not Observed	Ineffective	Apprentice	Professional	Master
Data Gathering and Assessing	Gathers various types of data for analysis.					
	Uses data to determine school effectiveness.					
	Influences staff to use data to make instructional decisions.					
Curriculum and Instruction Monitoring	Knows good instructional practices associated with different subject areas.					
	Makes sure curriculum standards are taught.					
	Models behavior expected of staff.					
	Discusses teaching practices with individual staff members.					
	Visits classrooms frequently to monitor teaching and learning.					

Checklist 2—Principal Skills Checklist

School Climate

Quality	Indicators	Not Observed	Ineffective	Apprentice	Professional	Master
Fostering and Sustaining School Climate	Involves all stakeholders in the school.					
	Creates a positive learning environment.					
	Models high expectations of staff and students.					
	Maintains a respectful relationship with staff, students, and parents.					
	Manages conflict and crisis in a timely and expert manner.					
Attending to Internal and External Dynamics	Establishes a climate of trust within the school.					
	Demonstrates honesty and credibility.					
	Monitors internal and external factors affecting school.					
Having High Expectations and Respect	Demonstrates caring, support, and respect for students.					
	Provides direction to staff and students.					
	Influences others' decisions.					
	Demonstrates concern for staff's personal needs.					
Handling Conflict and Crisis	Proactively establishes crisis management plans.					
	Keeps parents and community informed of safety issues.					
	Shares with parents and community how incidents are handled.					
Shared Decision Making	Distributes tasks within the school					
	Fosters multiple leaders in the school.					
	Empowers staff to make shared decisions.					
	Reviews school programs regularly.					

Checklist 3—Principal Skills Checklist

Human Resource Administration

Quality	Indicators	Not Observed	Ineffective	Apprentice	Professional	Master
Teacher Selection	Selects capable teachers.					
	Uses research-based interviewing practices.					
	Selects capable nonteaching staff.					
	Knows the hiring process in the school system.					
	Uses the school system hiring process as an advantage.					
Teacher Induction	Identifies strengths and weaknesses of new teachers.					
	Works with new teachers to improve their performance.					
	Creates a culture of support for new teachers.					
	Implements formal and informal procedures to help new staff members.					
Teacher Mentoring	Develops support for mentoring program.					
	Matches the right mentor with the right mentee.					
	Provides opportunities for new teachers to serve as experts in an area of strength.					
	Communicates expectations to new staff.					
	Serves as a role model to those mentoring new staff.					

(continued)

Checklist 3—Principal Skills Checklist

Human Resource Administration, *cont.*

Quality	Indicators	Not Observed	Ineffective	Apprentice	Professional	Master
Professional Development	Supports professional development initiatives.					
	Gains access to resources for professional development.					
	Matches needs of staff to professional development opportunities.					
	Solicits input from teachers in the design and implementation of professional development.					
	Fosters an atmosphere of professional learning among staff.					
Staff Retention	Promotes collaborative working relationships.					
	Supports positive working conditions.					
	Encourages innovation and risktaking.					
	Recognizes the importance of retaining quality staff.					

Checklist 4—Principal Skills Checklist

Teacher Evaluation

Quality	Indicators	Not Observed	Ineffective	Apprentice	Professional	Master
Evaluating Teachers	Focuses on both improvement and accountability in evaluating teachers.					
	Communicates with teachers throughout the evaluation process.					
	Informs teachers of elements related to the evaluation process.					
	Adheres to evaluation timeline.					
	Participates in programs designed to strengthen evaluation skills.					
	Conducts formal and informal conferences with teachers.					
Documenting Performance of Teachers[1]	Uses multiple data sources to evaluate teachers.					
	Conducts both formal and informal observations.					
	Considers student performance when evaluating teachers.					
	Provides feedback to teachers after observations.					
Adhering to Legal Considerations	Informs teachers of evaluation criteria prior to the evaluation process.					
	Follows state and local procedural process.					
	Maintains objectivity during evaluation process.					
	Documents patterns and effects of observed behaviors.					
	Provides clear descriptions of deficiencies, if they exist.					
	Provides clear remediable actions in case of deficiencies.					

[1]Documenting teacher performance is dependent on a school district's teacher evaluation system and cannot be applied without consideration of the unique requirements and methods included in the respective evaluation system.

Checklist 5—Principal Skills Checklist

Organizational Management

Quality	Indicators	Not Observed	Ineffective	Apprentice	Professional	Master
Coordination of Facilities and Operations	Provides procedures and routines to create an orderly environment.					
	Provides clear rules and routines for staff.					
	Provides clear rules and routines for students.					
	Ensures a trained crisis team is available.					
	Oversees routine maintenance of the facility.					
	Develops a master schedule that reflects state and local requirements.					
Allocation of Fiscal Resources	Reviews previous school budgets.					
	Develops a budget for each fiscal year.					
	Plans and prioritizes expenses.					
	Communicates distribution procedures to staff.					
	Creates procedures for reimbursement.					
	Follows board policy for vendors and bids.					
	Develops partnerships with community organizations.					
Use of Technology Resources	Provides training in technology to teachers.					
	Supports procurement of technology resources for use in instruction.					
	Uses technology effectively for administrative tasks.					

Checklist 6—Principal Skills Checklist

Communication and Community Relations

Quality	Indicators	Not Observed	Ineffective	Apprentice	Professional	Master
Effective Communication	Listens to stakeholder suggestions.					
	Applies stakeholder suggestions, if appropriate.					
	Maintains open lines of communication with all stakeholders.					
Communication with Parents and Families	Gathers input from parents and community members in making decisions.					
	Develops parent programs focused on instruction.					
	Fosters parental involvement.					
Communication with the Larger Community	Communicates positive image of school.					
	Cultivates partnerships with outside organizations.					
	Develops positive relationships with the media.					

Checklist 7—Principal Skills Checklist

Professionalism and the Principal

Quality	Indicators	Not Observed	Ineffective	Apprentice	Professional	Master
Standards and Ethical Behavior	Communicates beliefs and values to all stakeholders.					
	Balances responsibilities to students with needs of teachers.					
	Maintains a high ethical standard.					
	Performs duties with competence and integrity.					
Role Model	Models care for children.					
	Models desired characteristics for teachers.					
Professional Development	Participates in various types of professional development.					
	Talks with other principals regarding challenges.					
	Visits other schools.					
	Develops a network of support.					
	Participates in peer observation with other principals.					

Checklist 8—Principal Skills Checklist

Student Achievement

Quality	Indicators	Not Observed	Ineffective	Apprentice	Professional	Master
Behaviors Indirectly Influencing Student Achievement	Focuses on student learning in the school.					
	Focuses on implementing and achieving student performance standards.					
	Holds high expectations of teachers and students.					
	Protects academic learning time.					
	Emphasizes high-quality instruction related to the established curriculum.					
	Communicates to students a belief in their ability to succeed.					
Goal Setting and Student Achievement	Focuses on student achievement goals.					
	Makes decisions about school operations in terms of student academic goals.					
	Monitors school success based on student attainment of academic goals.					
Using Data to Guide Decision Making	Plans for an effective data collection and analysis system related to the school or program goals and objectives.					
	Analyzes student achievement data.					
	Ensures that student progress data are used to make instructional decisions.					
	Sets benchmarks to monitor progress toward school goals.					
	Takes midcourse corrective action to accomplish desired student outcomes.					
	Determines whether school goals were attained.					

Section II

Principal Quality Indicators and Red Flags

This set of principal responsibilities and behaviors, or qualities, is designed primarily to assist administrators and those who evaluate administrators in identifying key components of effectiveness as they visit schools and observe administrators in action. In essence, they are intended to facilitate a type of action research focused on behaviors that principals exhibit in their daily work. For some principals, the guidance that can emerge from feedback on the school qualities may be the impetus to refine a strategy or add something new to their toolkit of skills and techniques.

The positive and negative behaviors exhibited by principals determine, to a great extent, their effectiveness in leadership and, ultimately, the effect they have on teachers and student achievement. Several specific characteristics of principal responsibilities and behaviors that contribute directly to effective leadership are listed for each of the following categories:

- Instructional Leadership
- School Climate
- Human Resource Administration
- Teacher Evaluation
- Organizational Management
- Communication and Community Relations
- Professionalism and the Principal
- The Principal's Role in Student Achievement

Red flags signaling ineffective leadership are presented at the end of each section. Both positive and negative characteristics are based on a plethora of research-based studies that address the concept of improving the educational system for students, teachers, and schools. These qualities are general for any school level. The lists are provided as a vehicle to promote principal effectiveness.

Instructional Leadership

Instructional leadership leads to better learning experiences in schools.

Quality Indicators

- Building and Sustaining a School Vision
  - Has a clear vision for the school.
  - Strives to ensure quality instruction.
  - Holds high expectations for teachers and students.
  - Models confidence in the school to reach goals.
  - Focuses on school improvement.
  - Communicates to all stakeholders that learning is the school's most important mission.
- Sharing Leadership
  - Realizes he or she cannot reach instructional goals alone.
  - Attains school goals through individual and shared efforts.
  - Believes that staff should collaborate openly.
  - Discusses instruction and program administration collectively among all stakeholders.
  - Distributes leadership across the school.
  - Develops and counts on the expertise of teacher leaders to improve school effectiveness.
  - Creates opportunities for teachers to work together.
  - Functions as the chief instructional leader of the school while balancing multiple responsibilities.
- Leading a Learning Community
  - Tends to the learning of all members of a school community.
  - Serves as a participatory learner with staff.
  - Provides conditions through staff development that incorporate study of professional literature and successful programs, demonstration and practice of new skills, peer coaching, using action research focused on student data, and study of how new strategies affect students.
  - Provides staff development that is meaningful to teachers.
- Using Data to Make Instructional Decisions
  - Gathers data regarding student achievement.

- Uses student achievement data to determine school effectiveness.
- Influences school staff to actively analyze data for improving results.
- Monitoring Curriculum and Instruction
  - Possesses knowledge of the curriculum and good instructional practices.
  - Monitors the implementation of curriculum standards and makes sure they are taught.
  - Models behaviors that he or she expects of school staff.
  - Spends time in classrooms to effectively monitor and encourage curriculum implementation and high-quality instructional practices.
  - Steers the curriculum and prioritizes staff development.
  - Judges the quality of teaching.
  - Shares a deep knowledge of instruction with teachers.
  - Promotes coherence in the instructional program where teachers and students follow a common curriculum framework.
  - Trusts teachers to implement instruction effectively.

Red Flags of Ineffective Leadership

The following traits are pitfalls for those who wish to be effective instructional leaders:

- Lacks a clear vision.
- Fails to monitor the quality of instruction in the school.
- Fails to communicate high expectations to faculty and students.
- Lacks confidence in the school to reach its goals.
- Tries to implement policies to improve the school alone.
- Fails to provide opportunities for collaboration among faculty.
- Fails to provide opportunities to discuss instruction among faculty.
- Keeps leadership opportunities at a minimum for others.
- Fails to tap into the expertise of teachers in the building.
- Is unable to balance instructional responsibilities with other responsibilities.
- Spends little time monitoring instruction in the building.
- Is rarely seen in classrooms.
- Fails to provide engaging staff development to faculty.

- Makes decisions based on instinct rather than on data.
- Fails to encourage faculty to use data to make instructional decisions.
- Fails to monitor implementation of local and state curriculum standards.
- Fails to support teacher effectiveness through observations and conversations with teachers.
- Is unable to judge quality of teaching.
- Lacks trust in teachers' abilities to provide quality instruction.

School Climate

Fostering a positive school climate can greatly influence the effectiveness of teachers in the classroom, student attitudes toward the school, and program implementation.

Quality Indicators

- The Principal's Role in Fostering and Sustaining School Climate
  - Involves students, staff, parents, and the community to create and sustain a positive and safe learning environment.
  - Uses knowledge of the social, cultural, leadership, and political dynamics of the school community to cultivate a positive learning environment.
  - Models high expectations and respect for students, staff, parents, and the community.
  - Develops and implements a plan that manages conflict and crisis situations in an effective and timely manner.
  - Utilizes shared decision making to maintain positive school morale.
  - Builds relationships with all stakeholders.
- Internal and External Dynamics at Work in the School
  - Establishes a climate of trust.
  - Demonstrates honesty and credibility.
  - Monitors internal and external factors affecting the school.
- The Importance of High Expectations and Respect
  - Demonstrates respect, support, and caring for students.
  - Shapes teacher attitudes toward students and curriculum.

- Influences student opportunity to learn.
- Collaborates with others.

- School Climate, Conflict, and Crisis Management
  - Proactively develops crisis plans.
  - Regularly reviews and revises the crisis plans.
  - Assigns administrators to accessible locations.
  - Creates a school Incident Command Center.
  - Maintains communication devices.
  - Establishes evacuation and reunification procedures.
  - Debriefs stakeholders (parents and community) following an incident.
  - Keeps parents and community members informed of school safety issues.
  - Keeps parents and community members informed of how incidents are handled.
  - Communicates to parents and community that their children are safe.
- School Climate and Shared Decision Making
  - Distributes administrative tasks.
  - Creates multiple leaders within the school.
  - Empowers staff to engage in group decision making.
  - Reviews school progress collaboratively with all stakeholders.

Red Flags of Ineffective Leadership

There is a fundamental link that connects principals to school goals and attaining those goals. Success doesn't just occur through happenstance. Principals have a role in fostering and sustaining school climate. The following traits are pitfalls that will stand in the way of fostering and sustaining a positive school climate:

- Fails to involve students, staff, parents, and community in creating a positive and safe learning environment.
- Fails to use knowledge of the social, cultural, leadership, and political dynamics of the school community to cultivate a positive learning environment.
- Lacks plans to manage conflict and crisis situations in an effective and timely manner.

- Makes decisions without input from others.
- Fails to listen to others' views on school issues.
- Lacks credibility with stakeholders.
- Stays in the office most of the school day.
- Does not participate in school activities and operations.
- Fails to respect existing school and community cultures and traditions.
- Fails to put student safety and achievement above all else.
- Is unable to diagnose areas of change needed in the school.
- Tolerates ineffective teaching.
- Lacks confidence in school staff.
- Fails to keep others and self current with best practices.
- Fails to provide personal and professional support to staff.

Human Resource Administration

Hiring the best, keeping the best, and developing the best teachers are core responsibilities of any leader. Indeed, the school is only as successful as the people within the walls of the school building.

Quality Indicators

- Selecting Quality Teachers and Other Employees
  - Selects capable and committed teachers.
  - Selects capable and committed nonteaching staff.
  - Uses research-based interviewing practices.
  - Hires teachers based on qualities that make an effective teacher.
  - Seeks out training and makes justified legal decisions in the hiring process.
  - Knows the hiring system in the school district.
  - Uses knowledge of hiring system to gain access to the best possible candidates.
- Inducting and Supporting New Employees
  - Develops learning communities in which new teachers can grow professionally and advance.
  - Helps new teachers to develop a sense of cultural norms and traditions at the school.

- ○ Identifies strengths of new teachers.
- ○ Provides support in instruction to new teachers.
- ○ Provides opportunities for new teachers to collaborate with effective, veteran teachers.
- Mentoring Novice Teachers
  - ○ Establishes mentoring programs based on effective practices.
  - ○ Creates a culture in which new teachers are supported and mentored by others in the building and are not left to flounder alone in their classrooms.
  - ○ Knows own mentoring abilities and works to strengthen them.
  - ○ Provides the support structures for successful implementation of a mentoring program.
- Providing Professional Development Opportunities
  - ○ Supports professional development within the school that meets both teacher needs and school goals.
  - ○ Recognizes the teacher leadership within the building.
  - ○ Involves teachers in the design and implementation of professional development opportunities.
  - ○ Provides the time, resources, and structure for meaningful professional development.
  - ○ Is aware of the professional literature related to best practices and keeps staff informed as a part of professional development.
- Retaining Quality Staff
  - ○ Supports teachers in their work.
  - ○ Promotes collaboration and shared leadership.
  - ○ Takes risks and helps in problem solving with the staff.

Red Flags of Ineffective Leadership

The human resource role of the principal can be handled in a way that negatively affects teaching and learning as well as the school climate and culture. There are several common teacher hiring mistakes that principals and others are prone to make. These traits are pitfalls that may stand in the way of successful human resource management. The ineffective principal

- Lacks training in how to interview teacher candidates.
- Uses improper hiring criteria (e.g., important attributes ignored) or criteria unrelated to the job, or emphasis on a particular style.

- Fails to adequately assess the applicant's work with students.
- Relies on the interview only to make hiring decisions.
- Disregards the candidate's demonstrated effect on student achievement.
- Fails to check prejudices when making hiring decisions.
- Fails to adequately check candidate materials.
- Does not follow up with recommendations.
- Fails to adequately monitor new teaching staff.
- Lacks mentoring program for teachers who are new to the profession, new to the school system, or new to the school building.
- Assigns new teachers to the most difficult classes.
- Fails to provide professional development opportunities for staff.
- Does not involve staff in making decisions regarding professional development activities.
- Lacks knowledge of best practices in the field of education.
- Fails to inform staff of best practices in the field of education.

Teacher Evaluation

The effective principal recognizes the dual nature of teacher evaluation and sees the benefits in a system that both holds teachers accountable and provides for growth opportunities of the individual.

Quality Indicators

- What Are Good Practices in Teacher Evaluation?
    - Establishes clear goals for school improvement.
    - Determines how teacher evaluation relates to those goals.
    - Develops clear performance standards upon which teacher evaluation will be based.
    - Identifies acceptable standards of performance.
    - Builds clear and consistent procedural guidelines and safeguards for all evaluation procedures.
    - Establishes a reasonable evaluation timeline and sticks to it.
    - Communicates with the teacher throughout the evaluation process.
    - Recognizes that teacher supervision and evaluation are fundamental responsibilities of the principal.

- Participates in extensive training programs to increase his or her own skills in performance evaluation.
- Encourages substantial contributions to the evaluation process by the teacher.
- Talks about both strengths and areas for improvement during the evaluation conference.
- Seeks available resources to respond to individual needs.
- Involves teachers at every level in the evaluation process.
- Works to remove incompetent teachers.
- How Should Teacher Performance Be Documented?
  - Maintains accurate building-based personnel records.
  - Listens more than talks during the evaluation process to obtain more useful information about teachers' performance.
  - Balances review of past performance and future goals.
  - Recognizes teacher strengths and successes.
  - Provides specific commendations or recommendations for improvement.
  - Engages in problem solving to identify and analyze problems related to teacher performance.
- What Are the Legal Guidelines for Teacher Evaluation?
  - Informs teachers of all standards, criteria, and procedures for evaluation before implementation.
  - Follows any and all state and local procedural requirements.
  - Maintains objectivity throughout the evaluation process.
  - Documents patterns and effects of behavior.
  - Determines whether the educator's behavior is remediable or irremediable.
  - Where remediable deficiencies exist, provides clear descriptions of the deficiencies and clear, specific descriptions of the expected corrections or improvements in performance behaviors.
  - Where serious performance deficiencies have been cited, allows reasonable time to improve, and reasonable assistance in improving should be provided by the staff of the school or school district.

Red Flags of Ineffective Leadership

The teacher evaluation process can be a vehicle for professional growth, or it can be a source of mistrust and dissension between a principal and faculty. The following traits are pitfalls that may stand in the way of successful teacher evaluation by administrators:

- Bases performance evaluation of teachers on whether the individual is liked or disliked by the principal.
- Does not maintain accurate and complete personnel records.
- Fails to establish the expectation of teaching excellence.
- Fails to allocate adequate time and attention to implementing effective evaluation procedures.
- Lacks available resources or professional development funds to support the evaluation process and teacher improvement.
- Is not visible in the school and in teachers' classrooms.
- Does not have frequent contact with teachers and students.
- Fails to provide feedback to teachers in the spirit of coaching as well as evaluation.
- Is unaware of legal issues regarding evaluation.
- Disregards evaluation practices and legal issues surrounding these practices.
- Provides positive evaluations to ineffective teachers.

Organizational Management

Organizational management pertains to both short-range and long-term planning regarding the day-to-day school operations.

Quality Indicators

- Coordinating Safety, Daily Operations, and Maintenance of the Facility
  - Prepares, distributes, and updates school handbook.
  - Supervises operation, utilization, and upkeep of buildings and grounds.
  - Establishes routines for the smooth running of the school that staff members understand and follow.
  - Provides for the purchase, receipt, distribution, storage, care, repair, and inventory of school building supplies, materials, and equipment.

- Prepares miscellaneous requests, time sheets, absentee reports, memoranda, proposals, and correspondence, and various federal, state, and local reports and surveys.
- Maintains appropriate record-keeping system.
- Supervises maintenance of student enrollment, attendance, and cumulative records
- Provides and reinforces clear structures, rules, and procedures for staff.
- Provides and reinforces clear structures, rules, and procedures for students.
- Maintains a safe and orderly environment.
- Communicates expectations regarding behavior to students, teachers, and parents.
- Clearly communicates procedures for handling disciplinary problems.
- Implements and enforces disciplinary procedures in a timely and consistent manner.
- Realizes that the school and school leaders may be held liable if injury results due to negligence of school personnel.
- Collaboratively plans student grouping and development of the school master schedule.
- Facilitates professional learning communities focused on student learning.
- Coordinates transportation, custodial, cafeteria, and other supportive staff.
- Maintains discipline.
- Oversees student activities.
- Assigns and schedules building staff.
- Using Data in Organizational Management
  - Uses multiple forms of data in organizational management.
  - Develops school improvement plans collaboratively.
  - Monitors school improvement plans continually.
  - Allows for changes in school improvement plans, when needed.
- Seeking and Allocating Fiscal Resources
  - Makes creative use of all resources—people, time, and money—to improve teaching and learning.

- Involves all stakeholders in planning for school resources.
- Seeks input on the budget from all levels of affected staff.
- Prepares and defends annual school budget proposal.
- Manages budget allotments in accordance with building priorities.
- Maintains proper account ledgers and other financial records.
- Follows federal, state, and local policies with regard to finances.
- Establishes and uses an accepted procedure for receiving and disbursing funds.
- Audits fiscal records regularly to ensure the accountability of all funds.
- Keeps staff informed about status of budget requests, equipment purchases, and materials ordered.
- Organizing and Managing Technology Resources
  - Makes training opportunities available to teachers in the use of computer technology in schools.
  - Recognizes that technology can be used effectively in instruction.
  - Uses available technology to manage daily tasks more efficiently.

Red Flags of Ineffective Leadership

Organizational management can go awry if neglected by a principal. The following traits are pitfalls that will stand in the way of successful organizational management:

- Fails to review previous school budgets to discern patterns of expenditure and price fluctuations.
- Does not develop a budget for the fiscal year.
- Fails to involve all stakeholders in considering sources of school income and expenditures that come from other school district budgets (e.g., textbooks and school furnishings) or outside sources.
- Fails to plan and prioritize expenses.
- Fails to use school district budget categories and codes or provide any necessary breakdown of expenses (e.g., team or departmental budgets within the overall category of instruction).
- Does not communicate distribution procedures and timing.
- Does not ensure staff understanding of departmental or individual budgets.

- Does not create and adhere to procedures for reimbursement.
- Fails to monitor budget and adjust as needed.
- Fails to follow school board policy for bids and vendors.
- Lacks rotation for school capital expenses.
- Fails to create partnerships with community organizations.

Communication and Community Relations

Effective principals are effective communicators. Communicating effectively with internal and external constituents is important. Additionally, developing and maintaining positive relationships with students, staff, parents, and the greater school community is essential for a successful school.

Quality Indicators

- The Principal and Effective Communication
  - Incorporates stakeholder views in shared decision-making processes.
  - Is a good listener.
  - Engages in open and democratic dialogue with multiple stakeholders.
  - Distributes leadership to facilitate improved communication about the change process.
  - Holds periodic faculty and other staff meetings for the conduct of school business.
  - Disseminates needed information to faculty and staff in a timely fashion.
  - Encourages reciprocal communication within the school giving all staff members the opportunity for openness and collaboration.
  - Responds to staff requests, complaints, and grievances.
  - Counsels staff members regarding work-related problems.
- Communicating with Parents and Families
  - Spends a great deal of time working with parents.
  - Invites parents to visit the school and classrooms.
  - Develops positive relationships with parents.
  - Provides information to parents about their children's school progress.

- ◦ Understands that parents view their own involvement in different ways.
- • Communicating with the Larger Community.
  - ◦ Networks with individuals and groups in other organizations to build partnerships for pursuing shared goals.
  - ◦ Markets the schools to attract high-quality teaching staff.
  - ◦ Forms relationships with families and the larger community.
  - ◦ Develops external partnerships to support school improvement.
  - ◦ Recognizes the needs of the community.
  - ◦ Works effectively with parent, community, business, and government representatives.
  - ◦ Develops public support for the school.
  - ◦ Raises supplementary funds from parents, businesses, and other organizations.
  - ◦ Networks with people and groups in other organizations to solve common problems and pursue shared purposes.

Red Flags of Ineffective Leadership

A principal who fails to communicate effectively with all stakeholders, including staff, students, and parents, will find it difficult to support teaching and learning in the school. The following traits are pitfalls that will stand in the way of successful communication and community relations:

- • Lacks support from community organizations.
- • Fails to communicate consistently with families and community.
- • Does not know the needs of the community.
- • Is not admired by the teachers.
- • Does not "walk the talk."
- • Fails to understand his or her influence on others.
- • Fails to demonstrate core values in daily routines.
- • Is unavailable to parents and community members.

Professionalism and the Principal

Quality Indicators

- • Principal Performance Standards and Ethical Behavior
  - ◦ Is viewed as honest, with a high degree of integrity.

- Holds self to a high standard of ethics.
- Is morally centered.
- Communicates beliefs and values to the faculty, staff, parents, and students.
- Balances responsibilities associated with educating young people with the needs of teachers.
- The Principal as a Role Model
  - Models core values through interactions with students and teachers.
  - Models a sense of self-efficacy to staff.
  - Models care and genuine concern for children.
  - Contributes to the empowerment of teachers.
- Professional Development for the Principal
  - Recognizes the importance of his or her own professional development.
  - Participates in various types of professional development, including attending conferences, networking, mentoring, and peer observation.
  - Receives professional development that focuses on his or her roles and responsibilities as well as the nuances of context that affect decisions.
  - Serves on local, state, or national committees.
  - Maintains an active role in professional organizations.
  - Organizes, facilitates, and presents at local, state, or national conferences.

Red Flags of Ineffective Leadership

Professionalism communicates in ways that direct one-to-one communication cannot. Principals who hold themselves to a high professional standard communicate honesty, integrity, and confidence. Principals who do not adhere to professional performance standards and who are not ethical are not successful. These are some red flags of an ineffective leader:

- Does not promote the success of all students by facilitating the development, articulation, implementation, and stewardship of a vision of learning that is shared and supported by the school community.

- Does not promote the success of all students by advocating, nurturing, and sustaining a school culture and instructional program conducive to student learning and staff professional growth.
- Fails to ensure management of the organization, operations, and resources for a safe, efficient, and effective learning environment.
- Fails to collaborate with families and community members, respond to diverse community interests and needs, or mobilize community resources.
- Acts in an unethical manner.
- Is widely viewed as unfair and dishonest.
- Does not make the education and well-being of students the fundamental value of all decision making.
- Does not fulfill all professional duties with honesty and integrity, and does not act in a trustworthy and responsible manner.
- Does not support the principle of due process or protect the civil and human rights of all individuals.
- Does not implement local, state, and national laws.
- Does not pursue appropriate measures to correct those laws, policies, and regulations that are not consistent with sound educational goals or that are not in the best interest of children.
- Uses the position as principal for personal gain through political, social, religious, economic, or other influences.
- Accepts academic degrees of professional certification from any institution, whether accredited or not.
- Does not maintain standards and does not seek to improve the effectiveness of the profession through research and continuing professional development.
- Does not honor all contracts until fulfillment, release, or dissolution mutually agreed upon by all parties.
- Does not accept responsibilities and accountability for his or her own actions and behaviors.
- Does not commit to serving others above self.

The Principal's Role in Student Achievement

The purpose of schooling is to ensure that students learn and that they will be contributing, productive members of society. Indeed, the mission statements of many school districts say as much. The principal's role in student achievement is critical in setting the tone that student learning is the number one priority.

Quality Indicators

- The Principal's Indirect Influence on Student Achievement
    - Works to positively influence instructional practice.
    - Focuses on student learning and achievement of local and state standards.
    - Holds high expectations of teachers and students in regard to academic achievement.
    - Protects academic learning time through minimal disruptions during instructional time.
    - Ensures that all students have access to high-quality instruction and to the curriculum.
    - Communicates to students that every member of the school community believes that they can succeed.
- Focus on School Goals and Student Achievement
    - Focuses on goals such as increased graduation rates, heightened student reading ability, and so forth.
    - Believes that students will be successful only if the school is well run.
    - Maintains a focus on student achievement.
- The Principal's Use of Data to Guide School Success
    - Knows how to interpret student achievement data.
    - Knows how to use student achievement data to make curricular decisions.
    - Places less pressure on teachers to perform well on standardized testing.
    - Ensures that student progress data are used to make instructional decisions in the classroom and curricular decisions schoolwide.
    - Plans for an effective data collection and analysis system related to the school or program goals and objectives.
    - Sets benchmarks to monitor progress toward school goals.
    - Takes midcourse corrective action to accomplish desired outcomes.
    - Determines whether school goals were attained.
    - Debriefs on why goals were or were not attained.

Red Flags of Ineffective Leadership

There is a fundamental link that connects school goals and attaining those goals. That connecting thread is using data to make informed decisions. Success doesn't just occur through happenstance. Rather, it takes a commitment to data-informed decision making in order to assess. The ineffective leader

- Inaccurately interprets student achievement data.
- Uses one source of student achievement data to make changes to the instructional program.
- Fails to pre-assess student learning in the school.
- Sets unrealistic or easily attainable school goals.
- Attributes failure to meet goals to factors outside school.
- Fails to monitor progress toward goals.

Annotated Bibliography

Annotated Bibliography								
Reference	Instructional Leadership	School Climate	Human Resource Management	Teacher Evaluation	Organizational Management	Communication and Community Relations	Professionalism	Student Achievement
Barth, 2002	•	•						
Blase & Blase, 1999	•		•					
Boris-Schacter & Merrifield, 2000	•						•	
Catano & Stronge, 2006	•			•	•		•	
Charlotte Advocates for Education, 2004	•	•	•					
Cooper, Ehrensal, & Bromme, 2005	•		•	•				
Cotton, 2003	•	•	•		•	•	•	•
Elmore, 2005	•			•	•			
Fink & Resnick, 2001	•		•		•			
Fullan, 2002	•	•		•	•			
Fullan, Bertani, & Quinn, 2004	•			•	•		•	•

(continued)

Annotated Bibliography, cont.

Reference	Instructional Leadership	School Climate	Human Resource Management	Teacher Evaluation	Organizational Management	Communication and Community Relations	Professionalism	Student Achievement
Hallinger & Heck, 1996	•	•			•			•
Hargreaves & Fink, 2003	•		•					•
Kythreotis & Pashiardis, 1998a	•	•			•		•	•
Lashway, 2003	•		•		•			
Leithwood, Seashore Louis, Anderson, & Wahlstrom, 2004	•		•		•			•
Leithwood & Riehl, 2003	•	•	•		•	•	•	•
LoVette, Watts, & Hood, 2000		•	•		•		•	
Manasse, 1985		•			•		•	•
Marks & Printy, 2003	•		•		•			•
Marzano, Waters, & McNulty, 2005	•	•	•		•	•	•	•
Mazzeo, 2003	•				•		•	
McGhee & Nelson, 2005	•		•					•
Mendel, Watson, & MacGregor, 2002	•	•			•			
Painter, 2000				•				
Peterson, 2000b				•				
Portin, Schneider, DeArmond, & Gundlach, 2003	•	•	•		•	•		
Prestine & Nelson, 2003	•							
Reed, McDonough, Ross, & Robichaux, 2001	•				•			•

Reference	Instructional Leadership	School Climate	Human Resource Management	Teacher Evaluation	Organizational Management	Communication and Community Relations	Professionalism	Student Achievement
Ruebling, Stow, Kayona, & Clarke, 2004	•							•
Ruff & Shoho, 2005	•							
Simkins, 2005	•				•			
Spillane, 2005	•	•						
Spillane, Halverson, & Diamond, 2001					•			
Stronge, 2006a				•				
Tucker & Tschannen-Moran, 2002	•		•		•		•	
Usdan, McCloud, & Podmostko, 2000	•					•	•	
Villani, 1997	•	•						
Waters & Grubb, 2004							•	•
Witziers, Bosker, & Kruger, 2003							•	•

Barth, R. S. (2002, May). The Culture Builder. *Educational Leadership,* *59*(8), 6–11. [Journal article].

Keywords: Instructional Leadership, School Climate

Summary: The influence of school culture and the role of school leaders in changing toxic school cultures were reviewed. School culture has a huge influence that is immediately apparent to newcomers. School culture was defined as a deeply ingrained and complex combination of norms, beliefs, values, traditions, and myths regarding the organization that are often resistant to change. Among healthy cultural norms cited by the author were collegiality, trust, honesty, and open communication. The role of the instructional leader was described as facilitating with staff the continuous examination of cultural norms of the school, including discussing the nondiscussables, then keeping, re-examining, or discarding practices or behaviors based on the impact on student learning. Toxic cultures tend to associate learning and punishment. The challenge to instructional leaders is to uncouple these themes and encourage a message of learning not to avoid punishment but to improve oneself. Development of a school culture that encourages student and adult learning was noted to be a priority for school leaders.

Blase, J., & Blase, J. (1999). *Leadership for Staff Development: Supporting the Lifelong Study of Teaching and Learning.* Washington, DC: United States Department of Education, Education Resources Information Center (ERIC), (pp. 2–18). [Monograph].

Keywords: Instructional Leadership, Human Resource Management

Summary: A study examined the characteristics of instructional leaders that had a positive impact on classroom teaching. Instructional leadership is defined as coaching, reflection, collegial investigation, study teams, explorations into uncertain matters, and problem solving. The role of staff development as related to the instructional leader was also examined to determine if this was a factor in effective school leadership. An inventory was administered to 809 elementary and secondary teachers in the Southeast, Midwest, and Northwest who had various levels of teaching experience. Instructional leaders were found to significantly impact the classroom behaviors of teachers. Behaviors of effective instructional leaders included talking with teachers, promoting professional growth, and encouraging teacher reflection. Findings on staff development confirmed the value of professional growth and reflection for teachers. The authors described six elements of staff development:

1. The study of teaching and learning
2. Building a culture of collaboration
3. Promoting coaching
4. Using inquiry to drive staff development

5. Providing resources to support growth and improvement

6. Applying principles of adult development

The authors cited the importance of creating a culture of lifelong learning through the use of inquiry and collaboration.

Boris-Schacter, S., & Merrifield, S. (2000, January). Why "Particularly Good" Principals Don't Quit. *Journal of School Leadership, 10,* 84–98. [Journal article].

Keywords: Instructional Leadership, Professionalism

Summary: A study involving principals deemed particularly effective by their peers focused on principal professional learning. Conditions for principal learning exhibited by these principals revealed the broad themes of professional identity, influence of liberal arts, and personal identity. Specifically, these principals viewed professional development as an ethic and demonstrated a connection between their professional and personal lives. They modeled a deep interest in particular subjects and learning as well as a connection between their interests and profession, and they possessed a philosophy of continual improvement. Such principals, described as "self-directed learners," were aware of being unable to manage the principalship alone and the need to motivate and inspire others within the organization. They shared their interests and learning with others, modeling lifelong learning. Implications for recruitment of future leaders and professional development were described.

Catano, N., & Stronge, J. (2006, September). What Are Principals Expected to Do? Congruence Between Evaluation and Performance Standards. *NASSP Bulletin, 90*(3), 221–237. [Quantitative/qualitative content analysis].

Keywords: Instructional Leadership, Teacher Evaluation, Organizational Management, Professionalism

Summary: This study uses both quantitative and qualitative methods of content analysis to examine principal evaluation instruments, as well as state and professional standards for principals in school districts located in a Mid-Atlantic state in the United States. The purposes of this study were to

- Determine the degrees of emphasis that are placed on leadership and management behaviors expected of school principals.
- Explore the congruence of principal evaluation instruments to instructional leadership and management attributes.
- Explore the congruence of principal evaluation instruments with state and professional standards.

Findings revealed that school districts focused on instructional leadership, organizational management, and community relations as responsibilities for school principals. Principal evaluation instruments reflected common expectations for principals among school districts and state and professional standards.

Key Points:

- Principals are responsible for multiple goals, and there is pressure to attend to both the academic standards of the school and the social and emotional well-being of students. Strong working relationships with teachers and staff as well as parents and community are imperative.
- Principal roles are changing because accountability is changing. Principals are accountable not only to local, state, and national policymakers but also to parents and communities. Testing and test scores have become paramount to these groups, and principals are feeling the pressure.
- Public school districts must clearly communicate roles and expectations to principals.

The study raises several questions related to the responsibilities of school principals. These questions are centered around changing roles and job satisfaction, appropriate evaluation instruments, turnover rates, stakeholder understanding of increasing complexity, and the result of evaluation on principal effectiveness.

Charlotte Advocates for Education. (2004, February). *Role of Principal Leadership in Increasing Teacher Retention. Creating a Supportive Environment.* Charlotte, NC: Author (pp. 1–64). [Monograph].

Keywords: Instructional Leadership, School Climate, Human Resource Management

Summary: The relationship between principals, school culture, and teacher retention in the Charlotte-Mecklenburg Schools in North Carolina was studied. Twenty principals were identified who had been most successful at teacher retention. These principals completed surveys to determine whether there were common strategies, and focus groups were formed to address the teacher retention issue. Working conditions in five categories were assessed:

1. Time Management
2. Facilities and Resources
3. Leadership
4. Personal Empowerment
5. Opportunities for Professional Development

Effective principal behaviors included demonstrating strong leadership, relationship building, providing teacher support, teacher empowerment and leadership building, accessibility, protection of teacher time, and providing quality professional growth opportunities. The survey was then used at the state level to provide data on working conditions and the impact of leadership behaviors and school culture. Implications of results were also discussed.

Key Points:

- Successful principals have the following traits in common: visionary and entrepreneurial leadership style, risk taking, self-motivation and tenacity, problem solving, passion and commitment, strong attention to operational issues, an understanding of the value of people in terms of personal success and growth, preparation, and continued professional development.

- Results of the study include:
  - Principal experience: extensive, as both teachers and assistant principals.
  - Use of time: most are comfortable as instructional leaders; expectation is to spend 70 percent of time in instructional roles; half indicate that only 50 percent of time is actually spent in instructional roles, the other half being operations.
  - Principal preparation: most important is on-the-job training, experience as a teacher, and self-directed professional development. Least important are undergrad education and formal professional development.
  - Characteristics of effective principals: visionary leader, ability to synthesize, motivation, critical thinking, good and quick decision making, problem solving, self-reflection, organizational skills, articulate, ability to prioritize, confidence, trustworthy, risk taking, perseverance, drive, people skills, perceptive, listening skills, and sense of humor.

Cooper, B. S., Ehrensal, P. A., & Bromme, M. (2005, January/March). School-Level Politics and Professional Development: Traps in Evaluating the Quality of Practicing Teachers. *Educational Policy, 19*(1), 112–125. [Journal article].

Keywords: Instructional Leadership, Human Resource Management, Teacher Evaluation

Summary: Historical and structural factors affecting teacher supervision and evaluation were examined in several New York City schools. The micropolitical context affecting teacher-principal interactions was shaped by state and district policy, prior experiences with teacher dismissals, and contractual agreements with unions. The combination of these resulted in what is described by the authors as the following three traps of current teacher supervisory practices:

1. Reinforcement of top-down school management.

2. Treatment of teaching as a semi-profession.

3. Use of teacher empowerment and collegiality to restrain full participation and channel dissention.

Suggestions to avoid supervisory traps were provided, including

- Improvement of teacher evaluation techniques.
- Increasing teacher collegiality.
- Viewing teachers as self-directed professionals.
- Consideration of linking teacher salary to improvement in student learning outcomes.
- Leader awareness of when to lead and when to allow greater levels of teacher independence.

Key Points:

- Teacher evaluation is a major responsibility of principals. In New York City, relationships between teachers and principals are often guided by union contracts and local and state policies.
- *Trap 1: Bureaucratic Organization and Labor Management.* Reinforces top-down management. Teacher-supervisor relations are constrained by a long history of labor-management relations.
- *Trap 2: Teaching as a Semi-Profession.* The field of teaching is similar to other professional fields, yet the sense of professionalism is often different. This sense of professionalism can be shaped by the supervisory experience. With high-stakes testing there is enormous pressure to produce good results quickly and regularly. Having to teach to the test undermines and reduces teachers' autonomy and sense of professionalism.
- *Trap 3: Teacher Empowerment and the Collegiality of Leadership.* Teachers are encouraged to voice their opinions through structured and formalized means that reinforce the hierarchies set in place by administration. Empowerment is manipulated.
  Traps cannot completely disappear, but suggestions for improving them include
    - Improving evaluation techniques: Tucker, Stronge, Gareis, and Beers suggest portfolios and self-reflection as part of the evaluation process.
    - Increasing collegiality among teachers.
    - Viewing teachers as self-directed professionals; buffering teachers from organizational and external intrusions.
    - Tying salary and compensation directly to effort and success.

    ◦ Knowing when not to lead and when to empower others (senior teachers) to assume leadership roles.

Cotton, K. (2003). *Principals and Student Achievement: What the Research Says.* **Alexandria, VA: Association for Supervision and Curriculum Development. [Book].**

Keywords: Instructional Leadership, School Climate, Human Resource Management, Organizational Management, Communication and Community Relations, Professionalism, Student Achievement

Summary: An extensive review of post-1985 research examined principal behaviors as related to one or more student outcome measures. Principals of high-performing schools were found to exhibit 26 behaviors that affect student achievement positively, generally falling into seven categories:

1. Focus on Student Learning

2. Vision and goals focused on high levels of student learning
   - High expectations for student achievement
   - High levels of student learning

3. Interaction and Relationships
   - Communication and interaction
   - Emotional and interpersonal support
   - Parent and community outreach and involvement

4. Role modeling

5. School Culture
   - Recognition of student and staff achievement
   - Support of risk taking
   - Teacher autonomy
   - Collaboration
   - Shared leadership and decision making and staff empowerment
   - Positive and supportive school climate
   - Visibility and accessibility
   - Self-confidence, responsibility, and perseverance
   - Rituals, ceremonies, and other symbolic actions
   - Professional development opportunities and resources

6. Instruction
   * Importance of instructional leadership
   * Discussion of instructional issues
   * Instructional time

7. Accountability
   * Use of student data for program improvement
   * Classroom observation and feedback to teachers
   * Norm of continuous improvement
   * Safe and orderly school environment
   * Monitoring student progress and sharing findings

Differences between instructional leadership in several categories were explored, including principal gender, school socioeconomic status, and elementary-secondary leadership. Review of the literature concluded with the assertion that the effects of principal leadership on student learning, while indirect, are significant and positive.

Elmore, R. F. (2005, Winter). Accountable Leadership. *The Educational Forum, 69,* 134–142. [Journal article].

Keywords: Instructional Leadership, Teacher Evaluation, Organizational Management

Summary: The impact of performance-based accountability on school leadership practices was reviewed. Accountability was defined in terms of organizational response rather than compliance. Response, in turn, depended on the degree of agency exhibited by those in the organization. A model of leadership practice was proposed, focusing on internal accountability, improvement of agency, technical and social-emotional aspects of improvement, and distributed leadership. The authors indicated that the complexity of educational issues has forced educators to utilize new skills and distribute leadership throughout the organization.

Key Points:

* Changes in conditions lead to changes in leadership practices.
* Performance-based accountability was introduced to provide terms of accountability, not to create it where it did not previously exist.

- Three sources contribute to accountability: individual responsibility, collective expectations, and formal mechanisms.
- Internal accountability (alignment = individual values + collective expectations) is associated with greater success in terms of external accountability.
- Improvement is a process of individual and organizational learning. Improvement is not a linear process. Improvement includes using internal and external expertise and tailoring to specific needs.
- Improvement is both a technical and social-emotional process. It is not only improving old ideas or processes, but finding new ideas and processes.
- Accountable leadership stresses the importance of individual and collective agency.
- Accountable leadership is distributed leadership.

Fink, E., & Resnick, L. B. (2001, April). Developing Principals as Instructional Leaders. *Phi Delta Kappan, 82*(8), 598–606. [Journal article].

Keywords: Instructional Leadership, Human Resource Management, Organizational Management

Summary: A longitudinal study of an urban New York school district with a strong record of successful school improvement efforts over an 11-year period was described. The district sought to strengthen school leadership with a professional development program that emphasized continual learning, problem-solving strategies, professional support, and mentoring. A culture stressing the importance of teaching and learning was developed, and a connection between strong professional development and accountability has resulted in the district. Core beliefs central to the program are described.

Key Points:

- Though the ideal role for principals is instructional leader, most spend their time managing operations.
- Principals are primarily responsible for selecting and cultivating an effective teaching staff.
- Problem sharing is viewed as a positive process of professional engagement. This lends itself to creating a culture of mutual dependency and teamwork.

- Effective instructional leaders need to build intellectual capital as well as social capital
- Leadership skills and instructional knowledge must be developed concurrently.

Fullan, M. (2002, May). The Change Leader. *Educational Leadership, 59*(8), 16–20. [Journal article].

Keywords: Instructional Leadership, School Climate, Teacher Evaluation, Organizational Management

Summary: Leadership is needed at every level of school culture and during times of change. An organization cannot flourish on the actions of the top leader. Schools and districts need leaders at every level. This article describes the skills leaders must possess and the challenges they must face in order to provide for, protect, develop, and enhance their school environments.

Key Points:

- Effective leaders are the key to sustained, educational reform.
- Teachers must be mobilized for reform to happen.
- Five characteristics of effective leaders include moral purpose, an understanding of the change process, the ability to improve relationships, knowledge creation and sharing, and making processes coherent.
- Leaders with moral purpose seek to make a positive difference.
- Sustained improvement is impossible without the whole system moving forward.
- Understanding change requires selective innovation, realistic expectations, redefining of resistance, and reculturing.
- If relationships improve, schools get better. Building relationships and teams can be the most difficult work but will result in a resource that continues to give.
- Organizations must foster knowledge giving as well as knowledge seeking.
- Key components of sustainability are developing the social environment, learning in context, cultivating leaders at many levels, and enhancing the teaching profession.

Fullan, M., Bertani, A., & Quinn, J. (2004, April). New Lessons for Districtwide Reform: Effective Leadership for Change Has 10 Crucial Components. *Educational Leadership, 61*(7), 42–46. [Journal article].

Keywords: Instructional Leadership, Teacher Evaluation, Organizational Management, Professionalism, Student Achievement

Summary: The ability to implement and sustain systemic reforms in school districts was examined in several districts in Canada, Great Britain, and the United States. Ten critical components for successful change were identified:

1. A Compelling Conceptualization
   - Effective district leaders know how to use key advantages for implementing their vision.
   - Leaders must build a coalition of leaders who pursue the vision in practice.

2. Collective Moral Purpose
   - There must be an explicit goal of raising the bar and closing the gap.
   - Everyone has a responsibility for changing the education context.
   - Competition within districts is counterproductive.

3. The Right Bus
   - Structure must be right before anything else.
   - Structure must reflect the underlying principles of an organization

4. Capacity Building
   - Leaders should focus not only on achievement but also on development of future leaders.

5. Lateral Capacity Building
   - Connecting schools within a district is essential.
   - Team building also is critical.

6. Ongoing Learning
   - Effective districts continually analyze and refine strategies.
   - Assessment is essential.

7. Productive Conflict
    - Change will inevitably produce conflict. Leaders must balance resolving conflict with a commitment to the established vision.
    - Collaborative does not always mean being congenial and consensual.

8. A Demanding Culture
    - Competence is vital. Being well-intentioned is not good enough.

9. External Partners
    - Active external partners, including businesses and community organizations, are necessary.

10. Focused Financial Investments
    - Redeploying existing resources is valued.
    - Give financial backers (public and private) incentive to continue to invest.

District leaders require the daily, internal leadership of those within schools to facilitate change, including principals and teacher leaders. Four issues remained in large-scale change efforts:

1. Student achievement tends to reach a plateau.
    - Need stronger approaches.

2. More emphasis is needed on the study of change at the high school level.

3. State-level reform policies and strategies are needed.

4. Issues of centralization and decentralization must be addressed.
    - Districts must develop school capacity so schools can act more autonomously.
    - Districts have a moral obligation to intervene in underperforming schools.

The authors cited additional factors for consideration, including the obligation of districts to intervene when necessary to implement school change efforts.

Hallinger, P., & Heck, R. H. (1996, February). Reassessing the Principal's Role in School Effectiveness: A Review of Empirical Research, 1980–1995. *Educational Administration Quarterly, 32*(1), 5–44. [Journal article].

Keywords: Instructional Leadership, School Climate, Organizational Management, Student Achievement

Summary: Review of empirical literature examining the relationship between principal leadership behaviors and school effectiveness between the years of 1980 and 1995 was conducted. Forty studies met the following criteria for selection in the review:

- The studies were specifically designed to examine principal behaviors and the effects of principal leadership; that is, principal leadership was one of the independent variables.
- The studies were required to include an outcome measure of school performance as an independent variable.
- Efforts were made to include studies from outside the United States as well as those within the United States.

Previous research in the area of principal effectiveness centered primarily on student achievement outcomes. It was noted that this relationship is complex and difficult to validate empirically; however, overall small but positive indirect effects of principal leadership on student achievement have been demonstrated. Several theoretical models were used for examination of studies between the years of 1980 and 1995:

- The Direct Effects Model: antecedents of leadership include school context and personal characteristics of the principal
- The Mediated Effects Model
- The Reciprocal Effects Model

There is continued evidence that principal leadership impacts school effectiveness. Although it was noted that statistical methods for examination of empirical data have become more sophisticated following earlier studies, a move away from models examining student achievement as the primary measure of principal effectiveness is recommended. Principal effectiveness appears to be related to complex interactions between contextual variables within the specific school environment and is thus an area for further examination.

Hargreaves, A., & Fink, D. (2003, May). Sustaining Leadership. *Phi Delta Kappan, 84*(9), 693–700. [Journal article].

Keywords: Instructional Leadership, Human Resource Management, Student Achievement

Summary: The sustainability of educational change was examined in a five-year study of school improvement programs in New York and Canada. Historically, educational changes that have facilitated student learning over time have proven difficult to sustain. The authors differentiated between maintainability and sustainability, the latter referring to change that endures over time, promotes the growth of all, and is not dependent on a particular school leader or external resources. The primary responsibility of the school leader is to sustain learning, which is best accomplished with others. Several suggestions are provided:

- A culture of shared leadership and responsibility should exist within the school.
- Within a school district, leadership may be horizontal among leaders but should become a vertical system at the school level over time.
- The culture of distributed leadership should extend throughout the school community, "beyond the principal's office."

Key Points:

- Sustaining educational change over time has presented severe challenges for educators.
- A key challenge is in moving from the implementation to the institutionalization phase of change.
- Sustainable improvement is enduring, develops and draws on resources and support at a rate in pace with change, doesn't squander resources, and requires investment.
- Sustainability in educational change comprises five key characteristics:
    - Improvement that sustains learning.
    - Improvement that endures over time.

- ° Improvement that can be supported by available or achievable resources.
- ° Improvement that doesn't impact negatively on the surrounding environment of other schools and systems.
- ° Improvement that promotes ecological diversity and capacity throughout the educational and community environment.
- Three aspects of sustainable learning:
  - ° *Leading Learning:* Learning must be at the center of everything. High-stakes testing may result in improved results, but not better learning.
  - ° *Distributed Leadership:* This comprises a network of relationships among people, structures and cultures—an organic activity dependent on interrelationships and connections.
  - ° *Leadership Succession:* Sustainable leadership outlives individuals.
- School leadership is not the sum of its individual leaders.
- The efforts of all leaders are influenced by their predecessors and have implications for their successors.
- Distributed leadership creates a culture of initiative and opportunity.

Kythreotis, A., & Pashiardis, P. (1998a). *The Influence of School Leadership Styles and Culture on Students' Achievement in Cyprus Primary Schools.* **Nicosia, Cyprus: University of Cyprus (pp. 1–31). [Monograph].**

Keywords: Instructional Leadership, School Climate, Organizational Management, Professionalism, Student Achievement

Summary: A study conducted in Cyprus primary schools examined the relationship between school leadership, culture, and effectiveness. A sample of 49 principals was selected for participation on the basis of perceived levels of effectiveness. Semi-structured interviews, surveys, and observational data were used, with student achievement scores used as a dependent variable. Bolman and Deal's (1984, 1992, 1997) four leadership frames were used as a conceptual framework for the study. Seven results were revealed:

1. The direct model of principal influence on student achievement was supported.

2. Lack of influence of teacher leadership styles was noted.

3. The effects of school and classroom cultures were identified, consistent with results in other countries.

4. Principal leadership affected students at the class but not the school level.

5. Major response differences were noted between principal and teacher versions of the questionnaire, with principals supporting the generalizability theory in the four frames.

6. Agreement with previous studies examining multilevel models of school effectiveness was evident.

7. Agreement with previous school effectiveness studies was confirmed.

Analyses of the interview data revealed the following shared characteristics of primary school leaders in Cyprus:

- Love for the profession
- Continual learning
- Belief in the influence of the principalship
- Risk-taking
- Self-confidence
- Honesty
- Innovation
- Ambition
- Effectiveness in parent-school relations
- Belief in the trait-leadership theory

Recommendations for further study included obtaining additional empirical data on the direct effects model of principal leadership and considering the multilevel and multidimensional nature of school culture.

Lashway, L. (2003, July). Role of the School Leader. Eugene, OR: University of Oregon; and Washington, DC: U.S. Department of Education/ ERIC Clearinghouse on Educational Management. [Evaluative report, trends].

Keywords: Instructional Leadership, Human Resource Management, Organizational Management

Summary: Principals must define their role as a leader and use it to their advantage. In a standards-oriented age, contemporary visions of leadership can be easily found in the professional standards established by policy-makers and practitioners. School leaders in all settings face common challenges in meeting expectations. This article addresses these common challenges:

- Providing focused instructional leadership
  - There is unanimous agreement on the importance of instructional leadership, but there is no clearly articulated theoretical foundation for the construct.
- Leading change
  - School leaders are change agents.
- Developing a collaborative leadership structure
  - Collaborative leadership is necessary but can create ambiguity about authority and accountability.
  - For distributed leadership to flourish, principals must develop leadership capacity in teachers and others.
- Providing a moral center
  - It is important to listen to teachers' voices.
  - Principals must balance accountability with responsibility.

Today, leaders attend to the learning of all members of the educational community. This journey results in new approaches to student and adult learning, internal school accountability and shared responsibility, and a commitment to the decisions made for school improvement.

Leithwood, K., Seashore Louis, K., Anderson, S., & Wahlstrom, K. (2004). *How Leadership Influences Student Learning.* Learning From Research Project. St. Paul, MO: University of Minnesota Center for Applied Research and Educational Improvement (CAREI); Toronto, ON: Ontario Institute for Studies in Education at the University of Toronto (OISEUT); and New York: The Wallace Foundation. [Monograph].

Keywords: Instructional Leadership, Human Resource Management, Organizational Management, Student Achievement

Summary: Empirical research in effective practices in school leadership and the resulting effect on student learning was reviewed. Effective leadership

Was described as context-specific, dependent on organizational, student population, and policy contexts. A conceptual framework was presented, based on a systems perspective. In this framework, leadership was viewed as central to student learning but was mediated by multiple factors, including state and district policy and practices, leadership preparation, school and class conditions, stakeholder views, and teachers. Three categories of effective leadership practices were cited:

1. Setting Direction
   - Leadership practices in this category account for the largest proportion of a leader's impact.
   - People are motivated by goals that they find personally compelling, challenging, and achievable.

2. Developing People
   - Contribution of this set of practices is substantial.
   - Direct experiences with those in leadership roles have the most influence on motivation and performance.

3. Redesigning the Organization
   - Organizational conditions can blunt or wear down educators' good intentions and prevent the use of effective practices.
   - Successful educational leaders develop their districts and school as effective organizations that support and sustain the performance of administrators and teachers, as well as students.

The roles of policy and cultural context were examined with respect to leadership and student learning. The authors concluded that school leadership was second only to classroom instruction in the degree of impact on student learning, and that effective leadership is critical to school reform.

Leithwood, K. A., & Riehl, C. (2003, March). *What Do We Already Know About Successful School Leadership?* Washington, DC: AERA Division A Task Force on Developing Research in Educational Leadership (pp. 2–37). [Monograph].

Keywords: Instructional Leadership, School Climate, Human Resource Management, Organizational Management, Communication and Community Relations, Professionalism, Student Achievement

Summary: Empirical research was reviewed to describe what is known about successful school leadership. The core definition of leadership included the attributes of providing direction and exercising influence. It was noted that in order to positively influence school outcomes, leaders often acted through others; leadership effects were therefore primarily indirect in nature. Six assertions were made:

1. Effective school leadership contributes significantly to student learning.
   - Learning improves when teachers use appropriate, high-quality techniques and a well-crafted curriculum.
   - The impact of educational leadership on student achievement is demonstrable.

2. Principals and teachers are the primary leadership sources within a school.
   - Whether principal or teacher, the effect of leadership on the school is evident.

3. Leadership should be distributed throughout the school and school community.
   - In addition to principals and teachers, other professionals in schools and school systems are sources of distributed leadership.
   - With the multilayered and multifaceted nature of the school system, distributed leadership is necessary.

4. A core set of leadership practices is valuable in multiple contexts.
   - Setting directions
   - Identifying and articulating a vision
   - Fostering the acceptance of group goals
   - Creating high performance expectations
   - Developing people
   - Offering intellectual stimulation
   - Providing individualized support
   - Providing an appropriate model
   - Redesigning the organization
   - Strengthening school cultures
   - Modifying organizational structures
   - Building collaborative processes

5. Effective school leadership practices must acknowledge and respond to accountability policies.
   * Market accountability: creating and sustaining a competitive school.
   * Decentralization accountability: empowering others to make significant decisions.
   * Professional accountability: providing instructional leadership.
   * Management accountability: developing and executing strategic plans.
6. Successful school leaders facilitate high levels of school quality, equity, and social justice.

The authors concluded that school leadership was a necessary but insufficient component of school improvement in isolation. School leadership practices were viewed as varying in different contexts and were most successful when the emphasis was on teaching and learning. Gaps in effective leadership literature were cited, including the examination of how school leaders can best balance school management and leadership responsibilities.

LoVette, O., Watts, S., & Hood, J. (2000, November). *An Investigation of Teachers' Perceptions of Their Principals' "Delegation" and "Relationships" Behavior.* **United States Department of Education: Education Resources Information Center (ERIC), (pp. 2–31). Paper presented at the annual meeting of the Mid-South Educational Research Association. [Monograph]**

Keywords: School Climate, Human Resource Management, Organizational Management, Professionalism

Summary: The delegation and relationship skills of principals were evaluated by 93 graduate students in a Louisiana school leadership program using a survey. Research questions were designed to differentiate between several comparison groups of principals—female and male, younger and older, elementary and secondary, principals of smaller and larger schools—as well as to determine whether those with strong "delegation" skills were also perceived as having stronger "relationship" skills. Results indicated that age was the most significant variable in the study, with younger principals exhibiting greater delegation behaviors as well as possessing characteristics that resulted in better relationships with their staffs. Female principals were perceived to possess a greater degree of delegation skills, but the difference between genders on relationships was not significant. School level and student enrollment did not significantly affect the delegation and relationship skills among principals. Recommendations for principal training programs were provided, including those that foster teacher empowerment.

Key Points:

- Top-down management can result in negative attitudes and less reception to reform initiatives.
- Teacher commitment is linked to supportive principal behaviors.
- Research suggests that delegating leadership and building relationships is the best way to engage teachers, which results in effectively reaching goals.

Manasse, A. L. (1985, January). Improving Conditions for Principal Effectiveness: Policy Implications of Research. *The Elementary School Journal, 85*(3), 339–463. [Journal article].

Keywords: School Climate, Organizational Management, Professionalism, Student Achievement

Summary: Research on principal effectiveness prior to 1985 was reviewed, including specific discussion regarding what principals do on a daily basis. Methodological problems in early studies were noted. Factors characteristic of effective schools were directly or indirectly related to principal effectiveness and included high expectations for student achievement, a conducive learning climate, emphasis on skills, monitoring of student progress, and a high level of administrative leadership. Early school leadership research revealed that approximately 80 percent of principals' work involved personal interaction with others, while approximately 20 percent involved administrative duties such as phone calls and desk work. While both elementary and secondary principals spent more time with students than others, elementary principals spent more time with students than secondary principals, and secondary principals spent more time in meetings. Similarities in studies indicated that principals' work was fragmented, with many unplanned verbal interactions and multiple demands on their time during a school day. Findings were conclusive regarding the importance of the principal during implementation of change. Educational policy implications were suggested based on review of the research.

Key Points:

- Though there is a lack of a single definition of effective principals, there is agreement about certain qualities that indicate effectiveness: strong academic performance, sense of purpose, and positive response among school communities.
- Characteristics of effective schools (directly related to principal effectiveness) are described as
  - Strong administrative leadership.
  - Climate conducive to learning.
  - Schoolwide emphasis on skills.
  - High teacher expectations for student achievement.
  - Systematic monitoring of pupil performance.
- Principal behavior can be categorized into three role clusters: interpersonal, informational, and decisional.
- Effective principals are likely to have a clear sense of their own strengths and weaknesses, high energy levels, strong communication skills, an analytic approach to problem solving, human relations skills, and a high tolerance for stress.

Marks, H. M., & Printy, S. M. (2003, August). **Principal Leadership and School Performance: An Integration of Transformational and Instructional Leadership.** *Educational Administration Quarterly, 39*(3), 370–397. [Journal article].

Keywords: Instructional Leadership, Human Resource Management, Organizational Management, Student Achievement

Summary: School leadership relations between principals and teachers were examined in a study designed to consider the effect of instructional collaboration on teaching quality and student performance. Qualitative and quantitative methods were used to study 24 restructured elementary and secondary schools. Considerable variation was found in the degree to which instructional and transformational leadership behaviors were exhibited in different schools. In schools that lacked transformational leadership, an absence of shared leadership was evident. The authors surmised that strong transformational leadership was essential in supporting teacher commitment. The importance of integrated leadership, a pairing of instructional and transformational leadership, was discussed. Effective integrated leadership was determined to enhance teacher leadership and school performance.

Key Points:

- Shared instructional leadership involves the active collaboration of principals and teachers on curriculum, instruction, and assessment.
- A broader view of instructional leadership includes all functions that contribute to student learning.
- Shared instructional leadership has teachers taking responsibility for their own professional growth and instructional improvement.
- The authors of the study hypothesize that transformational leadership is necessary but not sufficient for principal effectiveness.
- Transformational leadership emphasized the ingredients of change: ideas, innovation, influence, and consideration for the individual in the process.

Marzano, R. J., Waters, T., & McNulty, B. A. (2005). *School Leadership That Works: From Research to Results*. Alexandria, VA: Association for Supervision and Curriculum Development; and Aurora, CO: Mid-continent Research for Education and Learning (McREL). [Book].

Keywords: Instructional Leadership, School Climate, Human Resource Management, Organizational Management, Communication and Community Relations, Professionalism, Student Achievement

Summary: Meta-analysis of research over 35 years was conducted in order to quantify the relationship between school leadership and student achievement. Of approximately 5,000 articles and studies that addressed school leadership, 69 were quantitative in nature and included in the meta-analysis.

The authors noted that the previous estimated correlation between school leadership and student achievement (Leithwood et al., 2004) was between .22 and .25. Twenty-one responsibilities of school leaders were provided along with their correlations to student achievement. These were subsequently ranked by the degree of their relationships to first-order (incremental) and second-order (complex) change. Comparison was made between the 21 responsibilities and Cotton's (2003) 25 leadership practices. Based on the meta-analysis, a five-step plan for effective school leadership was described and included suggestions for distribution of leadership responsibilities throughout the organization.

Mazzeo, C. (2003). *Improving Teaching and Learning by Improving School Leadership.* Washington, DC: National Governors Association Center for Best Practices (pp. 1–10). [Issue brief].

Keywords: Instructional Leadership, Organizational Management, Professionalism

Summary: This issue brief summarized research on what effective school leaders do and the continued need for school leaders. The author called for enhanced licensure, preparation, and principal professional development, indicating that most state leadership policies and practices are outdated and inadequate for the needs of current leaders. Three primary leadership roles were suggested that promote student learning: Principal as Entrepreneur, Principal as Organizer, and Principal as Instructional Leader. Reform efforts in several states were described, with recommendations on immediate and long-term actions for policymakers provided. The importance of revisions in principal leadership development was described. The author indicated that states should hold providers accountable for linking principal training, school change and improvement, and consequently, student learning.

Key Points:

- Policymakers have recommended three key areas for improvement in preparing and developing principals:
  - Licensure: remove barriers so talented individuals can enter the profession.

- ○ Preparation: allow and expand alternative preparation programs and develop a system of accreditation.
- ○ Professional development: use No Child Left Behind legislation to assess practices in low-performing schools and move toward more effective, research-based professional development.
- Three primary roles that promote student learning:
  - ○ Principal as Entrepreneur: develop and sustain a focus on instructional improvement while protecting teachers from outside intrusions.
  - ○ Principal as Organizer: bring innovative individuals and ideas, programs, and strategies that can improve teaching while also reforming. Engage internal and external partners in improvement efforts.
  - ○ Principal as Instructional Leader: build data-driven professional communities where every individual is committed to and accountable for improving student learning.
- Professional development for school leaders must be a priority and should include a focus on
  - ○ Student learning and problems practitioners face.
  - ○ Reinforcing and sustaining group work and collaboration among teachers.
  - ○ Linking directly with day-to-day practices in schools and classrooms.
  - ○ Sustaining a consistency of focus over time.
  - ○ Using feedback from teaching and learning to inform program development and evaluation.

McGhee, M. W., & Nelson, S. W. (2005, January). Sacrificing Leaders, Villainizing Leadership: How Educational Accountability Policies Impair School Leadership. *Phi Delta Kappan, 86*(5), 367–375. [Journal article].

Keywords: Instructional Leadership, Human Resource Management, Student Achievement

Summary: The impact of high-stakes accountability on school leaders was described, based on the accounts of three accomplished Texas principals who were removed from their positions based on preliminary standardized test scores. From their experiences, three themes emerged: Accomplished Careers, Without Warning, and From Collaboration to Isolation. All of the principals had exhibited impressive accomplishments, were not employed under performance contracts, and were suddenly removed from their jobs based on data from a single test. In two of three cases, the preliminary data were incorrect and the schools were not in fact "low-performing." Each principal noted lack of shared accountability from division staff and lack of access to their superintendents. Because the schools served diverse student populations, the authors speculated that such principals may be more vulnerable in terms of job security. Likewise, the authors speculated on the possible differences in job security in labor union states and those with strong professional organizations.

Key Points:

- The professional isolation of principals can be devastating.
- The study emphasizes the negative implications of having test scores drive decision making with regard to principal effectiveness and job security.
- The Risk of Serving the At-Risk: suggests that principals serving more diverse populations are at a higher risk for removal if test scores are not acceptable. If this is the case, how will these schools attract high-quality, effective principals?
- Fall from Grace: shifting the focus to test scores shifts the focus away from collaboration, support, and professional development.

Mendel, C. M., Watson, R. L., & MacGregor, C. J. (2002, October 6). *A Study of Leadership Behaviors of Elementary Principals Compared with School Climate.* **Paper presented at Southern Regional Council for Educational Administration. Kansas City, MO. [Research report].**

Keywords: Instructional Leadership, School Climate, Organizational Management

Summary: This research report described a study of school leadership styles and the relationship to school climate in 34 southwest Missouri schools. Three leadership styles were described: directive, nondirective, and collaborative.

Surveys of 169 teachers were conducted. Teacher perception was that the majority of principals exhibited a collaborative style. Those principals also had the highest school climate scores. Directive principals were found to have the lowest average score for school climate. The importance of a collaborative leadership style was reiterated.

Key Points:

- A principal's leadership style may affect the morale and productivity of teachers, as well as the entire climate of the school.
- Collaborative leadership styles are the ones in which administrators and teachers routinely work together to promote effective teaching and learning.
- Directive leadership styles view the principal as having authority and knowing more about improving instruction than the teachers.
- Nondirective leadership styles are the ones in which teachers are left to observe, identify problems, and offer solutions about instruction, without any input from the principal.
- Based on the findings of the study, the author contends that collaborative leadership is the most desirable leadership style.

Painter, S. R. (2000). Principals' Efficacy Beliefs About Teacher Evaluation. *Journal of Educational Administration, 38*(4), 368–378. [Journal article].

Keywords: Teacher Evaluation

Summary: A survey of elementary and middle school principals was conducted to assess principal beliefs of self-efficacy in the evaluation of low-performing teachers. Principal surveys were administered to selected elementary and middle school principals in a western state, with a return rate of 38 surveys (54 percent). Principals confirmed the importance of handling low-performing teachers and were found to be confident in their supervisory skills. Although principals did not significantly endorse a tendency to avoid or delay difficult supervisory issues, there was a greater tendency to view this as an area of concern than the issue of self-efficacy ratings. Perception of support from higher administrative supervisory levels was rated as adequate, with a perception of slightly less support from school boards. Areas for future research were reviewed.

Key Points:

- The responsibility for remediating the performance of low-performing teachers or removing them falls on school principals.
- Regardless of the assessments of outside observers and evaluation experts about the factors that enable or disable effective evaluation, the beliefs and attitudes of principals themselves about these factors as well as their beliefs about their own skills and abilities are likely to impact substantially the effective implementation of evaluation policies for the removal of incompetent teachers.
- Self-efficacy on the part of the principal is considered to be a key factor in the principal's ability to manage low-performing teachers.
- Though the majority of principals expressed confidence in their own skills and abilities in executing the evaluation process, they indicated a number of reasons for delaying or avoiding action (most common to least common):
  - Demands on time
  - Legal requirements
  - Social factors
  - Personal adequacy
- Principals felt supported by their district offices.

Peterson, K. D. (2000b). *Teacher Evaluation: A Comprehensive Guide to New Directions and Practices* (2nd ed.). Thousand Oaks, CA: Corwin Press. [Book].

Keywords: Teacher Evaluation

Summary: A comprehensive review of theories, techniques, and practices for effective teacher evaluation. Five areas are discussed:

1. Thinking About Teacher Evaluation
2. Multiple Data Sources for Teacher Evaluation
3. Tools for Improved Teacher Evaluation
4. Evaluation of Other Educators
5. School District Responsibilities and Activities

Portin, B., Schneider, P., DeArmond, M., & Gundlach, L. (2003, September). *Making Sense of Leading Schools: A Study of the School Principalship*. Seattle, WA: Center on Reinventing Public Education. [Report].

Keywords: Instructional Leadership, School Climate, Human Resource Management, Organizational Management, Communication and Community Relations

Summary: This report on the nature of the principalship was one of five research projects funded by the Wallace Foundation to examine the behaviors necessary for leading a school. In-depth interviews were conducted with administrators and teachers in 21 schools across four cities and four states, and included elementary and secondary public, private, and magnet schools. The research was guided by three areas of inquiry: the core roles played by principals, how these roles varied across the different kinds of schools, and whether current principal preparation programs are adequate for addressing the demands of the role. Five major conclusions are described:

1. The core of the principal's role is to determine the unique needs of the school and find the resources to address them.

2. Seven leadership areas are suggested as critical, regardless of the type of school:
   - Instructional: guiding curriculum and modeling teaching practice.
   - Cultural: reinforcing the importance of creating a school climate and sense of tradition that supports the goals and commitments of the school.
   - Managerial: fiscal management.
   - Human Resource: getting and keeping the right staff, professional development.
   - Strategic: creating and promoting a vision and mission.
   - External Development: marketing and fundraising.
   - Micropolitical: "the strategies by which individuals and groups in organizational contexts . . . use . . . authority and influence to further their interests."

3. Principals have the responsibility of ensuring that all seven areas of leadership are addressed, but this may occur through delegation and shared leadership.
   - Jazz Band Leader: utilizes assistant principals and teachers

- Orchestra Conductor: utilizes headmasters, heads of upper and lower schools and other teachers

4. The governance structure of the school affects the way that leadership functions are performed.
   - Governance structure can limit the ability to share leadership.

5. Principals generally relate that they learned essential leadership skills "on the job."
   - Topics that principals wish had been covered in their training programs include conflict resolution, cultural sensitivity, problem diagnosis and solving, organizational theory, and most of all, business and financial administration.

The report suggests that a variety of school leadership skills are necessary for school success and may depend on the needs of the school. It is suggested that the findings of the report are appropriate for policymakers at various levels in order to support, rather than discourage, the development of effective school leaders.

Prestine, N. A., & Nelson, B. S. (2003, April). *How Can Educational Leaders Support and Promote Teaching and Learning? New Conceptions of Learning and Leading in Schools*. Task Force for the Development of an Agenda for Future Research on Educational Leadership. Paper presented at the Annual Meeting of the American Educational Research Association, Chicago. [Monograph].

Keywords: Instructional Leadership

Summary: Recent research was reviewed in teaching and learning as well as the ways in which involvement of school leaders promoted teaching and learning. Historically, varying views existed on the nature of teaching and learning and the definition of educational leadership. General consensus emerged of what leadership behaviors constitute instructional leadership, but less information was available on the *how* and *why* aspects of instructional leadership. The importance of "jointedness, or mutual participation of teachers and leaders in professional development," was discussed as well as the need for school leaders to possess some degree of content knowledge. The authors called for additional empirical research in distributed leadership and in teaching and learning issues. Additionally, they advocated construction of school organizational and leadership frameworks based on learning theory rather than the reverse, which has been the prevalent framework historically.

Key Points:

- New conceptions of learning and teaching in schools require new conceptions of leadership.
- Although the concept of instructional leadership seems to dominate the literature, a clear definition of instructional leadership is lacking. The authors suggest that until it is identified and articulated, instructional leadership will have little probative value for meaningful improvement in schools.

Reed, C. J., McDonough, S., Ross, M., & Robichaux, R. (2001, April). *Principals' Perceptions of High Stakes Testing on Empowerment*. United States Department of Education: Education Resources Information Center (ERIC), (pp. 2–26). Paper presented at the Annual Meeting of the American Educational Research Association, Seattle, WA. [Report].

Keywords: Instructional Leadership, Organizational Management, Student Achievement

Summary: The effect of high-stakes testing on principal perceptions of empowerment and morale was examined in a qualitative study with 26 principals in South Florida. The study was conducted to assess the influence of these accountability mandates on leadership, teaching and student learning, and school morale. The schools selected met specific criteria and had been given letter grades of A to F on student achievement. The importance of school leaders in establishing an effective learning environment was discussed. Principals' perceptions of their abilities to positively affect their respective schools significantly affect interactions with teachers and therefore student learning. Although differences were noted regarding the impact of standardized testing on individual schools, principals overwhelmingly indicated that it negatively influenced teaching and learning as well as their ability to lead their schools. Four conclusions were reached regarding the effect of high-stakes testing on principal empowerment and the learning environment:

1. The complexity of school leadership necessitates shared decision making.

2. Trust must be established among all stakeholders, including policy-makers, school leaders, teachers, parents, and students.

3. Despite the pressure of high stakes testing, many principals engage in shared decision making.

4. In the face of high-stakes accountability, principals are better able to maintain an optimistic outlook when potential problems are viewed as challenges.

Key Points:

- Most principals and teachers feel pressure to have their students do well on high-stakes standardized tests.
- High-performing schools place less pressure on their teachers to perform well on standardized tests.
- Moderately performing schools were greatly concerned about test scores.
- Low-performing schools spoke of high mobility rates and non-English-speaking students.
- Principals indicated that what happens every day in classrooms is not always reflected in test scores.
- How principals perceive their own ability to make a difference in their school greatly influences the way they interact with teachers and others.

Ruebling, C. E., Stow, S. B., Kayona, F. A., & Clarke, N. A. (2004, Spring). Instructional Leadership: An Essential Ingredient for Improving Student Learning. *The Educational Forum, 68,* 243–252. [Journal article].

Keywords: Instructional Leadership, Student Achievement

Summary: The role of school leaders in ensuring student achievement of curriculum was studied by reviewing curriculum development work that had been conducted nationwide in a number of school divisions. The study was designed to determine the degree to which mathematics and language arts curricula were being effectively implemented, and it consisted of three components: administrator interviews, teacher surveys, and classroom observations.

Results revealed poor teacher understanding and implementation of the new curricula and assessments. A follow-up study was then conducted two years later by trainers from the School Improvement Model Center (SIM) at Iowa State University. Curriculum implementation in the states of Florida, Georgia, Indiana, Arizona, and New York was examined. The absence of several leadership behaviors was evident and was likely to have affected the results. These included lack of leader participation in the curriculum development and implementation phases, not holding teachers accountable for implementation, and general lack of knowledge regarding assessment and student performance. The authors note several implications for school improvement related to the school leader's role in curriculum implementation, assessment, and student learning.

Key Points:

- The authors suggest that a necessary, but missing, ingredient for satisfactorily achieving learning results is effective leadership behavior related specifically to developing and monitoring the implementation of curriculum.
- The authors suggest a number of ways that principals can improve on the results of the study:
  - Participate actively in the development of curriculum.
  - Provide opportunities, tools, and resources for all teachers to understand and use new curriculum and assessments.
  - Hold teachers, students, and themselves accountable for achieving results.

Ruff, W. G., & Shoho, A. R. (2005, August). **Understanding Instructional Leadership Through the Mental Models of Three Elementary School Principals.** *Educational Administration Quarterly, 41*(3), 554–577. [Journal article].

Keywords: Instructional Leadership

Summary: An empirical case study of three urban elementary principals was conducted. It used a qualitative collective case study design to examine differences in mental models of experienced and novice principals. Leithwood's 1988 framework on principal duties was cited and indicated that the relationship between principal practices and internal mental processes is a critical but neglected area of study when examining the work of the principal. Of the four leadership dimensions described by Leithwood and Montgomery (1986), significant qualitative differences have been found between effective and typical principals. Effective principals exhibited student-centered goals and strategies focused on student achievement as well as proactive, consistent, and participatory decision making. Results of the case studies indicated that the mental model of the typical experienced principal reflects an internal locus of control, with a student-centered standard of assessment as opposed to external accountability measures guiding assessment. Results also showed an organizational rather than personal orientation toward school leadership. The importance of consideration of the mental models of all school leaders within a system is emphasized due to the potential ability to expand or limit organizational effectiveness and levels of student achievement.

Key Points:

- The construct of a mental model aligns with the phenomena previously observed by others in researching the cognitive processes of educational leaders.
- Research questions guiding this study were (1) What are the mental models used by urban elementary school principals? and (2) How, if at all, do mental models vary with differences in reputation and experience?
- Three levels of principal experience were defined as the "Rookie" (novice), the "Experienced School Captain" (typical), and the "Distinguished Principal" (effective).

Simkins, T. (2005). Leadership in Education: "What Works" or "What Makes Sense"? *Educational Management Administration and Leadership, 33*(1), 9–26. [Journal article].

Keywords: Instructional Leadership, Organizational Management

Summary: Traditional and emerging approaches to leadership were compared. In traditional views, leadership was considered to be individualistic, hierarchically based, and more important than management, and was the result of leaders "doing something" to followers. Emerging approaches of leadership recognized the importance of context and allowed that leadership is a complex process involving many individuals. Leadership was one of many factors affecting organizational performance. The leadership and management distinction was unnecessary because leadership was only one factor among others within a social system. The policy context of leadership was considered, concluding with identification of six dimensions of sense making for school leaders.

Key Points:

- Leadership is considered a key factor if not the only factor in the success or failure of an educational organization.
- Six areas of sense making include
    - Making sense of the ways in which leadership itself is conceived.
    - Making sense of the role and purposes of the organization within a dynamic and conflictual policy environment.
    - Making sense of the ways in which leadership roles are changing and should change.
    - Making sense of the ways in which power and authority are and should be constituted and distributed in educational organizations.
    - Making sense of "other worlds" across interprofessional and organizational boundaries.
    - Using leadership development to understand sense making itself.

Spillane, J. P. (2005, September). Primary School Leadership Practice: How the Subject Matters. *School Leadership and Management, 25*(4), 383–397. [Journal article].

Keywords: Instructional Leadership, School Climate

Summary: The Distributed Leadership study in Chicago elementary schools was used as a basis for examination of the degree and nature of differences in instructional leadership by subject area. Observational and interview data in K–5 and K–8 schools were reviewed, with the conclusion that subject matter had a significant influence on teacher practice and the nature of leadership involvement. Typical leadership descriptions have discussed responsibility for curriculum in "subject-neutral" terms, when in daily practice the areas of reading and mathematics predominate. Although leaders viewed reading and mathematics as the central elements in school curriculum, differences existed in the ways in which instructional leadership was implemented in the two subject areas. Reading was treated as subject matter that pervaded all other subjects and was therefore integrated throughout the day. Mathematics was viewed as important due to standardized assessment requirements and treated as a "stand-alone" subject. Teachers and leaders relied more on internal expertise and shared leadership in reading areas but more on external expertise and less shared leadership in areas of mathematics. The author concluded that in elementary school leadership practices, social structure must be considered and that there are differences in the types of leadership evident across different subject areas.

Spillane, J. P., Halverson, R., & Diamond, J. B. (2001, April). Investigating School Leadership Practice: A Distributed Perspective. *Educational Researcher, 30*(3), 23–27. [Journal article].

Keywords: Organizational Management

Summary: A four-year longitudinal study was conducted and analyzed in 13 Chicago elementary schools in order to gain understanding of how school leadership works in daily practice. Leadership practices in urban elementary schools were examined during changes in mathematics, science, and literacy instruction with leadership practice in the school being the unit of analysis rather than examination of the individual leader. The authors contended that the definition of leadership suggests a transformational leadership perspective, and they argued that school leadership is distributed over social and situational contexts within the school and across multiple leaders. The study analyzed school leadership practice through leadership functions at the school level, emphasizing the importance of the sociocultural context. Implications for future research are suggested, emphasizing development of leadership expertise that is context- and task-specific and distributed with several school leaders rather than an individual leader.

Key Points:

- Distributed theory of leadership is built around four ideas: leadership tasks and functions, task enactment, social distribution of task enactment, and situational distribution of task enactment.

- Leadership involves the identification, acquisition, allocation, coordination, and use of the social, material, and cultural resources necessary to establish the conditions for the possibility of teaching and learning.

Stronge, J. H. (Ed.). (2006a). *Evaluating Teaching: A Guide to Current Thinking and Best Practice* (2nd ed.). Thousand Oaks, CA: Corwin Press. [Book].

Keywords: Teacher Evaluation

Summary: Multiple authors discuss the importance of teacher effectiveness in overall school effectiveness and student achievement. The text is divided into three parts:

1. Designing a Teacher Evaluation System
   - Teacher roles and responsibilities
   - Personnel evaluation
   - Legal considerations
2. Assessing Teacher Performance
   - Classroom-based assessments
   - Client surveys
   - Student achievement
   - Portfolios
   - Self-evaluation
   - Use of multiple data sources
3. Implementing the Teacher Evaluation System
   - Conducting a successful evaluation conference
   - Dealing positively with a nonproductive teacher
   - Professional development

Tucker, P. D., & Tschannen-Moran, M. (2002). School Leadership in an Era of Accountability. Richmond, VA: Commonwealth Educational Policy Institute, Virginia Commonwealth University (pp. 1–21). [Monograph].

Keywords: Instructional Leadership, Human Resource Management, Organizational Management, Professionalism

Summary: An overview of the current status of principalship in Virginia and a synthesis of challenges in the field were presented. Based on national and state-level data, four major concerns regarding principalship and policy initiatives in each area were described:

1. Working conditions
   - Challenges include extensive time demands, increased expectations for instructional leadership and operational management, lack of administrative and clerical support, insufficient authority to effect change, increased organizational challenges, increased stress, and inadequate compensation.
   - Policy initiatives include: restructured roles, allocation of more personnel, increased authority and flexibility, salary benchmarks, portable benefits, incentives, and recognition programs.

2. Shortages
   - Challenges include anticipated shortages, retirements, attrition, difficulty attracting high-quality candidates, and lack of diversity.
   - Policy initiatives include identification of talent within schools, sponsorship of talented prospective leaders, financial support for training in exchange for service commitments, statewide recruitment efforts, establishment of a principal scholarship loan program, and strategies to retain excellent principals.

3. The need for adaptation of current administrator preparation programs to meet changing demands
   - Challenges include recognizing that leaders must be knowledgeable in the core technology of schools, preparation programs need to link theory to practice, novices need to complete enriched internship experiences, and prospective school leaders need to hone skills in distributed leadership.
   - Policy initiatives include redesigned university-based preparation programs, standards-based evaluation, use of performance-based assessments, and multiple licensure routes.

4. Professional development needs
   - Challenges include fast-paced changes in federal and state programs, new skills needed to support expanded role expectations, and lack of systematic coaching.

- Policy initiatives include induction year with mentorship, executive coaching, leadership academies, collaborative professional development councils, and improved support network.

Although effective instructional leadership was noted to be an essential part of the principal's role, multiple and increasing job demands often prevented principals from having enough time to devote to this area. The need for additional resources was cited to address increased responsibilities and time demands in order to focus on student learning. The authors called for multiple stakeholders to work collaboratively and systematically to address the challenges evident in leadership quality and quantity.

Usdan, M., McCloud, B., & Podmostko, M. (2000). *Leadership for Student Learning: Reinventing the Principalship.* Washington, DC: Institute for Educational Leadership (IEL). [Task force report].

Keywords: Instructional Leadership, Communication and Community Relations, Professionalism

Summary: The changing nature of school principalship and the need for qualified school leaders to strengthen student learning was supported in review of the literature. The traditional conception of principal as middle manager has evolved, and principals must now focus on student learning and find alternative ways to handle other building responsibilities. Although evidence has indicated that there is an adequate supply of trained candidates for the position of principal, many of those with credentials have declined to pursue the principalship. The task force recommended three critical changes:

1. Fill the pipeline with effective school leaders.

2. Support the profession.

3. Guarantee quality and results.

Although improvements and policymaking have traditionally taken place at the state and local levels, the Interstate School Leaders Licensure Consortium (ISLLC) has recently become actively involved in efforts to improve principal standards and practice. The authors indicated that new models of school leadership have become necessary to address the multiple job demands of principals.

Key Points:

- Twenty-first-century principals are called upon to adopt the roles of instructional, community, and visionary leadership. Leadership for student learning is the priority that connects and encompasses all three.
- Support the profession: areas of focus include professional development, better pay and recognition, "doability" of job, and autonomy and authority.
- Guarantee quality and results: areas of focus include principal evaluation, accountability, and lack of adequate data and knowledge.

Villani, C. J. (1997, March). *The Interaction of Leadership and Climate in Three Urban Elementary Schools.* Paper presented at the annual meeting of the American Educational Research Association, Chicago (pp. 3–35). [Evaluative report].

Keywords: Instructional Leadership, School Climate

Summary: The role of leadership behaviors of elementary principals and the effect on school climate were studied in three urban Connecticut schools. Climate surveys were administered, and schools were rated as "open" or "closed" in terms of climate. Qualitative methods, including field observations and interviews, were used to study leadership behaviors in relation to school climate in "open" and "closed" schools. The characteristics of principal strength and security were examined as well as principal influence on teacher behaviors and productivity. Results indicated that the factors of principal strength and security affected school climate and influenced teachers and their interactions. It was concluded that school climate affected teacher productivity and therefore also affected student learning.

Key Points:

- The following traits were found to be indicative of an open climate (strong and secure principals): vision with clear and reasonable goals, effectively utilized personnel, cohesive work environment, open communication, opportunities for collaboration, conviction in philosophy, ability to stand up for beliefs, and a buffer for staff from outside criticism.

- The study revealed that support, collegiality, and collaboration alone are necessary but not sufficient to create an open school climate. The attributes of strength and security have an effect on principal effectiveness.
- The climate of the school is directly related to teacher productivity, which directly affects the quality of education that students receive. Therefore, creating an open and productive climate is vital for principals.

Waters, T., & Grubb, S. (2004). *Leading Schools: Distinguishing the Essential from the Important.* Denver, CO: Mid-continent Research for Education and Learning (McREL) (pp. 1–12). [Report].

Keywords: Professionalism, Student Achievement

Summary: The importance of principals being able to differentiate between important and essential responsibilities related to student achievement was described. Principal standards developed in the 1990s identified responsibilities, functions, and practices important for principals. These standards reflected the complexity and number of tasks in which principals were engaged, but did not distinguish between those that were important and those that were essential to improving student learning. Through the use of meta-analysis, 66 leadership practices used to fulfill 21 school leadership responsibilities were obtained. Results revealed that both the positive and negative impact of principal leadership on student achievement was evident. The authors emphasized the importance of being able to identify practices that are most likely to improve achievement. The need for first-order and second-order changes, respectively consistent or inconsistent with current norms and knowledge, depended on the individual organization. Knowledge of which forms of change were needed was described as critical to whether achievement would be positively or negatively affected. The authors noted that current performance standards reinforce the view of the principal as solely responsible for school success. Implications for principal preparation programs were described.

Witziers, B., Bosker, R., & Kruger, M. L. (2003, August). Educational Leadership and Student Achievement: The Elusive Search for an Association. *Educational Administration Quarterly, 39*(3), 398–425. [Journal article].

Keywords: Professionalism, Student Achievement

Summary: An overview and meta-analysis of principal impact on student achievement was examined, including discussion of both the direct and indirect effect models. Results revealed an overall small direct effect of principal leadership, with no direct effect at the secondary level. Limitations of research on the direct effect model were discussed. Review of previous research revealed a greater degree of support for the indirect effects model. The authors suggested additional research to clarify the concept of instructional leadership, as well as to provide additional insight into the effect of school cultures on student outcomes and the school leader's role regarding school culture. Additional research is also needed in the indirect effect model, and the authors cautioned that improved methodology is needed in future studies. The article suggests that research over the past 20 years has raised more questions about the relationship between leadership and student achievement than it has clarified.

References

American Association for Employment in Education (AAEE). (2000). *Educator supply and demand in the United States.* Columbus, OH: Author. Retrieved November 12, 2007, from www.aaee.org.

American Association of School Administrators. (2007). *Code of ethics: AASA's statement.* Retrieved July 15, 2007, from http://www.aasa.org/about/content.cfm?ItemNumber=2157.

American Association of State Colleges and Universities. (2005). *The facts—and fictions—about teacher shortages.* Washington, DC: Author. Retrieved November 12, 2007, from http://www.aascu.org/policy_matters/pdf/v2n5.pdf.

Anderson, G. (2001). Disciplining leaders: A critical discourse analysis of the ISLLC national examination and performance standards in educational administration. *International Journal of Leadership in Education: Theory and Practice, 4*(3), 199–216.

Anthes, K. (2005, January). *Leader standards.* Denver, CO: Education Commission of the States (ECS). Retrieved October 6, 2007, from http://www.ecs.org.

Armstrong, T. (2007, May). The curriculum superhighway. *Educational Leadership, 64*(8), 16–20.

Ascione, L. (2005, September). Teachers' tech use on the rise. *eSchoolnewsonline, www.eschoolnews.com,* 1–5.

Association of Community Organizations for Reform Now (ACORN). (n.d.). *Where have all of the teachers gone?* Retrieved December 7, 2007, from http://www.acorn.org/index.php?id=322.

Barrios, L., Jones, S. E., & Gallagher, S. S. (2007). Legal liability: The consequences of school injury. *Journal of School Health, 77*(5), 273–279.

Barth, R. (2002, May). The culture builder. *Educational Leadership, 59*(8), 6–11.

Beck, L. G., & Murphy, J. (1994). *Ethics in educational leadership programs: An expanding role.* Thousand Oaks, CA: Corwin Press.

Bergert, S., & Burnette, J. (2001). *Educating exceptional children: A statistical profile.* (Report No. ED308407). Arlington, VA: ERIC Clearinghouse on Disabilities and Gifted Education. (ERIC Document Reproduction Service No. ED452649).

Betts, J. R., Rueben, K. S., & Danenberg, A. (2000). *Equal resources, equal outcomes? The distribution of school resources and student achievement in California.* San Francisco: Public Policy Institute of California.

Blank, M., Heifets, O., Shah, B., & Nissani, H. (2004). Community schools: Engaging parents and families. *Principal, 83*(3), 18–21. Retrieved May 18, 2007, from http//www.naesp.org/ContentLoad.do?conentId=1122&action=print. (Note: The full text of this article is available via Web link only through organizational membership.)

Blase, J., & Blase, J. (1999). *Leadership for staff development: Supporting the lifelong study of teaching and learning.* Washington, DC. U.S. Department of Education/Education Resources Information Center, 2–18.

Blase, J., & Blase, J. (2001). *Empowering teachers: What successful principals do* (2nd ed.). Thousand Oaks, CA: Corwin Press.

Bodily, S., Keltner, B., Purnell, S., Reichardt, R., & Schuyler, G. (1998). *Lessons from new American scale-up phase: Prospects for bringing designs to multiple schools.* Santa Monica, CA: Rand Corporation. Retrieved May 29, 2008, from http://www. Rand.org/publications/MR/MR942/.

Boreen, J., Johnson, M. K., Niday, D., & Potts, J. (2000). *Mentoring beginning teachers: Guiding, reflecting, coaching.* York, ME: Stenhouse Publishers.

Boris-Schacter, S., & Merrifield, S. (2000, January). Why "particularly good" principals don't quit. *Journal of School Leadership, 10,* 84–98.

Borko, H., & Livingston, C. (1989). Cognition and improvision: Differences in mathematics instruction by expert and novice teachers. *American Educational Research Journal, 26*(4), 473–498.

Bosher, W. C., Jr., Kaminski, K. R., & Vacca, R. S. (2004). *The school law handbook: What every leader needs to know.* Alexandria, VA: Association of Supervision and Curriculum Development.

Bossert, S., Dwyer, D., Rowan, B., & Lee, G. (1982). The instructional management role of the principal. *Educational Administration Quarterly, 18*(3), 34–64.

Bridges, E. M. (1992). *The incompetent teacher: Managerial responses.* Washington, DC: Falmer Press.

Brimijoin, K., Marquisse, E., & Tomlinson, C. A. (2003, February). Using data to differentiate instruction. *Educational Leadership, 60*(5), 70–73.

Brody, J. A. (1977). A good teacher is harder to define than find. *American School Board Journal, 164*(7), 25–28.

Brooks, K., Schiraldi, V., & Zeidenberg, J. (2000). *School house hype: Two years later.* Washington, DC: Justice Policy Institute.

Bryk, A. S., & Schneider, B. (2002). *Trust in schools: A core resource for improvement.* New York: Russell Sage Foundation.

Buck, F. (2007). Saving time and paper with basic technology. *Principal, 86*(30), 18–21.

Burnett, J. R., Fan, C., Motowidlo, S. J., & DeGroot, T. (1998). Interview notes and validity. *Personnel Psychology, 51*(2), 375–396.

Carroll, J. M., (1994). *The Copernican plan evaluated: The evolution of a revolution.* Topsfield, MA: Copernican Associates.

Catano, N. (2002). *Content analysis of principal job descriptions and principal evaluation* instruments of K–12 public education in Virginia. Doctoral dissertation, The College of William and Mary, Williamsburg, VA.

Catano, N., & Stronge, J. H. (2006, September). What are principals expected to do? Congruence between principal evaluation and performance standards. *NASSP Bulletin, 90*(30), 221–237.

Catano, N., & Stronge, J. H. (2007). What do we expect of school principals? Congruence between principal evaluation and performance standards. *International Journal of Leadership in Education, 10*(4), 379–399.

Cawelti, G. (1999). *Portraits of six benchmark schools: Diverse approach to improving student achievement.* Arlington, VA: Educational Research Service.

Charlotte Advocates for Education. (2004). *Role of principal leadership in increasing teacher retention: Creating a supportive environment.* Charlotte, NC: Author.

Chavkin, N. F., & Williams, D. L. (1993). Minority parents and the elementary school: Attitudes and practices. In N. Chavkin (Ed.), *Families and schools in a pluralistic society* (pp. 73–83). Albany, NY: State University of New York Press.

Cheney, S. (2001). *Keeping competitive: A report of a survey of 1,800 employees.* Washington, DC: Center for Workplace Preparation.

Christensen, J. (2007, March). *School safety in urban charter and traditional public schools.* NCSRP Working Paper #2007–1, 1–17. Seattle, WA: Center on Reinventing Public Education.

Collins, J. (2001). *Good to great: Why some companies make the leap and others don't.* New York: HarperBusiness.

Colvin, G. (2007, October 1). Leader machines. *Fortune,* 98–106.

Conley, D. T. (1987, April). Critical attributes of effective evaluation systems. *Educational Leadership, 44*(7), 60–64.

Cooper, B. S., Ehrensal, P. A., & Bromme, M. (2005, January/March). School-level politics and professional development: Traps in evaluating the quality of practicing teachers. *Educational Policy, 19*(1), 112–125.

Copland, M. A. (2002). *Leadership of inquiry: Building and sustaining capacity for school improvement in the Bay Area School Reform Collaborative.* San Francisco: Center for Research on the Context of Teaching.

Cornell, D. G., & Sheras, P. L. (1998). Common errors in school crisis response: Learning from our mistakes. *Psychology in the Schools, 35*(3), 297–307.

Cotton, K. (2003). *Principals and student achievement: What the research says.* Alexandria, VA: Association for Supervision and Curriculum Development.

Cotton, K., & Wikelund, K. R. (1989). *Parent involvement in education.* Washington, DC: Office of Educational Research and Improvement, U.S. Department of Education.

Council of Chief State School Officers. (2002, April). *Expecting success: A study of five high performing, high poverty schools.* Washington, DC: Author.

Covey, S. M. R., with Merrill, R. R. (2006). *The speed of trust: The one thing that changes everything.* New York: Free Press.

Covino, E. A., & Iwanicki, E. (1996). Experienced teachers: Their constructs on effective teaching. *Journal of Personnel Evaluation in Education, 11,* 325–363.

Cruickshank, D. R., & Haefele, D. (2001, February). Good teachers, plural. *Educational Leadership, 58*(5), 26–30.

Cuban, L. (1984). *How teachers taught: Constancy and change in American classrooms, 1890–1980.* New York: Longman.

Cuban, L. (1988). *The managerial imperative and the practice of leadership in schools.* Albany, NY: State University of New York Press.

Danielson, C. (2001, February). New trends in teacher evaluation. *Educational Leadership, 58*(5), 12–16.

Danielson, C. (2002). *Enhancing student achievement: A framework for school improvement.* Alexandria, VA: Association for Supervision and Curriculum Development.

Danielson, C. (2007, September). The many faces of leadership. *Educational Leadership, 65*(1), 14–19.

Darling-Hammond, L. (2000a). *Solving the dilemmas of teacher supply, demand, and standards: How we can ensure a competent, caring, and qualified teacher for every child.* New York: National Commission on Teaching & America's Future.

Darling-Hammond, L. (2000b). Teacher quality and student achievement: A review of state policy evidence. *Education Policy Analysis Archives, 8*(1). Retrieved March 21, 2000, from http://epaa.asu.edu/epaa/v8n1/.

Darling-Hammond, L. (2003, May). Keeping good teachers: Why it matters, what leaders can do. *Educational Leadership, 60*(8), 6–13.

Davis, S., Darling-Hammond, L., LaPointe, M., & Meyerson, D. (2005). *School leadership study: Developing successful principals.* Stanford, CA: Stanford Educational Leadership Institute, Stanford University.

Davis, S. H. (1998). Superintendents' perspectives on the involuntary departure of public school principals: The most frequent reasons why principals lose their jobs. *Educational Administration Quarterly, 34*(1), 58–90.

Davis, S. H., & Hensley, P. A. (1999). The politics of principal evaluation. *Journal of Personnel Evaluation in Education, 13,* 383–403.

Deal, T. E., & Kennedy, A. A. (1983, February). Culture and school performance. *Educational Leadership, 40*(5), 14–15.

DeAngelis, K. J., & Presley, J. B. (2007). *Leaving schools or leaving the profession: Setting Illinois' record straight on new teacher attrition.* Illinois Education Research Council,

Policy Research Report: IERC 2007–1. Retrieved December 7, 2007, from http://ierc.siue.edu.

DeBell, M. (2006, January 17). Rates of computer use by children in nursery school and students in kindergarten through twelfth grade. *Education Statistics Quarterly, 7*(1–2), 1–2. Retrieved November 8, 2007, from http://nces.cd.gov/programs/quarterly/vol_1_2/4_4.asp.

DiPaola, M., & Tschannen-Moran, M, (2003). The principalship at a crossroads: A study of the conditions and concerns of principals. *National Association of Secondary School Principals Bulletin, 81*(634), 43–65.

DiPaola, M. F., & Hoy, W. K. (2008). *Principals improving instruction: Supervision, evaluation, and professional development.* Boston: Pearson.

Donaldson, Jr., G. A. (2007, September). What do teachers bring to leadership? *Educational Leadership, 65*(1) 26–29.

Doyle, M. E., & Rice, D. M. (2002). Model for instructional leadership. *Principal Leadership, 3*(3), 49–52.

Dozier, T. K. (2007, September). Turning good teachers into great leaders. *Educational Leadership, 65*(1), 54–59.

Drago-Severson, E. (2004). *Helping teachers learn: Principal leadership for adult growth and development.* Thousand Oaks, CA: Corwin Press.

Driscoll, A., Peterson, K., Browning, M., & Stevens, D. (1990). Teacher evaluation in early childhood education: What information can young children provide? *Child Study Journal, 20,* 67–69.

DuFour, R. (2004, May). What is a "professional learning community"? *Educational Leadership, 61*(8), 6–11.

Duke, D. L. (1990). Developing teacher evaluation systems that promote professional growth. *Journal of Personnel Evaluation in Education, 4,* 131–144.

Duke, D. L. (1997). Seeking a centrist position to counter the politics of polarization. *Phi Delta Kappan, 78,* 120–123.

Dunklee, D. R., & Shoop, R. J. (2002). *The principal's quick reference guide to school law.* Thousand Oaks, CA: Corwin Press.

Eaker, R., DuFour, R., & DuFour, R. (2002). *Getting started: Reculturing schools to become professional learning communities.* Bloomington, IN: Solution Tree.

Ebmeier, H., Jenkins, R., & Crawford, G. (1991). The predictive validity of student evaluations in the identification of meritorious teachers. *Journal of Personnel Evaluation in Education, 4,* 341–347.

Edgar, E., & Pair, A. (2005). Special education teacher attrition: It all depends on where you are standing. *Teacher Education and Special Education, 28*(3/4), 163–170.

Education Commission of the States. (2002). *No Child Left Behind issue brief: Data-driven decision making.* Denver, CO: Author.

Education Review Office. (1998). *The capable teacher.* Retrieved November 12, 2007, from http://www.ero.govt.nz/Publications/eers1998/98no2hl.html.

Ellett, C. D., & Teddlie, C. (2003). Teacher evaluation, teacher effectiveness and school effectiveness: Perspectives from the USA. *Journal of Personnel Evaluation in Education, 17*(1), 101–128.

Elmore, R. F. (2000). *Building a new structure for school leadership.* Washington, DC: The Albert Shanker Institute.

Elmore, R. F. (2005, Winter). Accountable leadership. *The Educational Forum, 69,* 134–142.

English, F. W. (2006). The unintended consequences of a standardized knowledge base in advancing educational leadership preparation. *Educational Administration Quarterly, 42*(3), 461–472.

Esch, C. E., Chang-Ross, C. M., Guha, R., Humphrey, D. C., Shields, P. M., Tiffany-Morales, J. D., et al. (2005). *The status of the teaching profession.* Santa Cruz, CA: The Center for the Future of Teaching Learning.

Ferguson, R. F. (1991). Paying for public education: New evidence on how and why money matters. *Harvard Journal on Legislation, 28,* 465–498.

Fetler, M. (1999). High school staff characteristics and mathematics test results. *Education Policy Analysis Archives, 7*(9). Retrieved November 12, 2007, from http://epaa.asu.edu/epaa/v7n9.html.

Fibkins, W. L. (2002). *An administrator's guide to better teacher mentoring.* Lanham, MD: Scarecrow Press.

Fink, E., & Resnick, L. B. (2001, April). Developing principals as instructional leaders. *Phi Delta Kappan, 82*(8), 598–606.

Friend, M. (2007, February). The coteaching partnership. *Educational Leadership, 64*(5), 48–52.

Fullan, M. (1991). *The new meaning of educational change.* New York: Teachers College Press.

Fullan, M. (2001). *Leading in a culture of change.* San Francisco: Jossey-Bass.

Fullan, M. (2002, May). The change leader. *Educational Leadership, 59*(8), 16–20.

Fullan, M. (2005). *Leadership & sustainability: System thinkers in action.* Thousand Oaks, CA: Corwin Press.

Fullan, M. G. (1996). Turning systemic thinking on its head. *Phi Delta Kappan, 77*(6), 424–436.

Fullan, M., Bertani, A., & Quinn, J. (2004, April). New lessons for districtwide reform: Effective leadership for change has 10 crucial components. *Educational Leadership, 61*(7), 42–46.

Gallagher, D. R., Bagin, D., & Kindred, L. W. (1997). *The school and community relations.* Needham Heights, MA: Allyn & Bacon.

Garsten, E., & Buckley, F. (1999). *School lesson: Deflect bullies, prevent violence.* Retrieved November 12, 2007, from www.cnn.com.

Glidden, H. (1999). Making standards matter 1999: Executive summary. *PreK–12 Teachers.* Retrieved June 1, 2007, from http://www.aft.org/teachers/index.htm.

Goe, L. (2002). Legislating equity: The distribution of emergency permit teachers in California. *Education Policy Analysis Archives, 10*(42), Retrieved June 1, 2005, from http://epaa.asu.edu/epaa/v10n42.

Groff, F. (2001, October/November). Who will lead? The principal shortage. *State Legislatures, 27*(9), 16.

Guin, K. (2004). Chronic teacher turnover in urban elementary schools. *Educational Policy Analysis Archives, 12*(42). Retrieved July 15, 2007, from http://epaa.asu.edu/epaa/v12n42/.

Guskey, T. R. (2003, February). How classroom assessments improve learning. *Educational Leadership, 60*(5), 6–11.

Hallinger, P., Bickman, L., & Davis, K. (1996). School context, principal leadership, and student reading achievement. *The Elementary School Journal, 96*(5), 527–549.

Hallinger, P., & Heck, R. H. (1996, February). Reassessing the principal's role in school effectiveness: A review of empirical research, 1980–1995. *Educational Administration Quarterly, 32*(1), 5–44.

Hanushek, E. A., & Rivkin, S. G. (2004). The revolving door [Electronic version]. *Education Next, 4* (1). Retrieved June 2, 2008, from http://www.hoover.org/publications/ednext/3345156.html.

Hargreaves, A., & Fink, D. (2003, May). Sustaining leadership. *Phi Delta Kappan, 84*(9), 693–700.

Hargreaves, A., & Fullan, M. (2000). Mentoring in the new millennium. *Theory into Practice, 39*(1), 50–56.

Harris, S. (2007). The best from the best: Effective strategies of award-winning principals. *Principal, 87*(1), 17–22.

Harris, S. L., & Lowery, L. (2002, May). A view from the classroom. *Educational Leadership, 59*(8), 64–65.

Harrison, C., & Killion, J. (2007, September). Ten roles for teacher leaders. *Educational Leadership, 65*(1), 74–77.

Hehir, T. (2007, February). Confronting ableism. *Educational Leadership, 64*(5), 9–14.

Heller, D. A. (2004). *Teachers wanted: Attracting and retaining good teachers.* Alexandria, VA: Association for Supervision and Curriculum Development.

Helm, V. M. (1997). Conducting a successful evaluation conference. In J. H. Stronge (Ed.), *Evaluating teaching: A guide to current thinking and best practice* (pp. 251–269). Thousand Oaks, CA: Corwin Press.

Helm, V. M., & St. Maurice, H. (2006). Conducting a successful evaluation conference. In J. H. Stronge (Ed.) *Evaluating teaching: A guide to current thinking and best practice* (2nd ed.) (pp. 235–252). Thousand Oaks, CA: Corwin Press.

Henke, R. R., Chen, X., & Geis, S. (2000). *Progress through the teacher pipeline: 1992–93 college graduates and elementary/secondary school teaching as of 1997* (NCES 2000–152). Washington, DC: National Center for Educational Statistics.

Herzberg, F. (1966). *Work and the nature of man.* New York: World Publishers, Inc.

Herzberg, F. (1982). *The managerial choice: To be efficient and to be human* (Rev. ed.) Salt Lake City, UT: Olympus Publishing.

Hindman, J. L. (2004) *The connection between qualities of effective teachers and selection interviews: The development of a teacher selection interview protocol.* Williamsburg, VA: The College of William and Mary.

Howard, B. B., & McColsky, W. H. (2001, February). Evaluating experienced teachers. *Educational Leadership, 58*(5), 48–51.

Hussar, W. J. (1999). *Predicting the need for newly hired teachers in the United States to 2008–09.* (NCES Publication No. NCES 1999–026) Washington, DC: U.S. Government Printing Office.

Ingersoll, R. M. (2001a). Teacher turnover and teacher shortages: An organizational analysis. *American Educational Research Journal, 38*, 499–534.

Ingersoll, R. M. (2001b). *Teacher turnover, teacher shortages, and the organization of schools.* (Document R-01-1). Seattle, WA: Center for the Study of Teaching and Policy, University of Washington.

Ingersoll, R. M. (2002). The teacher shortage: A case of wrong diagnosis and wrong prescription. *NASSP Bulletin, 86*(6), 16–31.

Ingersoll, R. M., & Kralik, J. M. (2004). *The impact of mentoring on teacher retention: What the research says.* Denver, CO: Education Commission of the States. Retrieved November 12, 2007, from http://www.ecs.org/clearinghouse/50/36/5036.htm.

Institute for Educational Leadership. (2000). *Leadership for student learning: Reinventing the principalship.* Washington, DC: Author.

Interstate School Leaders Licensure Consortium (ISLLC). (1996). *Standards for school leaders.* Washington, DC: Council of Chief State School Officers. Retrieved June 1, 2008, from http://www.ccsso.org/content/pdfs/isllcstd.pdf.

Iwanicki, E. F. (1990). Teacher evaluation for school improvement. In J. Millman & L. Darling-Hammond (Eds.), *The new handbook for teacher evaluation.* Newbury Park, CA: Sage.

Jacobsen, D. M., & Gladstone, B. (1999). A report on educational partnerships supporting the Galileo at Banded Peak School in Rocky View School Division. *The International Electronic Journal of Leadership in Learning.* Retrieved November 12, 2007, http://www.ucalgary.ca/~iejll/volume3/gladstone2.html.

Jay, J. K. (2002). Points on a continuum: An expert/novice study of pedagogical reasoning. *The Professional Educator, 24*(2), 63–74.

Jeynes, W. H. (2003). A meta-analysis: The effects of parental involvement on minority children's academic achievement. *Urban Education, 40*(3), 202–217.

Johnson, J. (2004, April). What school leaders want. *Educational Leadership, 61*(7), 24–27.

Johnson, L. A. (2005). Why principals quit. *Principal, 84*(3), 21–23.

Joint Committee on Standards for Educational Evaluation (D. L. Stufflebeam, Chair). (1988). *The personnel evaluation standards: How to assess systems of evaluating educators.* Newbury Park, CA: Sage Publications.

Jonson, K. F. (2002). *Being an effective mentor: How to help beginning teachers succeed.* Thousand Oaks, CA: Corwin Press.

Kannapel, P. J., Clements, S. K., Taylor, P. J., & Hibpshman, T. (2005, February). *Inside the black box of high-performing high-poverty schools.* Lexington, KY: Prichard Committee for Academic Success.

Kaufman, D., Johnson, S. M., Kardos, S. M., Liu, E., & Peske, H. G. (2002). Lost at sea: New teachers' experiences with curriculum and assessment. *Teachers College Record, 104*(2), 273–300.

Kelly, L. K., & Lezotte, L. W. (2003). Developing leadership through the school improvement process. *Journal of School Improvement, 4*(1). Retrieved November 12, 2007, from http://www.ncacasi.org/jsi/2003v4i1/develop_leadership.

King, D. (2002, May). The changing shape of leadership. *Educational Leadership, 59*(8), 61–63.

Kouzes, J. M., & Posner, B. Z. (2002). *The leadership challenge* (3rd ed.). San Francisco: Jossey-Bass.

Kythreotis, A., & Pashiardis, P. (1998a). *The influence of school leadership styles and culture on students' achievement in Cyprus primary schools.* Nicosia: University of Cyprus.

Kythreotis, A., & Pashiardis, P. (1998b). Researching the characteristics of effective primary schools in Cyprus: A qualitative approach. *Educational Management and Administration, 26*(2), 117–130.

Langer, S., & Boris-Schacter, S. (2003). Challenging the image of the American principalship. *Principal, 83*(1), 14–18.

LaPointe, M., & Davis, S. H. (2006). Effective schools require effective principals. *Leadership, 36*(1), 16–38.

Lashway, L. (2001). Leadership for accountability. *Research Roundup,* Clearinghouse on Education Policy and Management, *17*(3), 1–14.

Lashway, L. (2002a, July). *Developing instructional leaders.* Eugene, OR: ERIC Clearinghouse on Educational Management. (ERIC No. ED466023).

Lashway, L. (2002b, Spring). Research roundup: Rethinking the principalship. *Clearinghouse on Educational Policy and Management (CEPM), 18*(3). Retrieved April 8, 2007, from http://eric.uoregon.edu/publications/roundup/Spring_2002.html.

Lashway, L. (2003, July). *Role of the school leader.* Eugene, OR: University of Oregon; and Washington, DC: U.S. Department of Education/ERIC Clearinghouse on Educational Management.

Leinau, P. (1997). Field trips that strengthen community relations. *Principal, 16*(2), 1–4. Retrieved May 18, 2007, from: http://www.naesp.org/ContentLoad.do?conentId=1122&action=print. (Note: The full text of this article is available via Web link only through organizational membership.)

Leithwood, K., Seashore Louis, K., Anderson, S., & Wahlstrom, K. (2004). *How leadership influences student learning.* St. Paul, MO: Learning From Research Project: University of Minnesota, Center for Applied Research and Educational Improvement

(CAREI), Toronto: Ontario Institute for Studies in Education at the University of Toronto (OISEUT); and New York: The Wallace Foundation.

Leithwood, K. A., & Riehl, C. (2003, March). *What do we already know about successful school leadership?* Washington, DC: AERA Division A Task Force on Developing Research in Educational Leadership.

Lieberman, A., & Friedrich, L. (2007, September). Teachers, writers, leaders. *Educational Leadership, 65*(1), 42–47.

LoVette, O., Watts, S., & Hood, J. (2000, November). *An investigation of teachers' perceptions of their principals' "delegation" and "relationships" behavior.* United States Department of Education: Education Resources Information Center (ERIC), (pp. 2–31). Paper presented at the annual meeting of the Mid-South Educational Research Association.

Luekens, M. T., Lyter, D. M., & Fox, E. E. (2004). Teacher attrition and mobility: Results from the teacher follow–up survey, 2000–01. *Education Statistics Quarterly, 6*(3). Retrieved November 20, 2005, from http://nces.ed.gov/programs/quarterly/vol_6/6_3/3_5.asp.

Madison, M., Marson, A., & Reese, K. (1999). Passageway: An avenue into the future. Retrieved September 10, 2007, from www.eric.ed.govERICdocs/data/ericdocs2sql/content_storage_01/0000019b/80/17/89/97.pdf.

Manasse, A. L. (1985, January). Improving conditions for principal effectiveness: Policy implications of research. *The Elementary School Journal, 85*(3), 339–463.

Manatt, R. P., & Benway, M. (1998). Teacher and administrator performance: Benefits of 360-degree feedback. *ERS Spectrum, 16*(2), 18–23.

Marks, H. M., & Printy, S. M. (2003, August). Principal leadership and school performance: An integration of transformational and instructional leadership. *Educational Administration Quarterly, 39*(3), 370–397.

Marshak, J., & Klotz, J. (2002). *To mentor or to induct: That is the question.* Paper presented at the annual meeting of the Mid-South Educational Research Association, Chattanooga, TN.

Marvel, J., Lytar, D. M., Pettola, P., Strizek, G. A., Morton, B. A., & Rowland, R. (2007, January). *Teacher attrition and mobility: Results from the 2004–05 teacher follow-up survey* (NCES 2007–307). Washington, DC: U.S. Department of Education, Institute of Education Sciences, National Center for Educational Statistics. Retrieved December 7, 2007, from http://nces.ed.gov/pubs2007/2007307.pdf.

Marzano, R., Waters, T., & McNulty, B. A. (2005). *School leadership that works: From research to results.* Alexandria, VA: Association for Supervision and Curriculum Development; and Aurora, CO: Mid-continent Research for Education and Learning.

Marzano, R. J. (2003). *What works in schools: Translating research into action.* Alexandria, VA: Association for Supervision and Curriculum Development.

Mazzeo, C. (2003). *Improving teaching and learning by improving school leadership.* Washington, DC: National Governors Association Center for Best Practices.

McConney, A. A., Schalock, M. D., & Schalock, H. D. (1997). Indicators of student learning in teacher evaluation. In J. H. Stronge (Ed.), *Evaluating teaching: A guide to current thinking and best practice* (pp. 162–192). Thousand Oaks, CA: Corwin Press.

McEwan, E. K. (2003). *Seven steps to effective instructional leadership* (2nd ed.). Thousand Oaks, CA: Corwin Press.

McGahie, W. C. (1991). Professional competence evaluation. *Educational Researcher, 20,* 3–9.

McGhee, M. W., & Nelson, S. W. (2005, January). Sacrificing leaders, villainizing leadership: How educational accountability policies impair school leadership. *Phi Delta Kappan, 86*(5), 367–375.

McGrath, M. J. (2006). Dealing positively with the nonproductive teacher: A legal and ethical perspective on accountability. In J. H. Stronge (Ed.), *Evaluating teaching: A guide to current thinking and best practice* (2nd ed.) (pp. 253–267). Thousand Oaks, CA: Corwin Press.

McGreal, T. L. (1988). Evaluation for enhancing instruction: Linking teacher evaluation and staff development. In S. J. Stanley & W. J. Popham (Eds.), *Teacher evaluation: Six prescriptions for success* (pp. 1–29). Alexandria, VA: Association for Supervision and Curriculum Development.

McLaughlin, M. W. (1990). Embracing contraries: Implementing and sustaining teacher evaluation. In J. Millman & L. Darling-Hammond (Eds.), *The new handbook of teacher evaluation: Assessing elementary and secondary school teachers* (pp. 403–415). Newbury Park, CA: Sage Publications.

Melaville, A. I., & Blank, M. J., (2000). It takes a whole community. *Principal, 80*(1), 18–25. Retrieved May 18, 2007, from http//www.naesp.org/ContentLoad.do?conentId=1122&action=print. (Note: The full text of this article is available via Web link only through organizational membership.)

Mendel, C. M., Watson, R. L., & MacGregor, C. J. (2002, October 6). *A study of leadership behaviors of elementary principals compared with school climate.* Paper presented at the Southern Regional Council for Educational Administration, Kansas City, MO.

Mendro, R. L. (1998). Student achievement and school and teacher accountability. *Journal of Personnel Evaluation in Education, 12,* 257–267.

Menuey, B. P. (2005). Teachers' perceptions of professional incompetence and barriers to the dismissal process. *Journal of Personnel Evaluation in Education, 18*(4), 309–325.

Miech, R. A., & Elder, G. H. (1996). The service ethic and teaching. *Sociology of Education, 69,* 237–253.

Million, J. (2002, February). Stressed, angry parents and the principal. *Communicator, PR Primer,* 5–7. Retrieved May 18, 2007, from http://www.naesp.org/ContentLoad.do?contentId=301.

Million, J. (2004). Are you really listening? *Communicator 27*(8), 5–6. Retrieved May 18, 2007, from http://www.naesp.org/ContentLoad.do?contentId=1228.

Moore-Johnson, S., & The Project on the Next Generation of Teachers. (2004). *Finders and keepers: Helping teachers survive and thrive in our schools.* San Francisco: Jossey-Bass.

Mullen, C. A., & Lick, D. W. (Eds.). (1999). *New directions in mentoring: Creating a culture of synergy.* New York: Falmer Press.

Murphy, J. (2003, September) *Reculturing educational leadership: The ISLLC standards ten years out.* Paper prepared for the National Policy Board of Educational Administration, 1–60.

National Commission on Teaching and America's Future (NCTAF). (2003). *No dream denied: A pledge to America's children.* Washington, DC: Author.

National Commission on Teaching and America's Future (NCTAF). (2007). *High teacher turnover drains school and district resources.* Washington, DC: Author. Retrieved December 7, 2007, from http://nctaf.org/resources/news/press_releases/CTT.htm.

National Staff Development Council (NSDC). (2001). *Standards for staff development.* Retrieved August 15, 2007, from http://www.nsdc.org/standards/about/index.cfm.

Nye, B., Konstantopoulos, S., & Hedges, L. V. (2004). How large are teacher effects? *Educational Evaluation and Policy Analysis, 26*(3), 237–257.

Painter, S. R. (2000). Principals' efficacy beliefs about teacher evaluation. *Journal of Educational Administration, 38*(4), 368–378.

Pajak, E., & McAfee, L. (1992). The principal as school leader, curriculum leader. *NASSP Bulletin, 7* (547), 21–29.

Parsons, B. A. (2003, February). A tale of two schools' data. *Educational Leadership, 60*(5), 66–68.

Perkins, M. Y. (1998). *An analysis of teacher interview questions and practices used by middle school principals.* Doctoral dissertation, Virginia Polytechnic Institute and State University, Blacksburg, VA.

Peterson, K. (2004). Research on school teacher evaluation. *NASSP Bulletin, 88*(639), 60–79.

Peterson, K., & Kauchak, D. (1982). *Teacher evaluation: Perspectives, practices, and promises* (Report No. SP 022 900). Salt Lake City, UT: Center for Educational Practice. (ERIC Document Reproduction Service No. ED 233 996).

Peterson, K. D. (2000a). Student surveys for school teacher evaluation. *Journal of Personnel Evaluation in Education, 14*(2), 135–154.

Peterson, K. D. (2000b). *Teacher evaluation: A comprehensive guide to new directions and practices* (2nd ed.). Thousand Oaks, CA: Corwin Press.

Peterson, K. D. (2002). *Effective teacher hiring: A guide to getting the best.* Alexandria, VA: Association for Supervision and Curriculum Development.

Peterson, K. D. (2006). Using multiple data sources in teacher evaluation systems. In J. H. Stronge (Ed.), *Evaluating teaching: A guide to current thinking and best practice* (2nd ed.) (pp. 212–232). Thousand Oaks, CA: Corwin Press.

Peterson, K. D., Wahlquist, C., & Bone, K. (2000). Student surveys for school teacher evaluation. *Journal of Personnel Evaluation in Education, 14*(2), 135–153.

Piltch, B., & Fredericks, R. (2005, January/February). A principal's guide to school politics. *Principal, 84*(3), 10–14.

Portin, B., Schneider, P., DeArmond, M., & Gundlach, L. (2003, September). *Making sense of leading schools: A study of the school principalship.* Seattle, WA: Center on Reinventing Public Education.

Portner, H. (2003). *Mentoring new teachers.* Thousand Oaks, CA: Corwin Press.

Poston, W. K., Jr., & Manatt, R. P. (1993). Principals as evaluators: Limiting effects on school reform. *International Journal of Educational Reform, 2*(1), 41–48.

Prensky, M. (2005, December/January). Listen to the natives. *Educational Leadership, 63*(4), 8–13.

Prestine, N. A., & Nelson, B. S. (2003, April). *How can educational leaders support and promote teaching and learning? New conceptions of learning and leading in schools.* Task Force for the Development of an Agenda for Future Research on Educational Leadership. Paper presented at the annual meeting of the American Educational Research Association, Chicago.

Price, L. (1999). *Study: Bullying rampant in U.S. middle schools.* Retrieved November 12, 2007, from www.cnn.com.

Protheroe, N. (2005, November/December). Technology and student achievement. *Principal, 85*(2), 46–48.

Reason, C., & Reason, L. (2007, September). Asking the right questions. *Educational Leadership, 65*(1), 36–47.

Redfern, G. B. (1980). *Evaluating teachers and administrators: A performance objectives approach.* Boulder, CO: Westview.

Reed, C. J., McDonough, S., Ross, M., & Robichaux, R. (2001, April). *Principals' perceptions of high stakes testing on empowerment.* Paper presented at the annual meeting of the American Educational Research Association, Seattle, WA.

Reeves, D. (2006). *The learning leader.* Alexandria, VA: Association for Supervision and Curriculum Development.

Reeves, D. B. (2003). *Assessing educational leaders: Evaluating performance for improved individual and organizational results.* Thousand Oaks, CA: Corwin Press.

Reeves, D. B. (2004). *Accountability for learning: How teachers and school leaders can take charge.* Alexandria, VA: Association for Supervision and Curriculum Development.

Revenaugh, M. (2005, December/January). K–8 virtual schools: A glimpse into the future. *Educational Leadership, 63*(4), 60–64.

Riggins-Newby, C., & Hayden, H. (2004, March). *The principal's leadership network: Focusing on the image of the principal.* The Education Alliance, Brown University: Northeast and Islands Regional Educational Library; Alexandria, VA: National Association of Elementary School Principals (NAESP). Retrieved June 2, 2008, from http://www.alliance.brown.edu/pubs/pln/focus_prncpl.pdf.

Ritter, S. H. & Gottfried, S. C. (2002). *Supporting children through family-school-community-business collaboration.* Greensboro, NC: The Regional Educational Laboratory for the Southeast, University of North Carolina at Greensboro.

Rivkin, S. G., Hanushek, E. A., & Kain, J. F. (2001). *Teachers, schools, and academic achievement.* Amherst, MA: Amherst College Press.

Rowley, J. (1999, May). The good mentor. *Educational Leadership, 56*(8), 20–22.

Ruebling, C. E., Stow, S. B., Kayona, F. A., & Clarke, N. A. (2004, Spring). Instructional leadership: An essential ingredient for improving student learning. *The Educational Forum, 68,* 243–252.

Ruff, W. G., & Shoho, A. R. (2005, August). Understanding instructional leadership through the mental models of three elementary school principals. *Educational Administration Quarterly, 41*(3), 554–577.

Schmoker, M. (2003, February). First things first: Demystifying data analysis. *Educational Leadership, 60*(5), 22–24.

Schmoker, M. (2006). *Results now: How we can achieve unprecedented improvements in teaching and learning.* Alexandria, VA: Association for Supervision and Curriculum Development.

Sergiovanni, T. J. (1984). Leadership as cultural expression. In T. J. Sergiovanni & J. E. Corbally (Eds.), *Leadership and organizational culture* (pp. 105–144). Urbana, IL: University of Illinois Press.

Sergiovanni, T. J. (1992). *Moral leadership: Getting to the heart of school improvement.* San Francisco: Jossey-Bass.

Shellard, E. (2003). Defining the principalship. *Principal, 82*(4), 56–59. Retrieved March 15, 2006, from http://www.naesp.org.

Shellard, E. (2005). How assessment data can improve instruction. *Principal, 84*(3), 30–32.

Shen, J., & Hsieh, C. (1999). The instructional goals of the school leadership program: Future leaders' and educational leadership professors' perspectives. *Journal of School Leadership, 9*(1), 79–91.

Sherrod v. Palm Beach County School Board. (2006). District Court of Appeals of the State of Florida, Fourth District (No. 4D06-590). November 8, 2006.

Shortt, T. L., Moffett, C. F., & Williams, S. J. (2001). A blueprint for action: Creating a school community with no bullies. *The Virginia Principal, 21*(3), 14–15.

Simkins, T. (2005). Leadership in education: "What works" or "what makes sense"? *Educational Management Administration and Leadership, 33*(1), 9–26.

Snipes, J., Doolittle, F., & Herlihy, C. (2002). *Foundations for success: Case studies of how urban school systems improve student achievement.* New York: Manpower Demonstration Research Corporation (MDRC).

Sobel, A., & Kugler, E. G. (2007, March). Building partnerships with immigrant parents. *Educational Leadership, 64*(6), 62–66.

Sorenson, R. (2005). The seven keys to effective communication. *Principal-Web Exclusive, 85*(2), 1–41. Retrieved May 18, 2006, from http://www.naesp.org/ContentLoad.do?contentId=1768. (Note: The full text of this article is available via Web link only through organizational membership.)

Spillane, J. P. (2005, September). Primary school leadership practice: How the subject matters. *School Leadership and Management, 25*(4), 383–397.

Spillane, J. P., Halverson, R., & Diamond, J. B. (2001, April). Investigating school leadership practice: A distributed perspective. *Educational Researcher, 30*(3), 23–27.

Standler, R. B. (1999–2000). *Injuries in school/college laboratories in USA.* Retrieved November 12, 2007, from http://www.rbs2.com/labinj.htm.

Stratham, D. S., & Torell, C. R. (1996). *Computers in the classroom: The impact of technology on student learning.* Boise, ID: Army Research Institute, Boise State University. Retrieved November 12, 2007, from http://www.temple.edu/lss/htmlpublications/spotlights/200/spot206.htm.

Stronge, J. H. (1991). The dynamics of effective performance evaluation systems in education: Conceptual, human relations, and technical domains. *Journal of Personnel Evaluation in Education, 4,* 405–411.

Stronge, J. H. (1995). Balancing individual and institutional goals in educational personnel evaluation: A conceptual framework. *Studies in Educational Evaluation, 21,* 131–151.

Stronge, J. H. (2002). *Qualities of effective teachers.* Alexandria, VA: Association of Supervision and Curriculum Development.

Stronge, J. H. (Ed.). (2006a). *Evaluating teaching: A guide to current thinking and best practice* (2nd ed.). Thousand Oaks, CA: Corwin Press.

Stronge, J. H. (2006b). Teacher evaluation and school improvement: Improving the educational landscape. In J. H. Stronge (Ed.), *Evaluating teaching: A guide to current thinking and best practice* (2nd ed.) (pp. 1–23). Thousand Oaks, CA: Corwin Press.

Stronge, J. H. (2007). *Qualities of effective teachers* (2nd ed.). Alexandria, VA: Association of Supervision and Curriculum Development.

Stronge, J. H., & Helm, V. M. (1991). *Evaluating professional support personnel in education.* Newbury Park, CA: Sage Publications.

Stronge, J. H., & Hindman, J. L. (2006). *The teacher quality index: A protocol for teacher selection.* Alexandria, VA: Association for Supervision and Curriculum Development.

Stronge, J. H., & Ostrander, L. P. (2006). Client surveys in teacher evaluation. In J. H. Stronge (Ed.), *Evaluating teaching: A guide to current thinking and best practice* (2nd ed.) (pp. 125–151). Thousand Oaks, CA: Corwin Press.

Stronge, J. H., & Tucker, P. D. (1995). Performance evaluation of professional support personnel: A survey of the states. *Journal of Personnel Evaluation in Education, 9,* 123–137.

Stronge, J. H., & Tucker, P. D. (2000). *Teacher evaluation and student achievement.* Washington, DC: National Education Association.

Stronge, J. H., & Tucker, P. D. (2003). *Handbook on teacher evaluation: Assessing and improving performance.* Larchmont, NY: Eye on Education.

Supovitz, J. A., & Poglinco, S. M. (2001). *Instructional leadership in a standards-based reform.* Philadelphia, PA: Consortium for Policy Research in Education.

Sweeny, B. W. (2001). *Leading the teacher induction and mentoring program.* Arlington Heights, IL: Skylight Professional Development.

Taylor, P. J., & Small, B. (2002). Asking applicants what they would do versus what they did do: A meta-analytic comparison of situational and past behavior employment interview questions. *Journal of Occupational and Organizational Psychology, 75*(3), 277–294.

Texas Center for Educational Research. (2002). *The cost of teacher turnover.* Austin, TX: Author.

Thomas, D. D., Grigsby, C. J., Miller, J. C., & Scully, III, W. M. (2003). Networking: A life net for embattled principals. *Principal, 83*(1), 40–44.

Tirozzi, G., & Ferrandino, V. (2001, January 31). How do you reinvent a principal? [Electronic version] *Education Week.* Retrieved October 6, 2007, from http://www.naesp.org/Contentload.do?contentId=902.

Togneri, W., & Anderson, S. E. (2003). *Beyond islands of excellence: What districts can do to improve instruction and achievement in all schools.* Alexandria, VA: Learning Alliance First.

Trump, K. S. (2007). A game plan for safety. *American School Board Journal, 194*(2), 26–29.

Tschannen-Moran, M. (2004). *Trust matters: Leadership for successful schools.* San Francisco: Jossey-Bass.

Tucker, M. S., & Codding, J. B. (2002). *The principal challenge: Leading and managing schools in an era of accountability.* San Francisco: Jossey-Bass.

Tucker, P. D. (1997). Lake Wobegon: Where all teachers are competent (Or, have we come to terms with the problem of incompetent teachers?). *Journal of Personnel Evaluation in Education, 11,* 103–125.

Tucker, P. D., & DeSander M. K. (2006). Legal considerations in designing teacher evaluation systems. In J. H. Stronge (Ed.), *Evaluating teaching: A guide to current thinking and best practice* (2nd ed.) (pp. 69–97). Thousand Oaks, CA: Corwin Press.

Tucker, P. D., & Stronge, J. H. (2005). *Linking teacher evaluation and student learning.* Alexandria, VA: Association for Supervision and Curriculum Development.

Tucker, P. D., & Stronge, J. H. (2006). Student achievement and teacher evaluation. In J. H. Stronge (Ed.), *Evaluating teaching: A guide to current thinking and best practice* (2nd ed.) (pp. 152–167). Thousand Oaks, CA: Corwin Press.

Tucker, P. D., & Tschannen-Moran, M. (2002). *School leadership in an era of accountability.* Richmond, VA: Commonwealth Educational Policy Institute, Virginia Commonwealth University.

Tyack, D., & Cuban, L. (1995). *Tinkering toward utopia.* Cambridge, MA: Harvard University Press.

Tyack, D., & Hansot, E. (1982). *Managers of virtue: Public school leadership in America, 1820–1980.* New York: Basic Books.

United States Department of Education. (2006, Fall). *Lessons learned from school crises and emergencies.* Washington, DC: Author. Retrieved November 12, 2007, from http://eric.ed.gov/ERICDocs/data/ericdocs2sql/content_storage_01/0000019b/80/27/fa/ec.pdf.

Usdan, M., McCloud, B., & Podmostko, M. (2000). *Leadership for student learning: Reinventing the principalship.* Washington, DC: Institute for Educational Leadership.

Villani, C. (1997, March). *The interaction of school leadership and climate.* Paper presented at the annual meeting of the American Educational Research Association, Chicago.

Virshup, A. (1997, November 9). Grading teachers. *The Washington Post Magazine: A Special Issue About Education,* 14–17, 31–34.

Waddopus, G. L. (2004). *Technology integration, curriculum, and student achievement: A review of scientifically-based research and implications for EasyTech* (Executive summary). Portland, OR: Learning.com.

Wade, C., & Ferriter, B. (2007, September). Will you help me lead? *Educational Leadership, 65*(1), 65–69.

Waters, T., & Grubb, S. (2004). *Leading schools: Distinguishing the essential from the important.* Retrieved June 30, 2007, from http://www.mcrel.org/PDF/Leadership OrganizationDevelopment/4005IR_LeadingSchools.pdf.

Waters, J. T., Marzano, R. J., & McNulty, B. (2003). *Balanced leadership: What 30 years of research tells us about the effect of leadership on student achievement: A working paper.* Aurora, CO: Mid-continent Research for Education and Learning (McREL).

Weiss, I. R., & Pasley, J. D. (2006). *Scaling up instructional improvement through teacher professional development: Insights from the local systemic change initiative.* (CPRE Policy Brief No. RB-44). Philadelphia, PA: Consortium for Policy Research in Education.

Wenglinsky, H. (2002, February 13). How schools matter: The link between teacher classroom practices and student academic performance. *Educational Policy Analysis Archives, 10*(12). Retrieved May 17, 2005, from http://epaa.asu.edu/epaa/v10n12/.

Wenglinsky, H. (2005–2006, December/January). Technology and achievement: The bottom line. *Educational Leadership, 63*(4), 29–33.

Wherry, J. H. (2002). Planning ahead for parent involvement. *Principal, 81*(5), 53–54. Retrieved on May 18, 2007, from http://neasp.org.ContentLoad.do?contentID=803.

Wilkerson, D. J., Manatt, R. P., Rogers, M. A., & Maughan, R. (2000). Validation of student, principal, and self-ratings in 360 degree feedback for teacher evaluation. *Journal of Personnel Evaluation in Education, 14,* 179–192.

Williamson, L. G., Campion, J. E., Malos, S. B., Roehling, M. V., & Campion, M. A. (1997). Employment interview on trial: Linking interview structure with litigation outcomes. *Journal of Applied Psychology, 82*(6), 900–912.

Wilmore, E. (2002). *Principal leadership: Applying the new educational leadership constituent council (ELCC) standards.* Thousand Oaks, CA: Corwin Press.

Wise, A. E. (2001, December/January). Creating a high-quality teaching force. *Educational Leadership, 58*(4), 18–21.

Witziers, B., Bosker, R., & Kruger, M. L. (2003, August). Educational leadership and student achievement: The elusive search for an association. *Educational Administration Quarterly, 39*(3), 398–425.

Wolf, K. (2006). Portfolios in teacher evaluation. In J. H. Stronge (Ed.), *Evaluating teaching: A guide to current thinking and best practice* (2nd ed.) (pp. 169–185). Thousand Oaks, CA: Corwin Press.

Wollmer, S. K. (March, 2000). Turning back the turnover tide. *NJEA Review.* Retrieved November 12, 2007, from http://www.abacusassoc.com/NJEAEarlyLeavers.pdf.

Wong, H. (2002, March). Induction: The best form of professional development. *Educational Leadership, 59*(6), 52–54.

Wright, S. P., Horn, S. P., & Sanders, W. L. (1997). Teacher and classroom context effects on student achievement. Implications for teacher evaluation. *Journal of Personnel Evaluation in Education, 11,* 57–67.

Yildirim, A. (2001, April). *Instructional planning in a centralized school system: An assessment of teachers' planning at primary school level in Turkey.* Paper presented at the annual meeting of the American Educational Research Association, Seattle, WA. (ERIC Document Reproduction Service No. ED 453192).

Young v. Palm Beach County School Board. (2006). District Court of Appeals of the State of Florida, Fourth District. (No. 4DO5–4308). November 29, 2006.

Young, I. P., Rinehart, J. S., & Baits, D. M. (1997). Age discrimination: Impact of chronological age and perceived position demands on teacher screening decisions. *Journal of Research and Development in Education, 30*(2), 103–112.

Zavadsky, H. (2006, November). How NCLB drives success in urban schools. *Educational Leadership, 64*(3), 69–73.

Zirkel, P. A. (2001). *A digest of Supreme Court decisions affecting education* (4th ed.). Bloomington, IN: Phi Delta Kappa Educational Foundation.

Zmuda, A., Kuklis, R., & Kline, E. (2004). *Transforming schools: Creating a culture of continuous improvement.* Alexandria, VA: Association of Supervision and Curriculum Development.

Index

Note: Page numbers followed by *f* indicate illustrations.

About the Authors

James H. Stronge is the Heritage Professor in the Educational Policy, Planning, and Leadership area at the College of William and Mary in Williamsburg, Virginia. His research interests include policy and practice related to teacher quality and teacher and administrator evaluation. His work on teacher quality focuses on how to identify effective teachers and how to enhance teacher effectiveness.

Dr. Stronge has presented his research at numerous national and international conferences such as the American Educational Research Association, University Council for Educational Administration, National Evaluation Institute, Association for Supervision and Curriculum Development, and European Council of International Schools. Additionally, he has worked extensively with local school districts on issues related to teacher quality, teacher selection, and teacher and administrator evaluation. Stronge has authored, coauthored, or edited 18 books and approximately 90 articles, chapters, and technical reports. Some of his recent books include

- *Qualities of Effective Teaching*, 2nd ed. (Association for Supervision and Curriculum Development, 2007).
- *The Teacher Quality Index: A Protocol for Teacher Selection* (Association for Supervision and Curriculum Development, 2006).
- *Linking Teacher Evaluation and Student Achievement* (Association for Supervision and Curriculum Development, 2005).
- *Evaluating Teaching*, 2nd ed. (Corwin Press, 2005).
- *Handbook for Qualities of Effective Teachers* (Association for Supervision and Curriculum Development, 2004).

Dr. Stronge has been a teacher, counselor, and district-level administrator. His doctorate in the area of Educational Administration and Planning is from the University of Alabama. He may be contacted at The College of William and Mary, School of Education, P.O. Box 8795, Williamsburg, Virginia 23187-8795; phone: (757) 221-2339; e-mail: jhstro@wm.edu; http://jhstro.people.wm.edu/.

Holly B. Richard is an elementary school principal in the Chesterfield County Public Schools in the Richmond, Virginia, area. A former speech and language pathologist, she has worked extensively in preK–12 school settings and with special education populations. She received her PhD at the College of William and Mary in the Educational Policy, Planning, and Leadership program, with a research interest in policy and practice related to the principalship. She may be contacted at Bettie Weaver Elementary School, 3600 James River Road, Midlothian, Virginia 23113; phone: (804) 739-4179; e-mail: Holly_Richard@ccpsnet.net.

Nancy Catano currently serves the Williamsburg–James City County Schools in Williamsburg, Virginia, as an elementary school principal. Her career in education began as an elementary school teacher after completing a bachelor's degree in education from the College of William and Mary. After teaching for several years, she continued her education at William and Mary, completing her MEd and EdD degrees in general administration and educational policy. She has been published on issues related to the principalship in the *NASSP Bulletin* and the *International Journal of Leadership in Education*. She may be contacted at Norge Elementary School, 7311 Richmond Road, Williamsburg, Virginia 23188; phone: (757) 564-3372; e-mail: catanon@wjcc.k12.va.us.

Related ASCD Resources: Principals

At the time of publication, the following ASCD resources were available; for the most up-to-date information about ASCD resources, go to www.ascd.org. ASCD stock numbers are noted in parentheses.

Print Products

Education Update, October 2005, *When the Principal Is the New Kid at School* (#105117)

Learning-Driven Schools: A Practical Guide for Teachers and Principals by Barry Beers (#106002)

The New Principal's Fieldbook: Strategies for Success by Pam Robbins and Harvey Alvy (#103019)

Principals and Student Achievement: What the Research Says by Kathleen Cotton (#103309)

Principals Who Learn: Asking the Right Questions, Seeking the Best Solutions by Barbara Kohm and Beverly Nance (#107002)

Staffing the Principalship: Finding, Coaching, and Mentoring School Leaders by Suzette Lovely (#104010)

Videos and DVDs

Leadership Strategies for Principals (one 70-minute DVD accompanied by the book *The New Principal's Fieldbook: Strategies for Success* by Pam Robbins and Harvey Alvy) (608033)

For additional resources, visit us on the World Wide Web (http://www.ascd.org), send an e-mail message to member@ascd.org, call the ASCD Service Center (1-800-933-ASCD or 703-578-9600, then press 2), send a fax to 703-575-5400, or write to Information Services, ASCD, 1703 N. Beauregard St., Alexandria, VA 22311-1714 USA.